READING AND HEARING
THE BOOK OF THE TWELVE

SOCIETY
OF BIBLICAL
LITERATURE

SBL
SYMPOSIUM SERIES

Christopher R. Matthews, Editor

Number 15
**READING AND HEARING
THE BOOK OF THE TWELVE**
edited by
James D. Nogalski and Marvin A. Sweeney

James D. Nogalski and
Marvin A. Sweeney, editors

READING AND HEARING
THE BOOK OF THE TWELVE

Society of Biblical Literature
Atlanta

READING AND HEARING
THE BOOK OF THE TWELVE

edited by
James D. Nogalski and Marvin A. Sweeney

Copyright © 2000 by the Society of Biblical Literature

Library of Congress Cataloging-in-Publication Data

Reading and hearing the book of the Twelve / James D. Nogalski and Marvin A.
  Sweeney.
    p. cm. – (SBL Symposium series ; no. 15)
    ISBN 0-88414-021-0 (pbk. : alk. paper)
    1. Bible. O.T. Minor Prophets – Criticism, interpretation, etc. I. Nogalski,
  James. II. Sweeney, Marvin A. (Marvin Alan), 1953- III. Symposium series
  (Society of Biblical Literature)
  BS1560.R43 2000
  224′.9066 – dc21   00-030813

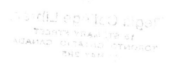

08 07 06 05 04 03 02 01 00   5 4 3 2 1

Printed in the United States of America
on acid-free paper

CONTENTS

PREFACE

Context, context, context. Something happens to the reader of biblical texts who learns to hear Hosea through Malachi as a corpus rather than as twelve independent writings. For more than a decade, scholars have mounted a concerted effort to evaluate the unifying features of biblical books. As part of that larger effort, an unprecedented amount of activity has focused on the implications of a long neglected, but ancient, tradition that "the Twelve," the collection of prophetic writings often called the Minor Prophets, was written on a single scroll and counted as a single book. Never before in the history of the discipline have so many people explored this tradition from so many different perspectives. This conversation about the Twelve, or the Book of the Twelve, needs to be heard in broader circles.

This collaborative effort has yielded significant insights, though by no means universal agreement on every issue. When one reads the essays in this volume, one is struck by recurring themes, dialogue among authors, and new avenues for interpreting the writings of the Twelve in a broader context. This interplay is not coincidental. The contributors to this volume have been actively involved in the Society of Biblical Literature (SBL) Seminar on the Formation of the Book of the Twelve (1997–1998) and/or a special session dedicated to this topic at the 1997 International Meeting of the SBL in Lausanne, Switzerland. These essays were all delivered in those settings. While the venues for these papers reflect recent trends in the discipline, the impetus for the study of the Book of the Twelve as a corpus derives from ancient traditions.

Background

For most of the nineteenth and twentieth centuries, modern critical scholarship has generally read the Twelve "Minor" Prophets as twelve individual prophetic books, interpreting each diachronically in relation to the individual historical settings or context in which each of the Twelve was deemed to have been written. But with the emergence of more recent impulses in the fields of redaction criticism, which call for an assessment of the final form of the biblical text as the initial basis for any attempt to recover the compositional history of the text, and newer forms of literary criticism that call for a synchronic reading of biblical literature, contemporary scholars are increasingly reading the Book of the Twelve as a single, unified biblical book.[1]

Indeed, there is a great deal of precedent for such readings. The Book of the Twelve Prophets functions simultaneously in Jewish and Christian versions of the Bible as a single prophetic book and as a collection of twelve individual prophetic books. Each of the twelve individual books — Hosea; Joel; Amos; Obadiah; Jonah; Micah; Nahum; Habakkuk; Zephaniah; Haggai; Zechariah; and Malachi, according to the Masoretic version of the Twelve — begins with its own superscription or narrative introduction that identifies the prophet and usually provides some details concerning the historical setting and overall concerns of the book. Each book is clearly distinguished from the others within the overall framework of the Twelve. There is generally no introduction or other common material that binds the works of the individual prophets that comprise the Twelve, but they almost invariably stand together as a clearly defined book with the other prophetic books of the Bible, that is, with Isaiah, Jeremiah, Ezekiel, and, in Christian Bibles, Daniel.

Although there is no single title for the Book of the Twelve as a whole, it is generally identified in Jewish tradition as *těrê* *ʿāśār*, Aramaic for "the Twelve," and in Christian tradition as *ʾoi dōdeka prophētai*, or *ton dōdekaprophēton*, Greek for "the Twelve Prophets." The deuterocanonical Wisdom of Jesus ben Sirach, or Ecclesiasticus, refers in 49:10 to "the bones of the twelve prophets," which suggests that Ben Sira knew the Twelve as a single book in the second century B.C.E. The first-century C.E. Jewish historian Flavius Josephus considers the Book of the Twelve as one of the twenty-two books of the Bible (*Ag. Ap.* 1.8). Likewise, *4 Ezra* 14:41 considers the Twelve to be one of the twenty-four holy books transcribed by Ezra. The Twelve is apparently omitted by accident from the canon list of the second-to-third-century church father Origen, who counts twenty-two Jewish books for the Old Testament but names only

---

[1] See Robert Morgan, with John Barton, *Biblical Interpretation* (Oxford: Oxford University Press, 1988); John Barton, *Reading the Old Testament: Method in Biblical Study* (rev. ed.; Louisville: Westminster/John Knox, 1996); Steven L. McKenzie and Stephen R. Haynes, eds., *To Each Its Own Meaning: An Introduction to Biblical Criticisms and Their Applications* (rev. ed.; Louisville: Westminster/John Knox, 1999); Odil Hannes Steck, *Old Testament Exegesis: A Guide to the Methodology* (trans. James D. Nogalski; 2d ed.; Resources for Biblical Study 39; Atlanta: Scholars Press, 1998).

twenty-one (Eusebius, *Hist. eccl.* 6.25). Most see this as evidence that he considered the Twelve to constitute a single book.[2]

The reading of the Twelve as a single book is evident in talmudic tradition, which considers the Twelve as a single prophetic book that follows Isaiah, Jeremiah, and Ezekiel (or alternatively, Jeremiah, Ezekiel, and Isaiah) in the "Latter Prophets" (*b. B. Bat.* 14b) and counts them as one book among the twenty-four of the Bible.[3] But the Talmud states that whereas the books of the Bible are to be separated in manuscripts by four blank lines, the individual books of the Twelve Prophets are to be separated from each other by three blank lines (*b. B. Bat.* 13b), which indicates their status as separate books as well. Likewise, the Masorah of the Twelve Prophets tallies the number of verses at the end of each individual prophetic book, but it also provides a count of verses for the Book of the Twelve as a whole.

Similar considerations appear in Christian tradition, which nearly consistently groups the Twelve Prophets together, but counts them as twelve individual books among the thirty-nine books of the Old Testament.[4] The first-century C.E. Bishop Melito of Sardis refers to the Twelve as *tōn dōdeka 'en monobiliōi*, "the twelve in one book" (Eusebius, *Hist. eccl.* 4.26). In his introduction to the Twelve Prophets of the Vulgate, Jerome states, *unum librum esse duodecim Prophetarum*, "the Twelve Prophets are one book." The term "Minor Prophets," *Prophetae minores* in Latin, first appears in Latin Christian patristic sources, such as the work of Augustine (*City of God* 18:29), and refers only to the relative length of the individual works of the Twelve Prophets when compared to the larger books of Isaiah, Jeremiah, Ezekiel, and Daniel.

Indeed, the term "Twelve Prophets" designates both the Book of the Twelve Prophets and the books of the Twelve Prophets, and scholars are

---

2 See Henry Barclay Swete, *An Introduction to the Old Testament in Greek* (1902; New York: Ktav, 1968) 203.

3 For general discussion of the canon in Jewish tradition, see Sid Leiman, *The Canonization of Hebrew Scripture: The Talmudic and Midrashic Evidence* (Hamden: Connecticut Academy of Arts and Sciences/Archon, 1976); Roger T. Beckwith, "Formation of the Hebrew Bible," in *Mikra: Text, Translation, Reading, and Interpretation of the Hebrew Bible in Ancient Judaism and Early Christianity* (ed. M. J. Mulder; CRINT 2/1; Assen: Van Gorcum; Philadelphia: Fortress, 1988), 39–86; Christian D. Ginsburg, *Introduction to the Massoretico-Critical Edition of the Hebrew Bible* (New York: Ktav, 1966).

4 For an overview of the form of the Bible in the Septuagint and patristic literature, see Swete, *Introduction*, 197–230; cf. Roger Beckwith, *The Old Testament Canon of the New Testament Church* (Grand Rapids: Eerdmans, 1986).

now beginning to discover what it means to read the Twelve as a single, prophetic book.[5]

Overview

The present volume is arranged in two parts, as reflected in the title. The contributions in Part One explore how and why one would read the Twelve Prophets as a corpus. The studies in Part Two ponder what happens when one listens to various elements in this larger corpus. The first part contains six conceptual essays, which examine various dimensions of the Twelve as a corpus, including the nature of the collection, its production, and the sequence of writings. The second part contains seven applied essays, which can broadly be labeled thematic explorations. These essays interpret motifs and/or paradigms that transcend the individual writings of the Twelve. A brief summary of

---

[5] Works in the first half of the last century and recent examples include, Karl Budde, "Eine folgenschwere Redaktion des Zwölfprophetenbuchs," *ZAW* 39 (1921): 218–229; Roland Emerson Wolfe, "The Editing of the Book of the Twelve," *ZAW* 53 (1935): 90–129; Peter Weimar, "Obadja: Eine redaktionskritische Analyse," *BN* 27 (1985): 35–99; Erich Bosshard-Nepustil, "Beobachtungen zum Zwölfprophetenbuch," *BN* 40 (1987): 30–62; Paul R. House, *The Unity of the Twelve* (Bible and Literature Series 27; JSOTSup 97; Sheffield: Almond Press, 1990); Erich Bosshard-Nepustil and Reinhold Gregor Kratz, "Maleachi im Zwölfprophetenbuch," *BN* 52 (1990): 27–46; Odil Hannes Steck, *Der Abschluss der Prophetie im alten Testament: Ein Versuch zur Frage der Vorgeschichte des Kanons* (Biblisch-theologische Studien 17; Neukirchen-Vluyn: Neukirchener, 1991); Terence Collins, *The Mantle of Elijah: The Redaction Criticism of the Prophetical Books* (Biblical Seminar 20; Sheffield: JSOT Press, 1993), 59–87; James Nogalski, *Literary Precursors to the Book of the Twelve* (BZAW 217; Berlin and New York: de Gruyter, 1993); idem, *Redactional Processes in the Book of the Twelve* (BZAW 218; Berlin and New York: de Gruyter, 1993); R. J. Coggins, "The Minor Prophets — One Book or Twelve?" in *Crossing the Boundaries: Essays in Biblical Interpretation in Honour of Michael D. Goulder* (ed. S. E. Porter, P. Joyce, and D. E. Orton; Biblical Interpretation Series 8; Leiden: Brill, 1994), 57–68; Barry Alan Jones, *The Formation of the Book of the Twelve: A Study of Text and Canon* (SBLDS 149; Atlanta: Scholars Press, 1995); John Barton, "The Canonical Meaning of the Book of the Twelve," in *After the Exile* (ed. J. Barton and D. J. Reimer; Macon, Ga.: Mercer University Press, 1996); James W. Watts and Paul R. House, eds., *Forming Prophetic Literature: Essays on Isaiah and the Twelve in Honor of John D. W. Watts* (JSOTSup 235; Sheffield: Sheffield Academic Press, 1996); Erich Bosshard-Nepustil, *Rezeptionen von Jesaja 1–39 im Zwölfprophetenbuch* (OBO 154; Fribourg, Switzerland: Universitätsverlag; Göttingen: Vandenhoeck & Ruprecht, 1997); Burkhard M. Zapff, *Redaktionsgeschichtliche Studien zum Michabuch im Kontext des Dodekapropheton* (BZAW 256; Berlin and New York: de Gruyter, 1997); Aaron Schart, *Die Entstehung des Zwölfprophetenbuchs* (BZAW 260; Berlin and New York: de Gruyter, 1998); Marvin A. Sweeney, *The Book of the Twelve Prophets* (2 vols.; Berit Olam; Collegeville, Minn.: Liturgical Press, forthcoming).

the articles in this volume will provide an overview for those who wish to join this conversation, perhaps for the first time.

In "A Book of the Twelve?" David L. Petersen questions terminology that refers to a "book" of the Twelve. He evaluates the rationale and implications of labeling these twelve prophetic texts as a book, using the lenses of scribal practice, size, order, formation, and literary features. Petersen's analysis leads him to conclude that ordering principles and/or redaction-historical evidence do provide evidence of a "very complicated process," but that the literary features are better classified as a "thematicized anthology" in which the Day of YHWH and the "liminality of time" play a crucial role.

In "The Production and Reading of the Book of the Twelve," Paul Redditt considers two questions: (1) Why is there a Book of the Twelve? (2) How has the Book of the Twelve been read? He organizes his response to the first question around five matrixes: theology, gender, class, political outlook, and a Jerusalemite orientation. Redditt concludes that the Book of the Twelve was produced for educated readers by custodians of prophetic voices influenced by Deuteronomy, Joel, and cultic language. These editors, likely upper-class males, focus on hopes for Jerusalem, but show little interest in structures of governance. As to the second question, Redditt documents that lack of awareness of the unifying features dominates the history of interpretation of the Twelve, but he suggests several benefits for reconsidering the Twelve as a redacted whole.

In "Reconstructing the Redaction History of the Twelve Prophets: Problems and Models," Aaron Schart considers recent treatments of the Twelve from five perspectives. He discusses the arguments for and against treating the Book of the Twelve as a redactional unity. He looks at how the orders of the writings have been treated as evidence. He examines recent suggestions of a global structure residing in the Twelve (plot, recurring themes, Day of YHWH, theodicy, similarity to Isaiah). Schart explores the similarities and differences of several recent redaction-historical models. Finally, Schart suggests five hermeneutical insights that can be derived from studying the Book of the Twelve.

In "Sequence and Interpretation in the Book of the Twelve," Marvin A. Sweeney evaluates the sequence of the writings as a potential clue to the hermeneutical interests of the LXX and MT. Since the sequence of writings varies in these two versions, Sweeney examines each writing for clues regarding how it could have functioned within each version. Sweeney concludes that both versions contain evidence of a deliberate, though not identical, arrangement that involves chronological and thematic considerations. Both versions display a general chronological movement from the eighth to the sixth centuries. Thematically, the LXX begins by emphasizing judgment against the northern kingdom (Hosea/Amos) and implications for the southern kingdom (Micah), before focusing on the Day of YHWH as a day of judgment on the nations and on restoration of Zion in a programmatic fashion (Joel). This emphasis is followed by treatment of specific nations (Obadiah, Jonah, Nahum). The last five writings focus on the judgment of Jerusalem by Babylon (Habakkuk, Zephaniah), Jerusalem's restoration (Haggai, Zechariah), and a review of the themes of the Twelve (Malachi). Sweeney theorizes that, at the beginning, the MT's sequence mixes the themes of the judgment on YHWH's people and on the nations with the two programmatic books (Hosea, Joel), while the remaining writings lay out the details of the two programmatic books.

In "The Book of the Twelve as a Witness of Ancient Biblical Interpretation," Barry A. Jones summarizes the debate over whether the Twelve represents a redacted whole or a collection of separate works. He argues that the diversity of textual traditions suggests an original diversity whose various arrangements shed light on the way the books were read and interpreted, which in turn affected the placement of certain books as the process of canonization moved toward uniformity. Using Obadiah and Jonah, Jones explores the ways in which the arrangement of these writings in three different versions follows interpretive clues furnished by the writings themselves.

In "How to Read the Book of the Twelve as a Theological Unity," Rolf Rendtorff accepts the premise that the Twelve constitutes a literary entity. He asks what unifies the individual writings once one assumes that the Book of the Twelve was intended to be read as a whole. He argues that the dated superscriptions of the writings provide a chronological framework for the corpus, while the themes of the Day of the Lord and the repentance of the nations play a central role in the undated superscriptions. Reading the writings of the Twelve sequentially allows one to trace the complex interrelationships of these themes.

In "Joel as 'Literary Anchor' for the Book of the Twelve," James D. Nogalski proceeds from a developing consensus that the Twelve exhibits a chronological framework, but that chronology alone is insufficient to explain the macrostructural principles. Nogalski raises questions about the character of the Twelve as a collection of twelve prophetic voices. He then examines the role of Joel as an interpretive key for major unifying *literary* threads in the Twelve. He explores Joel's literary function through its dovetailing of genres, its recurring vocabulary, and its paradigm of history. Hosea, Joel, and Amos are united by overlapping genres. The recurring vocabulary centers around several motifs (fertility language, the Day of YHWH, and theodicy), and can be seen in Joel's adaptation of other prophetic writings and in the implantation of Joel's vocabulary in other passages. Finally, Joel presents a historical paradigm that both presumes and transcends the chronological structure of the dated superscriptions in the Twelve.

In "Superscriptions and Incipits in the Book of the Twelve," John D. W. Watts analyzes every superscription and incipit, identifying three levels at which the introduction relates to subsequent material. At the basic level, the introduction functions closely with subsequent material; at secondary and tertiary levels, it does not. Watts concludes that incipits in three books (Jonah, Haggai, Zechariah) were not adapted for the Twelve while the majority of superscriptions show links to uniting the Twelve. Six of the writings (Joel, Micah, Nahum, Habakkuk, Zephaniah, Malachi) contain superscriptions that only relate to the building of the Twelve, while the introductory material in the other writings suggests that editorial work has expanded existing superscriptions in light of the context.

In "The Character of God in the Book of the Twelve," Paul R. House surveys the theological image of God through deliberation on theological method, evaluation of relevant texts, and a summary of ideas common to the individual writings. House calls for a canonical approach that can read the text as a coherent whole without losing the separate identity of the books. Reading the MT sequentially, House analyzes characteristic statements about God in the Twelve Prophets. He concludes that statements about the God who warns dominate the first six writings, while the God who punishes dominates the next three. Finally, the God who renews the temple, Jerusalem, and Israel takes center stage in the last three writings.

In " 'Israel' and 'Jacob' in the Book of Micah: Micah in the Context of the Twelve," Mark E. Biddle documents the ambiguous meanings for "Israel" and "Jacob" in Micah and then suggests relationships to the Twelve. Biddle notes that the core collection of Micah (chs. 1–3) uses these terms to designate the northern and southern kingdoms respectively, while manifesting links to texts in Hosea and Amos. Conversely, the eschatological texts of Mic 4–5 tend to use these epithets synonymously as references to the remnant, even while exhibiting different ideological positions on other themes in Micah. This tendency causes Biddle to classify chapters 4–5 as an anthology. These chapters share lexical and thematic connections with Zech 12–14. "Israel" and "Jacob" appear in Mic 6–7 in connection to terms associated with the twelve tribes. Finally, insertions in Micah (2:12–13; 1:2–4) exhibit links to the Edom polemic that runs through Joel, Amos, Obadiah, and Malachi.

In "The Zion-Daughter Oracles: Evidence on the Identity and Ideology of the Late Redactors of the Book of the Twelve," Byron G. Curtis builds on his earlier work by arguing that Zeph 3:14–20 exhibits connections to a Haggai-Zechariah-Malachi corpus. Curtis sees these three writings as a preexisting corpus, attached to the developing multivolume corpus as a single unit. Curtis maintains that Zeph 3:14–20 provides avenues into the agenda of the latter redactors of the Book of the Twelve. He reviews recent scholarship on the Twelve and clarifies his own model of its formation in relationship to those discussions. Next, he scrutinizes Zeph 3:14–20 using prose-particle analysis, demonstrating that 3:19–20 exhibits a high degree of prose characteristics when compared to the context. Curtis argues that these last two verses form a redactional bridge to Haggai-Zechariah-Malachi. Further, Curtis maintains that the Daughter Zion oracle in Zech 9:9–10 draws literarily on the Daughter Zion material in Zeph 3 to create a bridge from the early restorationist prophetic writings (Haggai, Zech 1–8) to the later restorationist writings (Zech 9–14, Malachi).

In "Remnant, Redactor, and Biblical Theologian: A Comparative Study of Coherence in Micah and the Twelve," Kenneth H. Cuffey suggests four categories to describe "coherence" in biblical studies before turning his attention to Micah and the Book of the Twelve. Cuffey labels these categories as coherence of internal linkage, structural linkage, perspective, and theme. In Micah, Cuffey finds the primary structural linkage in the four remnant promises, which link alternating sections of doom and hope. He finds the central thematic coherence in the God who punishes, yet restores. He notes how the internal linkage functions within and between the sections of doom and hope. He argues that the coherence of perspective only makes sense when one sees the data as material addressed to a group for whom restoration is an issue. Cuffey then analyzes the types of coherence suggested in recent treatments of the Twelve. He finds all four categories at work in various studies, but notes two important differences which need to be taken into account more fully. First, Cuffey argues that the scope of the Twelve exceeds the bounds of a self-contained and self-identified unit and that, second, this broader scope complicates the question of certainty regarding an author's or editor's intentions. Cuffey concludes by offering suggestions for evaluating the strength of arguments concerning links between texts and writings.

In "A Frame for the Book of the Twelve: Hosea 1–3 and Malachi," John D. W. Watts discusses literary framing techniques in the Hebrew Bible, then explains why he believes Hos 1–3 and Malachi function as a frame for the Book of the Twelve. In the Book of the Twelve, only these two passages directly and powerfully link YHWH and love (אהב). Watts argues that because these two texts constitute the beginning and end of the corpus, this theme functions similar to the rebellious-children frame in Isaiah. This frame provides a comforting rationale, using both positive and negative images, for YHWH's continued love in the face of Israel's ongoing disobedience. The images of YHWH's love are both theoretical and concrete. They undergird the presentation of a God who punishes and yet still remains intent on loving God's people.

The essays collected in this volume reflect diverse methodologies. They present a wide array of perspectives with which to consider the scroll of the Twelve as a single, albeit complexly unified, corpus. These essays exhibit common threads as well as contradictions, but such is the nature of multivocal dialogue. Taken as a group, the essays uncover a wealth of interpretive possibilities now receiving long-overdue attention. These essays document an ongoing conversation and invite others to participate. If and when one sees the value in reading the Twelve in context, one can begin to hear these prophetic texts in new ways.

JAMES D. NOGALSKI
Lombard, Illinois

MARVIN A. SWEENEY
Claremont, California

ABBREVIATIONS

*	= portions of text cited
AB	Anchor Bible
ABD	*Anchor Bible Dictionary*. Edited by D. N. Freedman. 6 vols. New York, 1992
AJSL	*American Journal of Semitic Languages and Literature*
ATD	Das Alte Testament Deutsch
AUSS	*Andrews University Seminary Studies*
AzTh	Arbeiten zur Theologie
BEATAJ	Beiträge zur Erforschung des Alten Testaments und des antiken Judentum
BETL	Bibliotheca ephemeridum theologicarum lovaniensium
BHK	*Biblia Hebraica*. Edited by R. Kittel. Stuttgart, 1905–1906, 1925², 1937³, 1951⁴, 1973¹⁶
BHS	*Biblia Hebraica Stuttgartensia*. Edited by K. Elliger and W. Rudolph. Stuttgart, 1983
BKAT	Biblische Kommentar, Altes Testament. Edited by M. Noth and H. W. Wolff
BN	*Biblische Notizen*
BZAW	Beihefte zur Zeitschrift für die alttestamentliche Wissenschaft
CBET	Contributions to Biblical Exegesis and Theology
CBQ	*Catholic Biblical Quarterly*
CRINT	Compendia rerum iudaicarum ad Novum Testamentum
DJD	Discoveries in the Judaean Desert
ExpTim	*Expository Times*
FAT	Forschungen zum Alten Testament

FOTL	Forms of the Old Testament Literature
HAT	Handbuch zum Alten Testament
JBL	*Journal of Biblical Literature*
JETS	*Journal of the Evangelical Theological Society*
JJS	*Journal of Jewish Studies*
JNES	*Journal of Near Eastern Studies*
JSOT	*Journal for the Study of the Old Testament*
JSOTSup	Journal for the Study of the Old Testament: Supplement Series
KAT	*Kommentar zum Alten Testament*
NICOT	New International Commentary on the Old Testament
OBO	Orbis biblicus et orientalis
OTG	Old Testament Guides
OTL	Old Testament Library
SBLDS	Society of Biblical Literature Dissertation Series
SBLEJL	Society of Biblical Literature Early Judaism and Its Literature
SBLSP	*Society of Biblical Literature Seminar Papers*
SBS	Stuttgarter Bibelstudien
SEÅ	*Svensk exegetisk årsbok*
ThWAT	*Theologisches Wörterbuch zum Alten Testament*. Edited by G. J. Botterweck and H. Ringgren. Stuttgart, 1970–
VT	*Vetus Testamentum*
VTSup	Vetus Testamentum Supplements
WBC	Word Biblical Commentary
WMANT	Wissenschaftliche Monographien zum Alten und Neuen Testament
ZAW	*Zeitschrift für die alttestamentliche Wissenschaft*
ZDMG	*Zeitschrift der deutschen morgenländischen Gesellschaft*

Part One

READING THE BOOK OF THE TWELVE

1

A Book of the Twelve?

David L. Petersen

Names and labels are powerful symbols. To describe a manuscript or any written material as a book gives it a special status, implying a certain level of coherence, authorial intent, and the like. To describe twelve biblical texts as a book is to do even more, suggesting that somehow these twelve texts belong together in a special, if not easily identifiable way. The matter is particularly complicated because the word "book," *Buch,* or *livre* in contemporary society bears even greater and specific connotations, for example, date of publication and copyright, which are not readily applicable to ancient documents. As a result, it is important for biblical scholars to be clear about the nature of their claims when using the phrase "the Book of the Twelve."

That ancient Israelite writers thought about texts as either a *seper* (ספר) or *megillah* (מגלה), I do not deny. Joshua 1:8 presents a parade example, when it refers to "this book of the law" (ספר התורה הזה). The phrase almost certainly refers to a form of Deuteronomy. Israel knew distinct or separate texts, one might even say "books," even if not the codex with which we are most familiar.

Only once, in all the Minor and Major Prophets, do we find the term ספר or מגלה; it appears in the title of one of the so-called Minor Prophets. Nahum 1:1 includes the phrase, "the ספר of the vision of Nahum of Elkosh." Apart from this phrase, the individual texts offer themselves as "words" ("the words of Amos," Amos 1:1); "the word" ("the word of Yahweh," Hos 1:1; Joel 1:1; Mic 1:1; Zeph 1:1); "vision" ("the vision of Obadiah," Obad 1); "oracle" ("an oracle concerning Nineveh," Nah 1:1; Hab 1:1). In the Major Prophets, we also hear about "the vision of Isaiah" (Isa 1:1) or "the words of Jeremiah" (Jer 1:1). These superscriptions typically refer to that which the prophet has seen, heard, or uttered, not to the writing's literary character, except in the aforementioned case of Nahum. Moreover, neither the word ספר nor מגלה is used with reference to all twelve books. In sum, to use the term "scroll" or "document," much

3

less "book," is several moves beyond the ways in which the documents refer to themselves, whether as individual texts or as the Twelve as a unit.

If there is no explicit textual warrant for viewing these twelve books as one literary entity, what case might be made for using the phrase "the Book of the Twelve"? In this essay, I analyze various claims for the existence of a Book of the Twelve and then propose another way by means of which one might construe these twelve documents as a thematized anthology that focuses on the *yom yhwh* (יום יהוה).

Scribal Practice

Ancient Hebrew and Greek texts have been discovered in which most or all of the Minor Prophets were written together on one scroll. The Greek Minor Prophets Scroll from Naḥal Ḥever (8ḤevXIIgr) and the Hebrew Minor Prophets Scroll from Wadi Murabbaʿat (MurXII) provide the key pieces of evidence.[1] Such scribal practice may presume but does not state explicitly that these books were viewed as one literary entity. The scrolls themselves do not preserve any titles apart from those of the individual canonical superscriptions.

Some scholars have deemed Sir 49:10 to offer some corroborating judgment: "May the bones of the Twelve Prophets send forth new life from where they lie. . . ."[2] However, Sirach seems to be referring to the prophets as individuals and not the books attributed to them. So, the aforementioned scrolls indicate that as early as ca. 200 B.C.E., these books were viewed as one scribal unit, but little more.

Several centuries later, certain rabbis thought that the Minor Prophets should be written together. As one rabbi put it, all the Twelve should be copied on one scroll so that the small books, such as Malachi, would not be lost (*B. Bat.* 13b). Jewish scribal practice, as stated in the Babylonian Talmud, required that four empty lines be left between biblical books, except between the Minor Prophets, where three lines were permitted.

Clearly, from a copyist's or scribal perspective, these twelve books belonged together on one leather scroll. But the most such practice

---

[1] E. Tov, *Textual Criticism of the Hebrew Bible* (Minneapolis: Fortress, 1992), 204.

[2] E.g., Herbert Marks writes, "The earliest mention of 'the twelve prophets' occurs in the deuterocanonical Wisdom of Jesus ben Sirach. . . . The collection is thought to have assumed its unitary form in the century before" ("The Twelve Prophets," in *The Literary Guide to the Bible* [ed. R. Alter and F. Kermode; Cambridge: Harvard University Press, 1987], 207). Marks appears to think that Sirach refers to the books, not the prophets.

might allow would be the claim that these books provide an anthology
or collection, not necessarily "a book."

Size

The second issue involves size. To speak of a book or ספר of the Twelve
suggests that this book is analogous to the other Latter Prophets, namely,
Isaiah, Jeremiah, and Ezekiel. Jeremiah is the longest prophetic book,
occupying 116 pages in one edition of the Hebrew Bible. Ezekiel is the
shortest, occupying ninety-five pages. The Twelve stands in between, with
ninety-six pages. (For the sake of completeness, Isaiah runs 105 pages.)
Simply in terms of mass or amount of text, the Twelve belongs in the
same league as the other exemplars of prophetic literature.[3] As a scroll,
probably a leather one, the Twelve would have been relatively long. For
example, 1QIsaa runs almost seven and one-half meters, whereas the
Naḥal Ḥever Minor Prophets scroll is more than ten meters long.[4] Relatively short books they might be, but when written together the Twelve
filled a scroll of a length similar to the Major Prophets.

Size alone, however, does not make a book. There is an obvious point
of contrast between the Twelve and the other three prophetic books: the
presence of an author to whom each of the other "Latter" Prophets may
be attributed. There is neither an Ezekiel nor an Isaiah to hold the
Twelve together. So the case for the Book of the Twelve will have to
rest elsewhere, either in the claim that these books were written and/or
edited with an eye to each other, or in the search for a theme or plot
that unifies this literature.

Order

The Twelve does not appear in random order. One may identify several principles at work to explain why the works appear in the order
in which they occur, even when the order varies. The discovery of such
principles suggests to some that the Twelve coheres as a book. What are
these principles, and what are their implications for the question we are
addressing?

---

[3] If M. Haran's thesis about the transition of writing on papyrus to leather is
correct, none of these prophetic texts would have been written on papyrus, but Tov
notes that the twelfth-century B.C.E. Harris papyrus (Egyptian) extends ca. 43 meters.
See "Book-Scrolls in Israel in Pre-exilic Times," *JJS* 32 (1982): 161–73.

[4] Tov, *Textual Criticism of the Hebrew Bible*, 204.

One of the principles that has affected the order of the Twelve is *chronology*. Hosea and Amos were probably the first books to be written and appear early in the collection, whereas Haggai and Zechariah were composed much later and appear near its end. Micah, due to the chronological note at its outset, must be placed after Hosea and Amos, and after Jonah, whose chronological roots are implied in 2 Kgs 14:25.

But there are troubling exceptions. Joel, which lacks any explicit historical allusion, is routinely dated to the Persian period. Yet this book appears second in the Masoretic Text. Moreover, even before Micah, whose superscription anchors it firmly to the eighth century, comes Obadiah, which dates to ca. 587. Though there is a temporal dynamic, the Twelve does not follow strict chronological order, whether putative or actual.

Another principle that has been used to explain the ordering of the Minor Prophets involves the so-called catchword. Here, the argument runs, certain books were conjoined due to comparable material near the beginning of one and the ending of another. That Amos should follow Joel may be explained in this way. The bicolon, "The Lord roars from Zion / and utters his voice from Jerusalem," occurs both near the end of Joel (4:16; Eng., 3:16) and near the beginning of Amos (1:2). Such proximity may be due to an editor placing these two books in their current order, based on this shared bicolon.[5] Habakkuk 2:20 and Zeph 1:7 offer a comparable case, with their admonition for "silence (הס)" before Yahweh.

Other factors may also have been at work. The issue of length probably played a role, moving from longer to shorter texts, as is particularly evident in the LXX order of the first five books.[6] One scholar has suggested that even geography, an alternating pattern between north and south in the first six books, affected their order.[7]

Finally, as is well-known, the LXX and the MT offer different orderings within the first six books of the Twelve. In contrast to MT, LXX reads Hosea, Amos, Micah, Joel, Obadiah, and Jonah. In LXX, Joel appears in the fourth as opposed to second position, and Jonah too is later,

---

[5] Cassuto has made this point in "The Sequence and Arrangement of the Biblical Sections," in *Biblical and Oriental Studies* (vol. 1; Jerusalem: Magnes Press, 1973), 5–6. Cf. James Nogalski, *Redactional Processes in the Book of the Twelve* (BZAW 218; Berlin: de Gruyter, 1993), 44–46.

[6] So, Marks, "Twelve Prophets," 208.

[7] Keil, as cited by R. van Leeuwen, "Scribal Wisdom and Theodicy in the Book of the Twelve," in *In Search of Wisdom: Essays in Memory of John G. Gammie* (ed. L. Perdue, B. Scott, and W. Wiseman; Louisville: Westminster/John Knox, 1993), 34.

sixth rather than fifth. By removing Joel from the early section, the LXX order more nearly mirrors the actual date of composition of the first four books. But thereafter, problems exist, since Joel and Jonah almost certainly postdate Habakkuk and Zephaniah.

The LXX evidence concerning order involves not only the ordering of the books themselves, but the ordering of the end of the Twelve, the final verses of Malachi. Of the three verses, Mal 3:22–24 (Eng., 4:4–6), the LXX places what is v. 22 in the MT, "Remember the torah of my servant Moses," after vv. 23–24, which allude to Elijah and the coming Day of Yahweh. Finally, the place of the Twelve in the Hebrew Bible is different in MT than it is in LXX, where it concludes the entire text.

In sum, several principles were apparently at work in the ordering of the Minor Prophets. That different orders achieved fixity in diverse canonical traditions does not, however, suggest that these books constitute "a literary unity."[8] To the contrary, diverse orderings argue in the direction of an anthology rather than a book.

Formation

The chronological and catchword principles can presume a situation in which the books already exist in a finished form, awaiting ordering by an editor. Is there, however, evidence that the books themselves were shaped so as to belong together?

James Nogalski has suggested as much. He has argued that an editor has revised portions of one book to enable it to be connected to another book, next to which it sits. He, too, attends to the catchword principle, but maintains that the catchwords were created for the current setting; they did not predate it. For example, Nogalski argues that Amos 9:12a reflects the vocabulary (ירשׁ) and focus on Edom and other nations that is more integral to Obad 16, 17–21. Hence, he suggests that this portion of Amos may have been introduced to help it fit better with Obadiah.[9] Similar processes were at work in the creation of Hos 14:8a (Eng., 14:7a), namely, to serve as a link to Joel through the catchwords of "grain," "vine," and "inhabitants."[10]

In a similar fashion, Jörg Jeremias has argued that an organic rela-

---

[8] So, contra B. Jones, *The Formation of the Book of the Twelve* (SBLDS 149; Atlanta: Scholars Press, 1994), 8, passim.

[9] Nogalski, *Redactional Processes in the Book of the Twelve*, 72–73.

[10] James Nogalski, *Literary Precursors to the Book of the Twelve* (BZAW 217; Berlin: de Gruyter, 1993), 69–70.

tionship existed between the earliest books of the Twelve.[11] He does not base his case on catchwords. Instead, he maintains that Hosea and Amos were created with an eye to each other. The book of Hosea exercised an influence on the composition of Amos (Amos 1:5; 2:8; 3:2; 5:25; 6:8; 7:9), whereas the book of Amos influenced late redactional additions to Hosea (e.g., Hos 4:15; 8:14).

A different sort of claim involving the formation of the Twelve has been advanced by those who suggest that a discernible editorial hand, for example, the Deuteronomist, shaped several of the Minor Prophets (Hosea, Amos, Micah, at a minimum), a collection that served as a generative core for the rest of the Twelve.

Finally, I have suggested elsewhere that the creation of the Twelve was in part accomplished by treating Malachi, which was originally one of three *maśś'ôt* that followed Zech 1–9, as a separate book. In so doing, this ancient editor construed *mal'aki* (מלאכי), which was originally a noun with pronominal suffix, "my messenger," as a proper name, Malachi. Thus, an ancient editor was able to create a roster of twelve individually named treatises, whereas earlier there had only been eleven.

So there is significant evidence that the formation of the Twelve was a complicated process, extending over a long period and attributable to many individuals. But do these developments allow for the judgment that the interrelated literatures comprise a book? Again, the answer is not self-evident.

Literary Features

Some scholars avoid discussion of the formation of the Twelve and instead attend to purely literary issues. They hold that it remains possible to read these twelve texts *as if* they were one book, though without attending either to ancient manuscript evidence or to redaction-critical issues.

If one thought that the Twelve constituted a book, one might analyze it as one would other books, assessing theme, plot, and so on. Such proposals are now being advanced. Herbert Marks has proposed the analytical vocabulary of multiple voices in one text. In his essay, however, the multiple voices overpower the notion of one text.[12] Paul House has suggested a threefold plot or movement, sin-punishment-restoration, which

[11] J. Jeremias, "Die Anfänge des Dodekapropheton: Hosea und Amos," in *Hosea und Amos: Studien zu den Anfängen des Dodekapropheton* (FAT 13; Tübingen: Mohr, 1996), 34–54.

[12] H. Marks, "Twelve Prophets" (see n. 2 above).

he links to a tripartite division of the Twelve: Hosea through Micah, Nahum through Zephaniah, and Haggai through Malachi. Nonetheless, many scholars believe that the suggestion clouds rather than reveals the secrets of the Twelve.[13] More successful, in my judgment, is Norman Gottwald's discussion of an implied narrative in the Latter Prophets, one that can be characterized as a comedy.[14] Ronald Clements's notion of patterns in the prophetic literature pushes in a similar direction.[15] The key issue is what critical vocabulary is salient — plot, point of view, imagery — and whether it is to be found in the text or imposed upon it.

I would suggest another option, namely, to assess the theme of the Twelve.[16] One phrase that occurs with striking prominence in the Twelve is יום יהוה, the Day of the Lord. It is present explicitly in all but two of the Twelve. Jonah and Nahum are the exceptions; and in Nahum the יום יהוה is implicit (Nah 1:7). In addition, references to the יום יהוה are relatively and surprisingly infrequent in the Major Prophets.[17]

The most important references to the יום יהוה in the Twelve are Hos 9:5; Joel 3:4; Amos 5:18–20; Obad 15; Mic 2:4; Hab 3:16; Zeph 1:7–16; Hag 2:23; Zech 14:1; and Mal 4:1.[18] In these and related texts, the Day of the Lord is more than just a phrase. The יום יהוה is a liminal moment when Yahweh will act as regent, often in a military manner. The day is ambiguous; it can offer weal or woe, depending on the historical circumstance. It is a day that Israel could use to interpret all of its significant historical moments.

---

[13] P. House, *The Unity of the Twelve* (JSOTSup 77; Sheffield: Sheffield Academic Press, 1990).

[14] N. Gottwald, "Tragedy and Comedy in the Latter Prophets," *Semeia* 32 (1985): 83–96.

[15] R. Clements, "Patterns in the Prophetic Canon," in *Old Testament Prophecy: From Oracles to Canon* (Louisville: Westminster/John Knox, 1996), 191–202.

[16] See T. Collins, "The Scroll of the Twelve," in *The Mantle of Elijah* (The Biblical Seminar 20; Sheffield; Sheffield Academic Press, 1993), 65, who identifies a plethora of themes: "The principal themes of the whole book are those of covenant-election, fidelity and infidelity, fertility and infertility, turning and returning, the justice of God and the mercy of God, the kingship of God, the place of his dwelling (Temple/Mount Zion), the nations as enemies, the nations as allies." This inventory neither characterizes the Twelve in distinction from other prophetic literature nor captures its essence.

[17] The phrase is considerably more prominent in Isaiah than it is in Jeremiah or Ezekiel. In Isaiah, the phrase יום יהוה appears primarily in oracles against foreign nations, e.g., 13:6; 22:5, and in later texts, e.g., 34:8, though Isa 2:11–12 may be compared with texts in the Twelve.

[18] Cf. R. Wolfe's notion of "The Day of Jahve Editor," which involves the judgment that many of these texts are secondary, in "The Editing of the Book of the Twelve," *ZAW* 12 (1935): 103–4.

Each of the Major Prophets includes a dominant theme. So, too, the Twelve. If Isaiah focuses on Zion, Jeremiah on the rhetoric of lament, and Ezekiel on the glory of Yahweh, the Twelve highlight Yahweh's day. Each of these four scrolls offers a distinctive theme.

The vocabulary of temporality — of time — is a key to understanding the Twelve, and for good reason, especially when one compares the other three prophetic books with the historical breadth offered by the Twelve. Isaiah's inaugural vision dates to 743 B.C.E. If one concludes that Isaiah 56–66 dates to the period immediately after completion of the second temple, then that book represents roughly 240 years. The chronological issue for Jeremiah is complicated due to the various ways in which Jer 1:2 may be understood. But the date itself is secure, namely, 627 B.C.E. Apart from the so-called historical appendix (ch. 52), the book appears to conclude soon after the defeat of Judah in 587. Here the chronological sweep is decidedly shorter than in Isaiah — more like forty years. Ezekiel presents the most compressed time frame, beginning in 593 and concluding in about 570 (see 29:17). So Ezekiel covers a little less than a quarter-century.

In contrast, the Twelve contains the earliest and the latest exemplars of prophetic literature. On the one hand, Amos reflects conditions of the mid–eighth century; on the other hand, Zech 9–14 stems from well into the Persian period. So, with the Twelve, we are dealing with a period of roughly four hundred years. None of the Major Prophets can compare with the historical sweep offered by the Twelve. Hence, it is utterly appropriate for these books to share a temporal lens — the Day of Yahweh — by means of which to focus their vision.

In conclusion, it is probably misleading to call the Minor Prophets a book. Something like Haran's "book-scroll" is probably more accurate, though infelicitous. I prefer to speak of a thematized anthology. This literature has been secondarily configured into twelve so-called books, with the separation of Malachi and the addition of Jonah. Moreover, they have, as a whole, been linked to other portions of the Hebrew Bible canon, overtly to the Pentateuch and the Deuteronomistic History, less explicitly to the Wisdom literature.[19] Finally, the predominant theme in this scroll is the יום יהוה, a tradition by means of which these prophets could explore both the devastation of judgment and possibilities of life beyond destruction, as they addressed Israel's existence for the better part of half a millennium.

---

[19] See van Leeuwen, "Scribal Wisdom and Theodicy" (cited above in n. 7).

2

The Production and Reading
of the Book of the Twelve

Paul L. Redditt

As of this writing, D. J. A. Clines has authored two articles under the heading, "Why Is There a Song/Book of... and What Does It Do to You If You Read It?"[1] Recent research on the Book of the Twelve suggests that Clines's questions are also appropriate for these writings. Scholars typically have acknowledged that the Twelve is reckoned as one book in the Hebrew Bible, but have continued to treat each of the Minor Prophets as a separate book or — especially in the case of Zechariah — as a collection in and of itself.

Two doctoral students have challenged that treatment with their dissertations. D. A. Schneider delineated four stages of growth for the Twelve: Hosea, Amos, and Micah were assembled first; Nahum, Habakkuk, and Zephaniah were added; then Joel, Obadiah, and Jonah; and finally Haggai, Zechariah, and Malachi. He also saw that many redactional comments within the Twelve belonged together as part of a systematic arrangement.[2] A. Y. Lee investigated the salvation passages in the Twelve for their insight into the overall understanding of the collection.[3]

Next, P. R. House studied the genre, structure, plot, use of characters, and point of view of the Twelve, concluding that the collection could and should be read as a single, literary construction.[4] O. H. Steck then compared the history of the redaction of the Twelve and of the

---

[1] D. J. A. Clines, "Why Is There a Song of Songs, and What Does It Do to You If You Read It?" *Jian Dao: A Journal of Bible and Theology* 1 (1994): 3–27, and "Why Is There a Book of Job, and What Does It Do to You If You Read It?" in *The Book of Job* (ed. W. A. M. Beuken; BETL 114; Louvain: Louvain University Press, 1994), 1–20.

[2] D. A. Schneider, "Unity of the Book of the Twelve" (Ph.D. diss., Yale University, 1979).

[3] A. Y. Lee, "Canonical Unity of the Minor Prophets" (Ph.D. diss., Baylor University, 1985).

[4] Paul R. House, *The Unity of the Twelve* (JSOTSup 97; Sheffield: Almond Press, 1990).

book of Isaiah, arguing that, at least by the final compilation of the Twelve, the books could no longer be read in isolation, but as a redacted composition.[5]

More recently, James Nogalski published a two-volume work[6] that (1) shows consistent editorial activity by means of catchwords inserted in passages at the beginnings and endings of the individual books; (2) points to two precursors of the Twelve, namely a "Deuteronomistic" collection consisting of Hosea, Amos, Micah, and Zephaniah, and the postexilic collection of Haggai/Zech 1–8;[7] (3) posits the addition of a group of books related to Joel, including Obadiah, Nahum, Habakkuk, and Malachi, which were merged into the previously existing corpora to form what might be called a "Book of the Eleven" (this author's title, not Nogalski's);[8] and (4) finds the conclusion of the process in the additions of Jonah and Zech 9–14.

Two scholars have attempted to refine some of Nogalski's conclusions. B. A. Jones argued that the Twelve originally ended with the book of Jonah, an ending preserved by 4QXII[a].[9] Aaron Schart traced seven stages in the growth of the Twelve — two stages prior to Nogalski's Deuteronomistic stage, a Deuteronomic corpus, and four subsequent stages: one adding Nahum and Habakkuk, another adding Haggai and

---

[5] O. H. Steck, *Der Abschluss der Prophetie im Alten Testament: Ein Versuch zur Frage der Vorgeschichte des Kanons* (Neukirchen-Vluyn: Neukirchener, 1991).

[6] James Nogalski, *Literary Precursors to the Book of the Twelve* (BZAW 217; Berlin and New York: de Gruyter, 1993), and *Redactional Processes in the Book of the Twelve* (BZAW 218; Berlin and New York: de Gruyter, 1993).

[7] Aaron Schart ("The Combination of Hosea, Amos, Micah, and Zephaniah on a Single Scroll: Unifying Devices and Redactional Intentions," paper presented at the Formation of the Book of the Twelve Consultation of the SBL, 1996) questioned whether the term "Deuteronomistic" should be used, while agreeing that the four belonged to a corpus, which well might be called "Deuteronomic." On the other hand, Ehud Ben Zvi ("A Deuteronomistic Redaction in/among 'The Twelve'? A Contribution from the Standpoint of the Books of Micah, Zephaniah, and Obadiah," *SBLSP, 1997,* 433–59) questions the very existence of a Deuteronomistic corpus.

[8] This aspect of Nogalski's reconstruction is unconvincing. It would seem more likely that Jonah was incorporated at the time of the Joel-related layer, forming a Book of the Twelve. If, as seems likely, Zech 9–14 was the latest addition, it came into a previously existing "Twelve" as an addition to Zechariah rather than as a thirteenth book.

[9] B. A. Jones, *The Formation of the Book of the Twelve* (SBLDS 149; Atlanta: Scholars Press, 1995), 7. On the text of the Twelve at Qumran and its fluidity, see Russell Fuller, "The Form and Formation of the Book of the Twelve: The Evidence from the Judaean Desert," in *Forming Prophetic Literature: Essays on Isaiah and the Twelve in Honor of John D. W. Watts* (ed. J. W. Watts and P. R. House; JSOTSup 235; Sheffield: Sheffield Academic Press, 1996), 86–101.

Zech 1–8 (and possibly much of Zech 9–13), a third adding Joel and Obadiah (along with Zech 14), and a fourth completing the Twelve with the addition of Jonah and Malachi.[10]

Finally, E. Bosshard-Nepustil published his dissertation investigating the intertextual connections among the prophetic books and their importance for the development of the prophetic corpus. The research proceeds from examination of important textual correlations between the Major and Minor Prophets. The correlations exhibit two main traits: on the one hand, they build connecting structures with chronological and thematic parallels and point to redactional activity that overlaps individual books; on the other hand, the correlations contain varied contents and therefore require a diachronic exegesis.

Bosshard-Nepustil identifies two exilic redactions in Isa 1–39. In the first redaction, Babel executes judgment (587/6 B.C.E.); in the second, judgment against Babel is awaited. Both redactions read Isa 1–39 and Jeremiah sequentially as consecutively ordered books. He also identifies two redactions of comparable content in the Minor Prophets. In the exilic and early postexilic periods, these redactions oriented the textual collections of, first, Hosea through Zephaniah and, later, Hosea through Zechariah, to the sequence of Isa 1–39 and Jeremiah. The latter redaction also alludes to Isa 40–66, yet presupposes that these chapters then followed Jeremiah and not Isa 1–39.[11]

These studies offer ample evidence that the Twelve underwent a series of redactions, culminating in a collection of prophetic voices, some well-known, some not, that spanned centuries.[12] This series of redactions appears to have been as deliberate as those of the Isaiah corpus, alongside of and in dialogue with which O. H. Steck and Erich Bosshard-Nepustil show the Twelve was shaped.[13]

---

[10] Aaron Schart, "Die Entstehung des Zwölfprophetenbuchs: Neubearbeitungen von Amos im Rahmen schriftenübergreifender Redaktionsprozesse" (Habilitationsschrift, Philipps-Universität Marburg, 1996), appendix 1.

[11] E. Bosshard-Nepustil, *Rezeptionen von Jesaja 1–39 im Zwölfprophetenbuch: Untersuchungen zur literarischen Verbindung von Prophetbüchern in babylonischer und persischer Zeit* (OBO 154; Fribourg, Switzerland: Universitätsverlag, 1997).

[12] Not all scholars are convinced of this point, of course. The case that the books constitute only an anthology placed together for convenience has been made by Ehud Ben Zvi ("Twelve Prophetic Books or 'The Twelve': A Few Preliminary Considerations," in Watts and House, *Forming Prophetic Literature*, 125–56).

[13] See Steck (*Abschluss der Prophetie*) and Erich Bosshard-Nepustil ("Beobachtungen zum Zwölfprophetenbuch," *BN* 40 [1987]: 36). Nogalski's Joel-related layer also exhibits knowledge of Jeremiah and Ezekiel, but those traditions do not affect the Twelve in a substantial way. See Nogalski, *Redactional Processes*, 280.

In light of this research, this essay, modeled after Clines's two studies, will address the Book of the Twelve as a redacted work by asking two questions: (1) Why is there a Book of the Twelve, and (2) How has the Book of the Twelve been read? In answer to the first question, this essay argues that the Twelve was produced for a readership of educated, literate purveyors of prophetic voices. The producers were male editors influenced by the messages of threat announced by various prophets, cultic language, and the book of Joel. These editors had connections to the upper class and centered their hopes for the future around Jerusalem, but gave little thought to how government might function properly. As the custodians of the authentic voice of God through earlier prophets, the editors were suspicious of the prophets of their own time. In answer to the second question, the article reviews selected readers, showing diverse reading agendas, but nowhere uncovering an interest in reading the Twelve as a connected discourse. The article concludes by giving three reasons for adopting that reading strategy.

Why Is There a Book of the Twelve?

The Implied Circumstances of the Text's Production

1. *The text.* Despite the modern convention, especially in connection with the Christian Old Testament, of speaking of twelve Minor Prophets, the Book of the Twelve has been recognized as a single volume as far back as 200 B.C.E., when Ben Sira mentioned the Twelve (Sir 49:10) in connection with the books of Isaiah, Jeremiah, and Ezekiel. The oldest manuscripts of the Twelve, from Qumran, show them collected into one scroll. In addition, *4 Ezra* 14 and apparently Josephus also reckon the Twelve as a single volume.[14] Likewise, in the Babylonian Talmud, *B. Bat.* 14b cites the Twelve as one book,[15] and the Masoretes added their notes to the collection as a whole.

The Twelve, however, was made up from a number of previously existing books. One of the techniques of the editors of the Twelve was to modify the endings of individual books and the beginnings of the fol-

---

[14] Josephus (*Ag. Ap.* 1.40) speaks of Moses and the prophets, who wrote thirteen books, apparently the five books of Torah, the four Former Prophets, and the four Latter Prophets (Isaiah, Jeremiah, Ezekiel, and the Twelve) familiar from the Hebrew Bible.

[15] Nogalski, *Literary Precursors,* 2–3. Cf. Jones, *Formation,* 2–13; Schart, "Entstehung des Zwölfprophetenbuchs," 8–10.

lowing books to make them fit together, as Nogalski has shown. That overall conclusion holds, even if one does not accept all of his examples.[16] The most obvious transitions include those between Hos 14:5–10 (Eng., 14:4–9) and Joel 1:2; Joel 4:16 (Eng., 3:16) and Amos 1:2; the emphasis on Edom in Amos 9:11–15 and Obadiah; Mic 7:8–20 and Nah 1:2–8; Nah 3:15–17 and Hab 3:17 (by means of allusions to Joel 1:4 and 2:25); Zeph 3:18–20 ("that time") to Hag 1 ("the time has come"); and Zech 8:9–23 and Mal 1:1–14.

Other techniques of production are also apparent. First is the use of thematic transitions between books as in the transition between Mic 7:18–19 (the destruction of Assyria) and Habakkuk (the coming of Babylon). Second, one finds echoes of striking verses reoccurring in the Twelve, such the phrase "depths of the Sea," which, in the entire Hebrew Bible, appears only in Jonah 2:4 (Eng., 2:3) and Mic 7:19. A second example is the use of Exod 34:6–7 in Joel 2:12–14 and 18; Jonah 3:9; 4:2; Mic 7:18–19; and Nah 1:3.[17] This last verse is part of an addition disrupting the alphabetical acrostic in 1:2–8 between letters *alef* and *bet*, and it provides almost indisputable evidence of redactional linking between Mic 7:8–20 and Nah 1:1–8.[18]

Schart argues that several passages long viewed as additions to their contexts can be explained as additions made during the growth of the corpus. Included among these additions are the hymns in Amos (added along with Nahum and Habakkuk); Amos 9:11–15 and Mic 4 and 5 (added along with Haggai and Zech 1–8); Zech 14 and Zeph 3:8–10 (added along with Joel and Obadiah); and Mal 3:22–24 (Eng., 4:4–6) to conclude the Twelve.[19] Katrina J. A. Larkin, in a study of Second Zechariah, points out that the Twelve opens with eschatological notes in Hos 2:2, 16–17, and 3:4–5 from the prophet himself. Other eschatological passages, often in the form of additions, include Joel 3 and 4; Amos 9:11–15; Obad 15–21; Mic 4:1–4; 4:6–8; 5:1–5; Hab 3:3–13; Zeph

---

[16] The passages are studied in Nogalski, *Literary Precursors*, 20–57.

[17] R. C. van Leeuwen, "Scribal Wisdom and Theodicy in the Book of the Twelve," in *In Search of Wisdom: Essays in Memory of John G. Gammie* (ed. L. G. Perdue, B. Scott, and W. Wiseman; Louisville: Westminster/John Knox, 1993), 39–46.

[18] Indeed, Nogalski (*Redactional Processes*, 104) points to a total of four irregularities in the half-acrostic with which Nahum opens, all of which tie directly to Micah 7. He expanded this work in "The Role of Nahum 1 in the Redaction of the Book of the Twelve, in *Among the Prophets: Language, Image, and Structure* (ed. Philip Davies and David D. J. Clines; JSOTSup 144; Sheffield: Sheffield Academic Press, 1993), 197–202.

[19] Schart, "Entstehung des Zwölfprophetenbuchs," 195–205, 210–15, 232, 248–53.

3:14–17, 18–20; Hag 2:20–23; Zech 8:20–23; much of Zech 9–14; and Mal 3:19–21, 22–24.[20]

Nogalski and/or Schart tie all but the verses in Hosea and Hag 2:20–23 to the redaction of the Twelve. For example, Nogalski shows that Obad 15a, 16–21, was composed to set the earlier Edom prophecy (1–14, 15b) in the larger redactional context of nations that had committed crimes against Jerusalem and Judah.[21] The oft-noted connection between Obad 17 and Joel 3:5 (Eng., 2:32) suggests that Larkin was correct to include Joel 3:1–5 (Eng., 2:28–32).[22] O. H. Steck also plausibly adds to these passages Zeph 3:8, 14–19, and Mal 2:10–12.[23]

In view of this redactional work, it is appropriate to raise Clines's first question: why was the Book of the Twelve produced? Clines reminds us that texts are public products, composed to be copied (i.e., published) and circulated. We may properly assume then that the Twelve was produced for a readership, likely consisting of people who already agreed with the point of view of the redacted whole, or who might be persuaded to agree with it.

2. *The public.* What might that readership look like? Again, Clines is helpful at this point. Its readers would have belonged to the literate minority in ancient Israel. They would have been wealthy enough at least to have the leisure time to read and ponder what they read. They also would have been voluntary readers; no ecclesial or political structure enforced reading, let alone adhering to, the traditions incorporated in the Twelve. Hence the book might suggest a readership that valued prophetic voices. On the other hand, the production of the book might imply that the redactors feared this prophetic community might abandon its heritage.[24]

3. *The authors/editors.* This study is concerned with the redactors of

---

[20] Katrina J. A. Larkin, *The Eschatology of Second Zechariah: A Study of the Formation of a Mantological Wisdom Anthology* (Kampen, the Netherlands: Kok Pharos, 1994), 218–19.

[21] Nogalski, *Redactional Processes,* 89–92.

[22] See Paul L. Redditt, "The Book of Joel and Peripheral Prophecy," *CBQ* 48 (1986): 230–31, where the argument is made that, except for 4:4–8, 3:1–5 constitutes the latest passage in Joel.

[23] Steck, *Abschluss,* 37 and 196–98. Cf. E. Bosshard-Nepustil and R. G. Kratz, "Maleachi im Zwölfprophetenbuch," *BN* 52 (1990): 29, who also add 1:14a.

[24] Rüdiger Lux concludes that the book of Jonah was written for a prophetic group and their sympathizers who saw prophecy in crisis and doubted their own commission (*Jona: Prophet zwischen 'Verweigerung' und 'Gehorsam'; Eine erzählanalytische Studie* [Göttingen: Vandenhoeck & Ruprecht, 1994], 208–9). Such a motivation could also underlie the collection of the Twelve itself.

the Twelve and the implications of their work. In particular, the study focuses on those editors whose work resulted in the collection of the Twelve as opposed to the individual books themselves. Even on that point, however, one must be cautious, since one cannot rule out the possibility that one or more of the books (e.g., Joel, Obadiah) adapted existing material for its position in the Twelve.[25] Nor will this study focus on the work of the Deuteronomistic editor[26] postulated by both Nogalski and Schart or on the editor of Haggai–Zech 1–8, whose works were precursors to the Twelve. As far as possible, this study will limit itself to the work of redactors who brought those corpora together and increased their number to twelve. The number and actual identity of those redactors will remain unknown, of course, but five matrices of their thought and work will be explored.

(a) *The theological matrix.* Three influences on the theology of the redactors can be inferred from what they included. First, in connection with his postulated "Deuteronomistic" corpus, Nogalski speaks of an emphasis on God's judgment, which ultimately became the basis for explaining Jerusalem's destruction.[27] Those motifs are crucial to Hosea, Amos, Micah, and Zephaniah, whether "Deuteronomistic" is the correct name for the corpus or not. Those motifs also carry through most of the other books of the Twelve, including even the postexilic prophets of Haggai, Zech 1–8, and Malachi, who had to explain the ongoing conditions of their day.

A second influence is cultic language, the clearest example of which is the confession in Exod 34:6–7, used by Joel 2:13, Jonah 4:2, Mic 7:18, and Nah 1:2–3a.[28] Not surprisingly, the redactors also betray a serious interest in Jerusalem, a theme to be explored in more detail later.

The third discernible influence is the theology of the book of Joel. Nogalski argues that the book may well have been compiled by a redactor for its place in the Twelve. If so, the entire book is evidence of his theology. Even if that is not so, however, the book exerted strong influence on the redactors of the Twelve. Nogalski notes, for example, that in

---

[25] See Nogalski, *Redactional Processes,* 276; so also Schart, "Entstehung des Zwölf-prophetenbuchs," 256.

[26] The distinction is simple. Since the books of Hosea, Amos, Micah, and Zephaniah are scattered from first to ninth among the Twelve, editorial additions in the seams between the books as they now stand were added subsequently to the composition of the Deuteronomistic corpus and belong to this study.

[27] Nogalski, *Literary Precursors,* 279.

[28] Van Leeuwen, "Scribal Wisdom and Theodicy in the Book of the Twelve," 31–49, esp. 39–48.

Nahum and Habakkuk the redactors interpret the locust plagues of Joel as the armies of Assyria and Babylon, and they see the reconstruction of the temple described in Haggai and Zech 1–8 as the beginning of the restoration of Yahweh's blessing.[29]

These three influences come together in the eschatology of the redactors of the Twelve. A strong note of judgment from the preexilic prophets combines with the postexilic hope for a better day. Redactional additions from Amos 9:12a through Mal 3:22–24 promise that new day, which will yet come if Israel will only heed God's word.

(*b*) *The gender matrix.* One should probably concede that from beginning to end the redactors (as well as the readers) of the Twelve were male. They may have exhibited less gender bias than the materials they inherited, however. A few examples of their differences must suffice. The book of Hosea opens with its depiction of the prophet's marriage to Gomer and her harlotry. To be sure her behavior is condemned less than Israel's idolatry, and Hosea even has God decline to punish the women for harlotry and adultery on the grounds that the men committed the same sins (4:14). Even so, Hosea and God are both portrayed as wronged males. Next, Amos spoke contemptuously of the women of Samaria, calling them "cows of Bashan" (4:1). Punishment for Amaziah's opposition to Amos includes Amaziah's death and his wife becoming a prostitute (7:17). Nahum 3:4–6 depicts the city Nineveh metaphorically as a prostitute, whose skirt God lifts up to expose her to all peoples, after which he throws filth at her. Finally, Zechariah's seventh vision (5:5–8) portrays wickedness as a woman in a basket, like a genie in a bottle.

One need only contrast these passages with Mal 2:10–16, which Steck derives from a redactor of the Twelve. There, without denigrating women, men are accused of infidelity to God and to their wives. Even if, as some scholars claim, the passage deals with idolatry and not adultery at all, its difference from Hosea is still marked.[30]

In Joel 3:1–2 (Eng., 2:28–29), a passage Larkin attributes to the editors of the Twelve, one encounters an agenda for the future in which women and men, young and old, servant and master receive God's charisma and have the same roles. That view, however, seems excep-

---

[29] Nogalski, *Redactional Processes,* 276.

[30] Even so, Mal 3:23 (Eng., 4:6) exhibits the use of male-gendered terms characteristic of the Bible: God "will turn the heart of the fathers with respect to the sons, and the heart of the sons with respect to the fathers."

tional in the Twelve and may belong to an earlier stage in the growth of Joel.[31]

(c) *The class matrix.* As noted above, one may assume that the Twelve emerged from a class with sufficient leisure to follow intellectual pursuits. Its readers, thus, would have had connections to the upper class and in some cases would have been wealthy. The Twelve never addresses the poor, who for the most part would have been illiterate anyway. Even the depiction in Zeph 3:11–13 of Jerusalemites as lowly and humble people who would one day "pasture and lie down" smacks more of the wealthy person's idealization of pastoral life than of the day-by-day labor and drudgery associated with it.[32]

The individual books among the Twelve arise from different types of social groups. Joel, Zech 9–14, and Malachi at least[33] appear to have originated among groups that moved to the periphery of Israelite life from positions within or close to the power structure. On the other hand, Nahum, Haggai, and Zech 1–8 appear to have emerged from the power structure and even to have supported it, though only Haggai and Zech 1–8 among them hitched their hopes directly to the temple and the house of David. While these observations do not allow more conclusive statements about the class matrix of the redactors of the Twelve, they do raise the issue of the redactors' political aspirations.

(d) *The political matrix.* Given the extensive criticism of kings (Hos 5:1; Amos 7:10), rulers (Mic 3:1–3, 9–11), priests (Hos 4:4–10; Mal 1:6–14), prophets (Mic 3:5–7; Zech 13:3–6), and other members of the power structure (Amos 6:1–7; Zeph 3:1–4) in the books making up the Twelve, however, one should admit the possibility that the Twelve was collected by people who either wished to correct the perceived shortcomings of Judah's leaders or perhaps even aspired to leadership in the postexilic community, but who were not actually part of the ruling structure, either politically or religiously.[34]

---

[31] Redditt, "Book of Joel and Peripheral Prophecy," 231–33.

[32] Nogalski, *Literary Precursors,* 203, n. 77, argues for a date well into the Persian period for these verses. While they might not derive from the same redactor as 3:18–20, with its connections to Mic 4:4–6 and Hag 1, they postdate the Deuteronomistic corpus.

[33] See Redditt, "Book of Joel and Peripheral Prophecy," 225–40; idem, "Israel's Shepherds: Hope and Pessimism in Zechariah 9–14," *CBQ* 51 (1989): 631–42; idem, "The Two Shepherds in Zechariah 11:4–17," *CBQ* 55 (1993): 676–86; and idem, "The Book of Malachi in Its Social Setting," *CBQ* 56 (1994): 240–55.

[34] Raymond F. Person (*Second Zechariah and the Deuteronomic School* [JSOTSup 167; Sheffield: Sheffield Academic Press, 1993], 154) called such dichotomization "sim-

Of the passages Nogalski studies for catchwords linking the individual books of the Twelve, only Amos 9:11–15 makes reference to the Davidic king. Amos 9:11, 12b, 13aα, 14–15 (reflecting the hopes of returning exiles) form part of a pro-Jerusalem addition to Amos, but are not part of the work of the redactors of the Twelve, who added 9:12a to anticipate Obad 17–21 and 9:13 employing the language of Joel.[35]

It is instructive to notice the difference between Amos 9:11 and 9:12a. Amos 9:11 (from returning exiles) looks forward to raising the fallen booth of David, while 9:12a (from the redactors of the Twelve) looks forward to the political domination of Jerusalem over Edom and others. Hence, the redactors are pro-Jerusalem, but the Davidic house seems no longer to have been an issue.[36] In fact, one finds little indication how the redactors thought government might function, implying perhaps a willingness to accept the prevailing arrangement, provided the rulers in Jerusalem paid more attention to God's word as expressed through past prophets.

If that is so, it raises the question of their view of the foreign power holding hegemony over Judah at that time. When was that? Nogalski argues that "the formative work on this larger corpus took place in the latter part of the Persian period, while the subsequent additions (Jonah, Zech 9–14) did not enter the corpus until after 332."[37] His dates are based on his view that Joel dates from the late Persian period, while Jonah and Second Zechariah come from the Greek period. It is, however, possible to date Joel between 515 and 445[38] and the redaction of

---

plistic," and indeed it would be if one supposed that there were only two groups in postexilic Judah, one ruling and the other opposing. In fact, there seem to have been a number of peripheral groups producing literature in opposition to the religious and/or political elite. Person himself agrees that Second Zechariah was an eschatological response of a disillusioned group distancing itself from the hierarchy in light of unmet expectations. Further, one must reckon with the possibility that the power structure itself was not always united. The redactors of the Twelve showed no interest in a restored Davidic king, even though *some* of the futuristic passages in the Twelve from the early years after the exile certainly did (e.g., Amos 9:11, 9:14–15, and Zech 9:1–10).

[35] Nogalski, *Literary Precursors*, 121–22.

[36] K. E. Pomykala argues that early Judaism exhibited no continuous, widespread, or dominant expectation of a Davidic Messiah (*The Davidic Dynasty Tradition in Early Judaism: Its History and Significance for Messianism* [SBLEJL 7; Atlanta: Scholars Press, 1995], 270). Rather, such an expectation can be dated only from the middle of the first century B.C.E.

[37] Nogalski, *Redactional Processes*, 280.

[38] Redditt, "Joel and Peripheral Prophecy," 233–35.

Zech 9–14 soon after the career of Nehemiah, perhaps by 400.[39] Nor does the existence of Greek parallels to the sea episode in Jonah necessitate a date during the Greek period for Jonah since Wolff adduces parallels from the Greek singer Arion, who flourished ca. 620.[40] Thus, the addition of the Joel-related layer (including Jonah, contra Nogalski) could have come in the late fifth century and the addition of Zech 9–14 anytime after ca. 400.

Relations between Persia and Palestine were probably not always smooth, though one would not know that from the Hebrew Bible, which reports only positive events like the Edict of Cyrus, the rebuilding of the temple, the repair of Jerusalem's wall with Persian permission, and Ezra's mission. Difficulties within the community, as late as the first year of Xerxes, typically are blamed on people in Samaria (Ezra 4:6). Both Ezra and Nehemiah claim to have come to Jerusalem under Persian appointment, and it seems likely that rebuilding the wall signaled Persian plans to elevate the status of Jerusalem as a commercial and/or political center, which Samaria and her Judean sympathizers would naturally have opposed. No later than the time of Nehemiah, Judah had its own governor, appointed by the Persians.[41]

One may infer that the redactors of the Twelve had no fundamental objection to that arrangement. A similar attitude is observable in narratives from the Diaspora during the reign of Xerxes and later. The book of Esther and especially the court narratives of Dan 1–6 show that while things could go badly wrong for Jews in the Diaspora, some educated Jews considered it possible not only to get along but even to prosper.[42]

Finally, one should recognize that among literati the ability to read and write is a form of power. The redactors of the Twelve, then, may have been satisfied with the opportunity to compile, edit, and "publish" their prophetic traditions alongside those of Isaiah. Their work as curators of those traditions, which granted them the power to influence the thinking and behavior of other people, may have seemed a congenial or even superior alternative to the powers of procurators.

---

[39] Paul L. Redditt, "Nehemiah's First Mission and the Date of Zechariah 9–14," *CBQ* 56 (1994): 675–77.

[40] H. W. Wolff, *Dodekapropheten 3: Obadja und Jona* (BKAT 14/3; Neukirchen-Vluyn: Neukirchener, 1977), 86.

[41] On the issue of governors before Nehemiah, see the opposing views of S. E. McEvenue, "The Political Structure in Judah from Cyrus to Nehemiah," *CBQ* 43 (1981): 353–64, and C. L. Meyers and E. M. Meyers, *Haggai, Zechariah 1–8* (AB 25B; Garden City, N.Y.: Doubleday, 1987), 13–17.

[42] J. J. Collins, *Daniel* (Hermeneia; Minneapolis: Fortress, 1993), 194, 273.

(*e*) *The Jerusalem matrix.* The overwhelming interest in Jerusalem among most of the latest books among the Twelve (e.g., Obadiah, Haggai, Zech 1–8, Joel, Malachi, and Zech 9–14) and in redactional seams between the books suggests that the Twelve was edited there. Again, a search of the passages in those seams is the place to study the redactors' view of Jerusalem. The first seam to address the issue is Joel 4:16a/Amos 1:2a, which reads:

> The Lord roars from Zion,
> and utters his voice from Jerusalem.... (NRSV)

Jerusalem and the temple function here as the holy city and sanctuary (Joel 4:17),[43] the abode of God on earth, that is, as Judah's version of the center or navel of the earth, the place from which God administers both blessing (4:18) and punishment (4:19). This idea is neither new nor unique to the redactors of the Twelve; it continues the temple tradition in a postmonarchical time. The monarchy, in both the north and the south, may have failed, resulting in subjugation to foreign kingdoms and even exile, but God would avenge the destruction of Jerusalem, become a refuge for God's people, and both Jerusalem and Judah would be reinhabited (Joel 4:16, 20–21). In Amos the same roar of Yahweh that *would* mean life and blessing to the people of postexilic Jerusalem/Zion *had* meant punishment to preexilic Israel, for reasons Amos 1:3–9:10 would make perfectly clear.

Obadiah 15–21 again takes up the Zion motif. In contrast with Edom, which God would punish for its actions during the sack of Jerusalem by Nebuchadnezzar, a holy remnant of exiles would survive (Obad 17) and go up to Jerusalem, from which they would rule Mount Esau (Obad 21).[44] Two other texts in particular work with the alternative fates of Jerusalem/Judah and Edom. The first is Joel 3:5 (Eng., 2:32), which cites Obad 17. The difference between them was that Obad 17–21 thought in terms of returnees from the exile, whereas Joel 3:5, presumably written later, focused instead on a group that called upon the Lord.

---

[43] Jonah 2:3, 5 also refers to the temple as holy, but Nogalski's catchwords between Jonah and other texts are not as clear as here.

[44] These sentiments may have been superimposed over older, somewhat conflicting traditions. One tradition (Obad 18) saw the Joseph tribes capturing Esau, while a second (Obad 19) saw Judeans in the Negev capturing Esau, as well as the Shephelah, Ephraim, and Samaria, while Benjamin captured Gilead. Yet a third (Obad 20) envisioned some northern Israelites (obscurity in the text precludes saying who) taking possession of much of Phoenicia, while exiles from Jerusalem in Sepharad (location uncertain) repossessed the Negev.

They would be numbered among the survivors. The second text to explore this issue is Mal 1:2–5,[45] in which the steps toward recovery made by Judah are contrasted with the present and future destitution of Esau as evidence of God's continued love for Jacob/Judah and God's power beyond the borders of Judah. The extent to which the redactors of the Twelve reworked this passage may be left open; its content resonated with theirs.

As mentioned earlier, the emphasis on "time" in Zeph 3 and Hag 1 connects those two books. In other words, the temple was essential to the fruition of God's promises to the people. When, however, it was completed, the new day anticipated in Zech 8 did not dawn, and the book of Malachi was added to Haggai/Zech 1–8 to show why: the priests and the people alike had defiled the sanctuary and broken their covenant with God. The new day had to wait for the rectification of those wrongs. The redactor of the book of Malachi anticipated God's coming to the temple to purge it (Mal 3:1–4), while the redactors of the Twelve looked for God to send Elijah back to rectify matters lest God again put the people under the ban (Mal 3:23–24 [Eng., 4:5–6]).

In view of this interest in Jerusalem and the temple, it is surprising that the redactors of the Twelve did not have more to say about temple personnel. How should one read that phenomenon? Since the collection obviously implies a group interested in prophets and prophecy, a lack of interest in assuming priestly prerogatives or functions might not be surprising. Possessing God's word, they did not need further instruction; they needed to obey the teaching they had instead of repeating the mistakes of their predecessors (cf. Mal 3:16, 18). Further, the subsequent inclusion of Zech 9–14 implies that the redactors perhaps shared the mistrust of contemporary prophecy voiced in Zech 13:2–5. If so, they would scarcely have desired to hold a prophetic office either, if such an office even still existed. Instead, the redactors of the Twelve served as curators of the word of God through the line of prophets showcased in the Twelve.

---

45 These verses also presuppose a later time period than the book of Obadiah, in that Edom in Obadiah appears still to have been standing, but to have fallen already in Malachi. This sequence seems to corroborate the general consensus that Obadiah was composed in the sixth century not long after the destruction of Jerusalem, while Malachi was written in the fifth century. Julia M. O'Brien disagrees with this conventional date for Malachi (*Priest and Levite in Malachi* [SBLDS 121; Atlanta: Scholars Press, 1990], 113–33). Even if she is correct, the conclusions drawn here about the redaction of the Twelve would not be affected.

4. *The question of canon.* Two passages in particular raise the question
of canon. The first is Zech 13:2–5, which recasts Amos 7:14, in which
Amos denies that he is a prophet. Zechariah 13:5 reiterates Amos's de-
nial with the intention of showing that prophetic contemporaries were
illegitimate, presumably because authentic prophecy had been vouch-
safed to the faithful. This redactor echoes the sentiment of the redactor
of Haggai/Zech 1–8, who said (Zech 1:5–6) that while neither the fathers nor the prophets had survived, the word of God that came to the
fathers through the prophets had survived and would continue to guide
God's people if they would obey. The redactors of the Twelve would have
had no difficulty agreeing with these sentiments and seeing themselves
as the custodians of the words of the prophets.

The second passage is Mal 3:22–24 (Eng., 4:4–6), penned by the
redactors of the Twelve.[46] Those verses indeed look forward to a new
Elijah, who would come before the Day of the Lord, but for all their op-
timism about a future Elijah, they say nothing about present prophets.
More important, they had in view Moses and the original Elijah, representatives of the Law and the Prophets. In other words, those verses
presuppose a canon including at least Deuteronomy (if not the whole
Pentateuch), the Former Prophets including Elijah (in other words the
Deuteronomistic History), and the Twelve. Until Elijah should return,
the word of God was available to be read.

The Implied Psychological or Inner Circumstances of the Text's Production

Clines advocates sifting a text for the implied inner conflicts of its
author. To do so one could ask such questions as: What does the author
seem to fear? What does he wish for? What inner needs does writing this
text meet? Clearly these are not the questions of a clinical psychologist
working with a patient, but questions for exploring a piece of literature
in an attempt to articulate motives for its production.

---

[46] This point has been adequately argued elsewhere. See Wilhelm Rudolph,
Haggai—Sacharja 1–8—Sacharja 9–14—Maleachi (KAT 13/4; Gütersloh: Mohn,
1976), 291. On the other hand, Joyce Baldwin (*Haggai, Zechariah, Malachi* [Tyndale
Old Testament Commentaries; London: Tyndale, 1972], 251), Beth Glazier-
McDonald (*Malachi, the Divine Messenger* [SBLDS 98; Atlanta: Scholars Press, 1987],
245, 262, 267), and Pieter A. Verhof (*The Books of Haggai and Malachi* [NICOT; Grand
Rapids: Eerdmans, 1978], 163, 337) argue that the verses are authentic. Either way,
the point being made here is that the redactor was looking elsewhere than the book
of Malachi.

One would surmise that the redactors of the Twelve, these curators of the collected word of God, might well fear new prophetic voices. T. W. Overholt observes that the genuineness of prophecy lies in the eye of the beholder. That is, prophecy did not die out in the fifth or fourth century B.C.E.; rather, Israelite society ceased, "at least for the moment, to credit (authorize) specific incidences of prophetic behavior."[47] Zechariah 13:2–5 is evidence that people still styled themselves as prophets, and the passage cautioned its readers against heeding them. Perhaps the redactors of the Twelve shared that fear.

It might be worth venturing a couple of guesses about the nature of challenges from the new prophets. Perhaps they advocated acceding to Persian directives that the redactors deemed counter to Israelite faith or practice. Or perhaps they advocated novel "messages from God" that were theologically unacceptable to the redactors. In other words, perhaps the redactors feared that the community as a whole, or even their readers, would seek other authorities than themselves and the prophets they so treasured.

Whatever the precise nature of their fear, the act of collecting the Twelve would seem to have met their need and their perception of the larger community's need for an authoritative voice from God that stood above competing voices. People typically fear new ideas if they perceive themselves to be holding their own or improving in areas of life that matter to them, or if they fear the new ideas will threaten them. In either situation, they seek support for their interests in their received traditions and values.

Judging by the eschatological tone of their work, the redactors thought the future could be better than the present. Judging by the tone of warning in Mal 3:23–24 (Eng., 4:5–6; cf. Mal 3:16, 18 again), they feared the ruin of the Israelite community if it did not mend its ways and avoid the mistakes of earlier generations that had failed to live as God had directed through Moses and the prophets. By publishing the Book of the Twelve, they meant to aid in averting God's wrath in the future.

How Has the Book of the Twelve Been Read?

Until now this essay has dealt with the redactors of the Twelve, who were themselves readers and shapers of the written text. Now it turns to

---

[47] T. W. Overholt, "The End of Prophecy: No Players without a Program," *JSOT* 42 (1988): 112. Cf. F. E. Greenspahn, "Why Prophecy Ceased," *JBL* 108 (1989): 42–47.

generations of other people who have read the Book of the Twelve with this question in mind: what happens to you if you read the Book of the Twelve? Lest this essay become a multivolume book, it will be possible to survey only a few readers and merely to suggest their reading strategies and results. What is clear is that readers historically have approached the Twelve as independent works, not as a collected whole.

The Earliest Readers

1. *The readers implied by the Book of the Twelve.* House points to three differences between the redactors and their readers. (*a*) The norms of the reader are not always those of the various authors. In the Twelve, he notes, Israel never repents, never changes, and never follows Yahweh. In Jonah, Nineveh does, but in Amos, Hosea, Micah, and Zephaniah, Israel and Judah do not. Even in Haggai, Zechariah, and Malachi, it is not clear whether the postexilic community embraces God's ways as set forth by the Twelve Prophets. (*b*) Unlike the prophets and redactors, the people behaved as if the nation had no future. They failed to understand the ramifications of the Day of Yahweh and to live accordingly, and they never understood that they (or at least part of them) were the remnant God would restore (Mal 3:16–18). (*c*) The readers also failed to grasp the significance of their own history. All they could see was their present. In the postexilic period, they lost sight of God's historical covenant with Israel (Mal 1:2–5), the sanctity of temple worship (Mal 1:6–14), and their obligation to keep the commandments (Mal 2:10–16; cf. Zech 1:1–6; 7:1).[48]

2. *Sirach.* The earliest external witness to the Twelve is Sir 49:10, which reads: "May the bones of the Twelve Prophets send forth new life from where they lie, for they comforted the people of Jacob and delivered them with confident hope" (NRSV). Not only does that passage treat the prophets as a group, it also emphasizes what House called the collection's *U*-shaped comic framework, which ends on a note of triumph.[49] What should happen to readers of the Twelve, according to Sirach, is that they should take hope from God's message to the people.

3. *The biblical commentaries among the Dead Sea Scrolls.* Another early reader of the Twelve is the author(s) of a series of biblical commentaries among the Dead Sea Scrolls. They include commentaries on four books among the Twelve, specifically Hosea (4Q166–7), Micah (1Q14),

---

48 House, *Unity of the Twelve*, 238–39.
49 Ibid., 123.

Nahum (4Q169), and Habakkuk (1QpHab), and exhibit a common concern with the earlier history of their own community. Their reading strategy consisted of finding key terms or catchwords with which they could apply a passage under discussion to the past or future of Israel in general, or to their own movement in particular.

One example must suffice. Habakkuk 1:6a, in which God promised Habakkuk he would send the Chaldeans to Judah, became a prediction of the coming of the Kittim (or Romans). In the succeeding verses of Hab 1, the commentator scoured the text for correspondences between the two peoples, in particular their prowess in war, their haughtiness, even a metaphor about eagles. Indeed, the point of sending the Chaldeans, namely to punish the wicked in Israel, became lost in the *Habakkuk Commentary,* which interpreted 1:12–13a to mean that God would punish the nations through the hand of the community itself. This example shows that the text lost its rootedness in the past struggles among Israelites, between Israelites and non-Israelites, informed the author's community about its own struggle for identity, and bolstered their struggle for survival.

Selected Early Christian Writers

1. *Readings from the New Testament.* New Testament authors, naturally, read the Twelve from a different perspective, namely in light of the experience of the early church. Three books, Matthew, Romans, and Revelation, will be reviewed for their authors' reading strategy and use of the Twelve. A few examples from each must suffice.

One of the special interests of the gospel of Matthew was to show that Jesus was the Jewish Messiah promised in the Hebrew Scriptures. The author of Matthew read the Twelve from that perspective, and used several verses to help make that point.[50] In the birth narrative, Matt 2:6 cites Mic 5:2 as proof not only that Jesus descended from David, but also that the Messiah would be born in Bethlehem. Next, Matt 2:15 says that the return of the infant Jesus and his family from Egypt fulfilled Hos 11:1, a verse that reminded Israel about the exodus. Last, Matt 21:5 says that Jesus' triumphal entry fulfilled Zech 9:9.

The gospel of Matthew also portrayed Jesus as a teacher. In doing so, it twice had Jesus quote the Twelve to make a point. In 9:13 (cf. 12:7) he directs the Pharisees, who had criticized him for eating with sinners,

---

[50] Scholars long have questioned the historicity of several of the events that will be discussed. The issue in this essay is not whether the events happened, but how the gospel of Matthew used the Twelve.

to learn the true meaning of Hos 6:6: "I desire mercy, not sacrifice." Likewise, in 11:10, Jesus says that John the Baptist was the messenger predicted in Mal 3:1, and in 11:14 he equates that messenger with Elijah in Mal 4:5 (MT 3:23). These references to the Twelve show the author's concern to present Jesus as the one who fulfilled and taught Scripture, but they give little insight into how the evangelist viewed the Book of the Twelve itself.

In various places in the book of Romans, the Apostle Paul drew upon the Twelve. Probably the most famous instance was his use of Hab 2:4 in Rom 1:17 (cf. Gal 3:11): "The one who is righteous will live by faith." In doing so, Paul makes the verse say something quite different than other Jewish readers might have said. Anders Nygren may overstate the difference between Paul and the synagogue on the issue of faith and works, but he expresses Paul's use of the text succinctly: "He takes it out of the hands of the representatives of the righteousness of the law and makes it the motto and crowning expression of a view which is the direct opposite, of the righteousness of faith."[51] In 10:13, Paul also used Joel 2:32 ("Then everyone who calls on the name of the Lord shall be saved") as evidence that faith in God was sufficient for salvation.

In Rom 9, Paul used three different passages from the Twelve in dealing with Israel's refusal to accept Christian faith. In 9:13, he quotes Mal 1:2b–3a ("I have loved Jacob, but Esau I have hated") as evidence that the chronological priority of Israel was no evidence that Jews were God's elect. In 9:25 he quotes Hos 2:23 ("and I will say to Lo-ammi, 'You are my people'"), words addressed by God to Israel, to the effect that God called Gentiles to be among God's people. In 9:26, Paul used Hos 1:10 to the same effect. Other examples could be cited, but these will suffice. As with the author of Matthew, Paul's treatment of texts from the Twelve gives little indication of how he viewed the collection.

If the gospel of Matthew and the Apostle Paul used the Twelve as evidence for their claims vis-à-vis Judaism, the book of Revelation used the Twelve in a more congenial fashion. Revelation 1–4 employs in its imagery the motif of the golden candlestick with seven lamps from Zech 4, although it modified the candlestick into seven candlesticks, one for the "angel" of each of the seven churches. Similarly, Rev 5:6 lifts the motif of seven eyes from Zech 4:10, and the four horsemen of Rev 6:1–8 derive from Zech 1:8. The description of opening the sixth seal (Rev 6:12) includes catastrophes to the sun and moon similar to those described

---

[51] Anders Nygren, *Commentary on Romans* (Philadelphia: Fortress, 1949), 82–83.

in Joel 3:4 (Eng., 2:31). Talk of the "great day of...wrath" in Rev 6:17 is borrowed from Zeph 1:14–15. These examples show the author of Revelation drawing upon prophetic and proto-apocalyptic imagery of the Twelve in developing the book's own symbolism, but do not reflect either a systematic reading of the Twelve or a treatment of it as one volume.

2. *Jerome and John Chrysostom*. Among the early Christian theologians, Jerome and John Chrysostom may be taken as typical. In his preface to the Twelve Minor Prophets, Jerome at least notes that Jews count the Twelve as one book. John Chrysostom, in his extant works, comments on all of the Twelve except Obadiah, but only in a piecemeal fashion. The Twelve is cited about half as often as Isaiah, about as frequently as Jeremiah, and far more often than Ezekiel.[52] Typical is his use of passages from Habakkuk, Haggai, Hosca, Malachi, and Micah as proof texts for Jesus' second coming.[53]

Readings from the Talmud

The rabbis recognized that a late hand redacted the Twelve, and they ascribed the book (along with Ezekiel, Daniel, and Esther) to the Men of the Great Assembly, but they never seemed to base their reading strategies on that observation.[54] One place they might have done so was at the beginning of Hosea. Indeed, they read Hos 1:2 to the effect that Hosea was the first (and thus the greatest) prophet with whom God spoke, and asked why the book of Hosea did not come first in the prophetic corpus, that is, in front of Isaiah (*B. Bat.* 14b). Their answer was that such a small book might well have gotten lost that way. By implication so might all of the others. Hence the rabbis concluded that the Twelve were joined together to prevent their being lost (*Pesaḥ.* 87b).

If one looked elsewhere for a discussion of the Twelve as a whole, its conclusion in Mal 3:22–24 (Eng., 4:4–6), with its retrospective look at Moses and Elijah, might fit the bill. Such was not the case, however. *M. 'Ed.* 8:7 simply observes that 3:23–24 predicts that Elijah will return to bring peace to the world. *'Erub.* 43b cites v. 23 in connection with

---

[52] See R. A. Krupp, *Saint John Chrysostom: A Scripture Index* (New York, London, and Lanham, Md.: University Press of America, 1984), 89–94.

[53] See John Chrysostom, *Manual of Christian Doctrine* (Philadelphia: John Joseph McVey, 1906), 64–67.

[54] *B. Bat.* 15a

the subject of whether one should drink wine on the Sabbath! *Šabb.* 89a, commenting on v. 22, observes that the law was named after Moses because he disparaged himself. Comments on the verses immediately preceding vv. 22–24 yield similar findings. *Roš Haš.* 17a applied v. 21 to sinners who go to Gehinnom; their body will be consumed, their soul burned, and the wind will scatter their remains. *'Abod. Zar.* 4a applies 3:21 to the future world, and *Ned.* 8b relates 3:19 to the profanation of the name of God. In short, the Talmud records only interpretation of individual verses, not comments on the Twelve as a whole.

In other places, the Talmud cites verses from the Twelve as proof texts for various doctrines. A glance at two texts important to Christian interpreters will illustrate typical rabbinical readings of the Twelve. *Sanh.* 99a gives Zech 9:9 a messianic interpretation, but *Bek.* 56b relates that verse to dreams by saying that if one dreams of a donkey one may hope for salvation. *Sanh.* 98b interprets Mic 5:2 as a reference to Roman power over Israel, which was necessary before the son of David could return. *Sukkah* 52b names the seven shepherds of Mic 5:4: David will stand in the middle with the pre-Israelite figures Adam, Seth, and Methuselah on his right and the Israelite heroes Abraham, Jacob, and Moses on his left. The eight princes of Mic 5:4 are identified as Jesse, Saul, Samuel, Amos, Zephaniah, Zedekiah, the Messiah, and Elijah. While such interpretations reflect the rabbis' obvious mastery of Torah and Nebiim, they give no indication that the rabbis read the Twelve as a single book. Indeed, the topical structure of the Talmud precludes their treating any book as a connected whole.

On the other hand, Schart points to the nontalmudic *Pirqe Eliezer* 43 as one place at which he can show a rabbi reading two books among the Twelve in canonical order. In Jonah 3:4, the prophet predicts the destruction of Nineveh in forty days, but that disaster was averted by the penance of its inhabitants. Nahum 2 and 3 likewise predict the overthrow of Nineveh, a prediction which exercised Eliezer in light of God's decision to spare the city, as reported in Jonah 3:10. In other words, his reading of Jonah created a problem in reading Nahum, two books later. His solution, by the way, was to posit a period of forty years (derived from Jonah's mention of forty days) between the career of Jonah and that of Nahum, during which time the inhabitants of Nineveh had backslidden.[55]

---

[55] Schart, "Entstehung des Zwölfprophetenbuchs," 26.

The Reformers Luther and Calvin

Both Martin Luther and Jean Calvin lectured on the books of the Bible, including the Twelve. Neither reformer, however, read the Twelve as an integrated compilation. Their reading strategies can be reviewed quickly.

1. *Martin Luther.* In his lectures on the Minor Prophets, Luther claimed that "all the prophets have one and the same message, for this is their one aim; they are all looking toward the coming of Christ or to the coming kingdom of Christ. All their prophecies look to this, and we must relate them to nothing else."[56] Not everything in a prophetic book constituted prophecy, of course, and Luther thought some prophecies dealt with events leading up to Jesus. Even so, every prophetic message in some way pointed to Jesus. His handling of the book of Joel will make his reading strategy clear. Luther understood Joel 1 to refer to the events of the prophet's own time. With Joel 2, however, prophecy began, in this case the prophecy of a locust plague upon the Jews. At 2:28 (MT 3:1) the words no longer applied to ancient Israel; rather, the prophet spoke of the Holy Spirit. The final chapter applied to the kingdom of Christ.[57]

2. *Jean Calvin.* Calvin's lectures on the Minor Prophets, committed to writing by his students, open with these words: "[The Twelve Minor Prophets] have been long ago joined together, and their writings have been reduced to one volume; and for this reason, lest by being extant singly in our hands, they should, as often happens, disappear in the course of time on account of their brevity."[58] Calvin was simply reiterating — knowingly or not — the opinion voiced in *B. Bat.* 14b about the preservation of the Twelve. In the lectures, Calvin introduced each of the Twelve, but never as part of a continuing plot. He adopted a reading strategy common to that which he employed in the Major Prophets, in which he also spoke of the Jewish community as a church, and offered christological interpretations of the passages predominantly used by the Christian church as predictions of Jesus.[59]

---

[56] Martin Luther, *Luther's Works: Eighteen Lectures on the Minor Prophets* (ed. Hilton C. Oswald; St. Louis: Concordia, 1975), 1.79.

[57] Ibid., 405–6.

[58] Jean Calvin, *Hosea* (vol. 1 of *Commentaries on the Twelve Minor Prophets;* Grand Rapids: Eerdmans, 1950), 35.

[59] In connection with Isaiah, Calvin translates *'almāh* in 7:14 as "virgin" and understands "Immanuel" as Christ (*Commentary on the Book of the Prophet Isaiah* [5 vols.; Grand Rapids: Eerdmans, 1948], 1.247–48). In 9:6–7, the child born "unto us" is Jesus (1.306–17); in 11:1–12 the branch is Christ (1.372). Verse 11 is understood to deal with the future glory of the church (1.389), and the "dispersions of Judah" were

Representative Modern Scholars

The readers surveyed to this point preceded the rise of critical scholarship. Modern scholars, however, have until very recently paid as little
attention as their predecessors to the redaction of the Twelve. Julius
Wellhausen may be taken as fairly representative. He paid so little attention to the canonical order of the Twelve that his commentary dealt with
the prophets by and large in chronological order: Amos, Hosea, Micah,
Zephaniah, Nahum, Habakkuk, Haggai, Zechariah, Malachi, Obadiah,
Joel, and Jonah.[60] What is more, he saw no single thread running
through them as Luther had. Rather, he saw the great preexilic prophets
as the heart of the Hebrew Scriptures. He found the Torah to be without
light,[61] and the cultus to be "heathen" (in what he called a nonpejora-
tive sense of the term!).[62] This reading of the history of Israel left little
room to appreciate works like Haggai, Zech 1–8, and Malachi, precisely
because of their involvement with the cultus, and no real interest in pur-
suing the late, scribal editing of the book that included them. Amos and
Hosea were read in their "purity," without recourse to their meaning in
their larger, canonical position.

While most scholars today would disagree with Wellhausen about the
relative worthlessness of the Torah, their preference for the preexilic
prophets matches his. Many still denigrate Haggai and Zech 1–8 for
hitching their hopes for the future to the second temple, and most continue to read the Twelve as individual books rather than as a redacted
whole. Indeed, B. S. Childs concludes his remarks under the heading
"Introduction to the Latter Prophets" with this comment: " . . . the order

taken to be Christians (1.391). The one mentioned in Isa 53:8 as stricken for the
transgression of his people was Jesus (4.120–22).

Other prophets were treated similarly. The Branch in Jer 23:5 was seen as Jesus
(*Commentaries on the Book of the Prophet Jeremiah and the Lamentations* [5 vols.; Grand
Rapids: Eerdmans, 1950], 3.136–37), and Calvin often equated Israel with the
church. The description of God as one having "the likeness of the appearance of
a man" in Ezekiel's call vision led Calvin to read the passage in Trinitarian terms and
to write: "[T]he prophet saw God only in the person of Christ" (*Commentaries on the
First Twenty Chapters of the Book of the Prophet Ezekiel* [2 vols.; Grand Rapids: Eerdmans,
1948], 1.98). The fourth kingdom in Dan 2 was Roman (*Commentaries on the Book of
the Prophet Daniel* [2 vols.; Grand Rapids: Eerdmans, 1948], 1.162), and the son of
man in 7:14 was Christ when he returns at the end of time as judge (2.44).

[60] Julius Wellhausen, *Die Kleinen Propheten: Übersetzt und erklärt* (4th ed.; Berlin: de
Gruyter, 1963).
[61] Julius Wellhausen, *Prolegomena to the History of Israel* (Edinburgh: Adam & Charles
Black, 1895), 3.
[62] Ibid., 422–23.

of the prophetic books within the collection of the Latter Prophets assumed no great canonical significance and thus differed from the attitude shown to the order within the Pentateuch."[63]

What Benefits Accrue
from Reading the Twelve as a Whole?

If readers from antiquity until the present have read the Twelve individually, why should people today follow the lead of scholars like House, Nogalski, Steck, and Schart and read it as a redacted whole? Three reasons readily come to mind. First, reading the Twelve as a book forces one to recognize the pervasiveness of the redactional processes. Redaction occurred not just at the level of the individual books themselves, but at the level of the Twelve as a whole and at intermediate stages in between. Reading the Twelve this way reminds the reader of the persons who molded and shaped the materials between their earliest, typically oral stage and the final stage seen in the text. Such a reading is the richer, precisely because it is attuned to the redactional nuancing of the individual writings that make up the Twelve.

Second, such a reading is a canonical reading, which offers glimpses into the canonical process.[64] The Twelve may well have been redacted with Deuteronomy and the Deuteronomistic History in view as a conclusion to the Law and the Prophets. Further, the Twelve may have been redacted quite consciously alongside the emerging Isaiah corpus, as Steck and Bosshard-Nepustil have shown.

Third, such a reading shows that in the Twelve, as in many other cases, the whole is greater than the sum of its parts. Read as a continuous narrative it offers a prophetic critique of history that parallels the Deuteronomistic History and the history of the Chronicler plus Ezra and Nehemiah, offering prophetic explanations for the sweep of events from the eighth through the fifth centuries.

---

[63] B. S. Childs, *Introduction to the Old Testament as Scripture* (Philadelphia: Fortress, 1979), 309–10.

[64] M. S. Odell, responding to this paper at the 1997 Society of Biblical Literature meeting, noted that holistic readings are not necessarily the only canonical reading. The rabbis were perfectly aware of the canonicity of the Twelve, but did not read it holistically. Nor, Odell said, are holistic readings mandated by the text; no ancient reader had to read it in its entirety in order to appropriate it as the word of God. On the other hand, she agreed, the canonical reading advocated here provides yet another valid approach for reading the text.

3

Reconstructing the Redaction History
of the Twelve Prophets:
Problems and Models

Aaron Schart

The *Introduction to the Old Testament as Scripture* by Brevard S. Childs represents an important shift in the research on prophetic books.[1] In the legacy of Hermann Gunkel, the main interest had been in the small units which could be perceived as delivered in an oral setting. It was common to imagine the prophet standing somewhere in the streets confronting his hearers with the divinely inspired message. In his commentary on Hosea, for example, Hans W. Wolff considered many texts to be *Auftrittsskizzen,* written hastily during or immediately after the oral communication.[2] Wolff impressively presented Hosea, Amos, and Micah as participants in the social conflicts of their historic societies, trying to make the conflicting parties hear the unambiguous word of God. At the same time, he noted in his commentary on Amos that many passages, including important ones, were written by redactors from different times.[3] Since then, interest in the historical prophet has declined. Instead, the canonical prophetic book has become more and more important.[4] Prophetic books include the original prophetic oracles in such a fashion that it is, in most cases, almost impossible to reconstruct the oral set-

---

[1] B. S. Childs, *Introduction to the Old Testament as Scripture* (Philadelphia: Fortress, 1979).

[2] H. W. Wolff, *Hosea* (vol. 1 of *Dodekapropheton;* BKAT 14/1; Neukirchen-Vluyn: Neukirchener, 1961), xxv.

[3] Compare H. W. Wolff, *Joel und Amos* (3d ed.; vol. 2 of *Dodekapropheton;* BKAT 14/2; Neukirchen-Vluyn: Neukirchener, 1985), 129–38.

[4] As an example one may quote O. H. Steck, *Die Prophetenbücher und ihr theologisches Zeugnis: Wege der Nachfrage und Fährten zur Antwort* (Tübingen: Mohr, 1996), who states that "durch die heutige Zeit donnernder Amos seine unmittelbare Stunde längst gehabt habe" (124). In English, the quotation reads, "...Amos thundering through the present time, when his time has long since passed" (*The Prophetic Books and Their Theological Witness* [trans. James D. Nogalski; St. Louis: Chalice Press, 2000], 114).

ting.[5] The final text is, for the most part, the result of many different redactional activities, which wanted to focus the prophetic claims on new generations. Within this new stream of research the fact was registered with fresh insight that, in antiquity, the Book of the Twelve Prophets was considered as one book. It seems appropriate to reserve the word "book" to denote the collection as a whole and to speak of the twelve units ascribed to different prophets as "writings."[6]

The Book of the Twelve as a Redactional Unit

E. Ben Zvi has vehemently disagreed that the Book of the Twelve was originally meant to be a unit.[7] He conceives of the book as a collection of writings, some of which may indeed manifest thematic overlaps, or even allude to one another, but which have no redactional sense as a whole. A reader may impinge meaning upon the whole, but one should be clear that this is not what the final redactors had in mind. They wanted to preserve the individual writings. Ben Zvi rightly emphasizes the problem of discerning that the redactors wanted to present the Twelve Prophets as part of a larger unity. The most unambiguous evidence is lacking: the Book of the Twelve has no superscription. So what else can be accepted as signal of redactional purpose?

Widely acknowledged is the *Stichwortverkettung* (catchword chain) phenomenon. F. Delitzsch noted that the ending of one writing and the beginning of the adjacent one often share significant vocabulary.[8] The following instances were considered significant: Hos 14:2 // Joel 2:12; Joel 4:16 // Amos 1:2; Amos 9:12 // Obad 19; Obad 1 // Jonah (as messenger to the nations); Jonah 4:2 // Mic 7:18–19 // Nah 1:2–3; Nah 1:1 // Hab 1:1 (מַשָּׂא); Hab 2:20 // Zeph 1:7. Some assumed that redactors grouped together that accidentally contained such *Stichwörter*. Others postulated that the *Stichwörter* were implemented to stitch together writings that the redactors wanted to place in sequence. This second hypothesis is strongly supported by J. Nogalski, who has thoroughly treated the *Stichwort* phenomenon and discovered *Stichwörter*

---

[5] Steck is very skeptical in this respect (ibid., 120–23).

[6] That is the way J. Nogalski has done it.

[7] E. Ben Zvi, "Twelve Prophetic Books or 'The Twelve'? A Few Preliminary Considerations," in *Forming Prophetic Literature: Essays on Isaiah and the Twelve in Honor of John D. W. Watts* (ed. J. W. Watts and P. R. House; Sheffield: Sheffield Academic Press, 1996), 125–56.

[8] F. Delitzsch, "Wann weissagte Obadja?" *Zeitschrift für die gesammte Lutherische Theologie und Kirche* 12 (1851): 92–93.

that had been overlooked. For example, the inconspicuous word "time" (עת) connects Zeph 3:20 with Hag 1:2, 4. The glorious future envisioned in Zeph 3:9–20 is contrasted with the unsatisfactory state of the people living around the ruins of the temple.[9]

B. A. Jones and Ben Zvi doubt that the *Stichwörter* can provide evidence for the redactional linking. One problem is that shared vocabulary exists between writings that do not stand adjacent. Obadiah, for example, could as easily follow Joel 4:19 (where Edom is mentioned) as Amos 9:12, especially since the decisive term "Edom" in Amos 9:12 is (according to Jones) lacking in the Hebrew *Vorlage* of the Septuagint.[10] Jones and Ben Zvi rightly argue that in many cases the *Stichwörter* are not significant enough to preclude accidental allusion of the respective passages. The *Stichwörter*, however, especially if additional cases are found, are still valuable clues to the redactional plan. Most important are source-critical observations. If, to use a disputed example of Nogalski, almost all differences between Obadiah and its *Vorlage* in Jer 49 pick up vocabulary and themes present in Amos 9, it is probable that Obadiah was designed to fit into its position after Amos.[11] Jones too easily dismisses the arguments of Nogalski when he states: "Even if Nogalski's conclusion is correct, however, that Obadiah has been shaped redactionally under the influence of Amos 9, again this may explain but does not *require* the arrangement of Amos and Obadiah in the MT Book of the Twelve. One should not be surprised that a relatively late book such as Obadiah has been influenced by the Book of Amos."[12] It is unjustified to require this high degree of probability from the proponents of redactional unity only. For too long, the Book of the Twelve as a whole was ignored. One should challenge this commonly held reading by inverting the burden of proof and start with the assumption that the Book of the Twelve is a unit; the assumption should only be relinquished if the opposite can be demonstrated.[13]

A further question for detecting redactional intention is whether the reading process sees small units as parts of a global discourse structure. One has to ask, for example, if a unit presupposes a thought from a

---

[9] J. D. Nogalski, *Literary Precursors to the Book of the Twelve* (BZAW 217; Berlin: de Gruyter, 1993), 215.

[10] B. A. Jones, *The Formation of the Book of the Twelve: A Study in Text and Canon* (SBLDS 149; Atlanta: Scholars Press, 1995), 175–91.

[11] J. D. Nogalski, *Redactional Processes in the Book of the Twelve* (BZAW 218; Berlin: de Gruyter, 1993), 61–74.

[12] Jones, *Formation of the Book of the Twelve*, 211–12.

[13] Steck, *Prophetenbücher*, 30.

previous text or uses a lexeme whose connotation was established in an earlier passage. Frames are also important. For example, Hosea starts with a *Fremdbericht* (Hos 1), and Amos included one in the final vision cycle (Amos 7:10–17). Likewise, a meaningful superstructure points toward a deliberate ordering, for example, the historical ordering of the writings with Hosea first (because it mentions the "House of Jehu" in Hos 1:4) and Malachi last (because it presupposes an operative second temple).[14]

The Order of the Writings

Manuscript evidence of the Book of the Twelve has been investigated by Jones, Fuller, and Steck.[15] So far, three variants are known. In the Hebrew tradition, all manuscripts follow the Masoretic order with the exception of one of the oldest scrolls, 4QXII[a], in which the most plausible reconstruction is that Jonah followed Malachi.[16] In the Septuagint tradition we find a third option. The first six writings are arranged Hosea, Amos, Micah, Joel, Obadiah, Jonah. Whether we have enough evidence to reconstruct the goal of the final redactors comes up again. Do the different variants signal that the order of the writings was meaningless, or, to the contrary, that the sequence was important to express a new understanding of the whole by the redactors and/or translators? The consensus so far is that the Masoretic order was the original one.[17] By contrast, Jones considers the Septuagint order to be older,[18] who states that the aim was to group writings similar in content; this is, for example, why Obadiah immediately follows Joel. The main problem with Jones's hypothesis is that it does not explain how the Masoretic order came into being. Much more convincing is that the Septuagint placed Amos and Micah immediately after Hosea and left all other writings in

---

[14] Compare A. Schart, *Die Entstehung des Zwölfprophetenbuchs: Neubearbeitungen von Amos im Rahmen schriftenübergreifender Redaktionsprozesse* (BZAW 260; Berlin: de Gruyter, 1998), 133–50.

[15] Jones (see n. 10); R. E. Fuller, "The Form and Formation of the Book of the Twelve: The Evidence from the Judean Desert," in Watts and House, *Forming Prophetic Literature*, 86–101; O. H. Steck, "Zur Abfolge Maleachi–Jona in 4Q76 (4QXIIa)," *ZAW* 108 (1996): 249–53.

[16] Russell E. Fuller, "The Minor Prophets Manuscripts from Qumran, Cave IV," in *The Prophets* (ed. Eugene Ulrich; vol. 10 of *Qumran Cave 4;* DJD 15; Oxford: Clarendon Press, 1997), 221–318 + plates xl–lxiv.

[17] D. A. Schneider, "The Unity of the Book of the Twelve" (Ph.D. diss., Yale University, 1979), 224–25; Nogalski, *Precursors*, 2.

[18] Jones, *Formation of the Book of the Twelve*, 218–20.

the Masoretic order. The reason probably was the historical setting given by the superscriptions; since Hosea, Amos, and Micah prophesied partly under the same kings, they form a closed group to which Joel, Obadiah, and Jonah do not belong.

More convincing is Jones's hypothesis that the oldest order had Jonah after Malachi, as represented by 4QXII[a]. Since Jonah has a different position in each of the three variants, Jones argues that it came into the collection last.[19] One can imagine that this strange writing was first attached to the end of the collection, and, because Jonah ben Amittai had lived under Jeroboam II (2 Kgs 14:25), in a second step found its place close to the prophets from the eighth century.

The Global Structure of the Twelve

If the Book of the Twelve is purposefully arranged, one should expect a coherent global structure that directs the reading process.[20] Most important in this respect are the beginnings of the writings, of which nine contain superscriptions.[21] Since the dated beginnings follow in historical sequence, the reader gets the impression that the collection intends to unfold part of the history of prophecy. The deepest break is between Zephaniah and Haggai, where the Babylonian exile is presupposed, but not mentioned.

According to P. House, the implied picture of the history of Israel follows the scheme "sin-punishment-restoration."[22] Hosea, Joel, Amos, Obadiah, Jonah, and Micah belong to the first topic. These writings are mainly, although not exclusively, concerned with the sin of Israel and the nations. Nahum, Habakkuk, and Zephaniah describe the punishment for that sin. Haggai, Zechariah, and Malachi envision the restoration of Israel within the nations. Although House's description of the global

---

[19] Ibid., 129–69; Schart, *Entstehung des Zwölfprophetenbuchs,* 290.

[20] T. Collins, *The Mantle of Elijah: The Redaction Criticism of the Prophetical Books* (The Biblical Seminar 20; Sheffield: JSOT Press, 1993), 65; P. R. House, *The Unity of the Twelve* (Bible and Literature Series 27; JSOTSup 97; Sheffield: Almond, 1990), 67–71.

[21] Schart only wants to speak of a superscription if "die Informationen, die sie enthält, auf einer Metaebene zum restlichen Textkorpus liegen und sie weder grammatisch noch semantisch eine lineare Anknüpfung an den folgenden Text aufweist" (*Entstehung des Zwölfprophetenbuchs,* 32). "The information that [the superscription] contains transcends the rest of the corpus, while, grammatically and syntactically, it shows no linear connection to the following text" [editor's translation]. This is true only for Hos 1:1; Joel 1:1; Amos 1:1; Obad 1a; Mic 1:1; Nah 1:1; Hab 1:1; Zeph 1:1; and Mal 1:1.

[22] House, *Unity of the Twelve,* 63–109.

structure of the Twelve contains many insights into the intertextual relationships among the different writings, his scheme seems too imprecise.[23] At first glance, it is obvious that all three, sin, punishment, and restoration, are part of all the single writings. Malachi, for example, contains more numerous and more specific accusations than Joel. As a result, it is difficult to limit the aim of Joel to disclosing the sin of Israel or to limit the aim of Malachi to Israel's restoration.[24]

T. Collins presents a more complex model. He identifies a set of recurring themes. "The principal themes of the whole book are those of covenant-election, fidelity and infidelity, fertility and infertility, turning and returning, the justice of God and the mercy of God, the kingship of God, the place of his dwelling (Temple/Mt. Zion), the nations as enemies, the nations as allies."[25] Every prophet adds to the topics, sometimes in accordance, sometimes in opposition to other writings. Collins tries to find the unity which can make sense of all the different aspects. How this works may be illustrated from passages dealing with the temple. Hosea accuses the temple of northern Israel of idolatry, because a calf is worshiped there. In contrast, Joel's call to repentance makes clear that the true worship of YHWH is taking place at the temple in Jerusalem. It is not until Mic 3:12 that the temple on Mount Zion is condemned. Immediately thereafter, however, it is envisioned that Mount Zion will once again be the center of the world, to which all nations will come spontaneously in order to accept the Torah as the way to universal peace. Zephaniah 3:9–20 further explores this topic. In order to fulfill its eschatological responsibility, Mount Zion must be cleansed and must be the home of holy community. This thought sets the stage for Haggai, Zechariah, and Malachi. Zechariah 8, especially, which once formed the end of a smaller collection, reminds the reader of Zeph 3 (cf. Zech 8:3 with Zeph 3:11, 15). Malachi then recognizes that the promised, glorious

---

[23] As examples of observations, which have been picked up by others, one may name the following: House perceives the summons to hear in Hos 4:1 as the opening of an accusation speech, which ends in Mic 6:2–16. In both passages the lexeme *ryb* (lawsuit) plays an important role (ibid., 87; cf. Schart, *Entstehung des Zwölfprophetenbuchs*, 191–92). Another observation is that the prominent role that the "love of God" plays in Malachi refers back to Hosea (House, *Unity of the Twelve*, 108; cf. Collins, *Mantle of Elijah*, 81).

[24] House does implicitly admit the difficulty: "Unlike the recipients of Hosea's condemnation, the sin of God's people in Joel is much more subtle. Judgment is fast approaching, but is not coming because of an obvious rejection of Yahweh and a subsequent embracing of idolatry. Rather, the religion pictured in Joel has lost its vitality. The Lord and His presence are taken for granted" (*Unity of the Twelve*, 76).

[25] Collins, *Mantle of Elijah*, 65.

future of Zion "is still impeded by the unworthy behaviour of the priests in the temple, the very place where God's name should be honored most."[26] Collins's model is certainly more complex than House's model, but it does more justice to the variety of topics and to the sometimes striking differences between writings than to the unity.

A prominent topic of the Twelve is the Day of YHWH. No other prophetic book contains as many passages about this day, which are at the same time central for the overall structure. In addition, the Day of YHWH is the concept which integrates basic topics into one scenario. Joel impressively introduces the Day of YHWH into the collection, and the reader is forced to follow within this framework.[27] Amos 5:18–20 implies that the opponents of Amos are longing for the Day of YHWH. Since Amos himself never spoke about this day, the hearers must know about it from elsewhere. From the perspective of the reader of the Twelve, it is obvious that the opponents have already heard Joel's message. From reading in this manner, one gets the impression that the contemporaries of Amos used Joel's prophecy to evade the call to turn back to God (Amos 5:4–6, 14–15). How they evaded the call is not spelled out. Amos restates the severe scenario of Joel: for those who do not repent, the coming day will bring complete darkness. Likewise, this reading sets the stage for understanding the Day of YHWH in Obad 18, where it is announced that the "House of Jacob" will burn the "House of Esau." According to Amos 5 and 9:8–10, this eschatological "House of Jacob" will comprise only those who did not reject the message of Amos and who, at the same time, belong to those persons called by God, as stated in Joel 3:5. Rendtorff rightly observes that the nearness of the Day of YHWH inspires a call to repentance (Joel 2:12–14; Amos 5:4–6, 14–15; Zeph 2:1–3; Mal 3:24). The reader may also infer that every reference to a decisive day, on which YHWH will punish sin and restore the true Israel — for example, "on that day" (Amos 2:16; 8:3) or "day of trouble" (Nah 1:7) — points toward the one Day of YHWH.

R. C. van Leeuwen observes how the first six writings make use of Exod 34:6–7, a text that contains "an elaboration of the name YHWH expressing the bipolar attributes of mercy and retributive justice."[28] The first allusion he sees already in Hos 1:6, where it is unambiguously

---

26 Ibid., 81.

27 R. Rendtorff, "Alas for the day! The 'Day of the LORD' in the Book of the Twelve," in *God in the Fray: A Tribute to Walter Brueggemann* (ed. Tod Linafelt and Timothy K. Beal; Minneapolis: Fortress, 1998), 186–97.

28 R. C. van Leeuwen, "Scribal Wisdom and Theodicy in the Book of the Twelve,"

declared that the merciful character of God is no longer operative. However, Hos 14:10 implies that the wise know that God forgives those who repent. The redactors seem to exploit the tension God's between mercy and justice in order to show that different prophets emphasized various attributes of the very same God. Joel 2:12 cites Exod 34:6–7. Jonah cites the same verse in 3:9 and 4:2. Micah cites it in 2:8 (conjectured) and 7:18–20. Finally, Nahum cites Exod 34:6–7 in 1:2–3a. The tensions between the different writings are deeply rooted within God. Only a multiplicity of approaches does justice to the mystery of God's personality.

The Book of the Twelve shares certain features with the book of Isaiah. One may note, for example, that the Judean kings listed in Isa 1:1 (Uzziah, Jotham, Ahaz, and Hezekiah) are identical with the ones listed in Hos 1:1. Also, Isa 2:2–4 and Mic 4:1–4 are almost identical. For these and other reasons Bosshard-Nepustil has closely examined the relationship between both books. It is remarkable how many cross-references he detects in different layers. He proposes that the main redactions in the Book of the Twelve, which he calls the "Assur/Babel-Redaktion[XII]" and the "Babel-Redaktion[XII]," were influenced by similar redactions in the book of Isaiah.[29] Although he tries to display his results in well-structured tables, the sheer complexity of his reconstructions is overwhelming. Many of his source-critical decisions appear problematic, and one often has the feeling that the intertextual allusions cannot be controlled.

Models for the Redaction History of the Book of the Twelve

There is no question that a simple synchronic approach is insufficient. The superscriptions already make it unambiguously clear that the different writings originated in different centuries. All of the redaction-critical models proposed so far assume that smaller collections predated the final book. It is highly unlikely from the outset that twelve independent books were combined for the first time in Hellenistic times.

---

in *In Search of Wisdom: Essays in Memory of John G. Gammie* (ed. L. G. Perdue, B. B. Scott, and W. J. Wiseman; Louisville: Westminster/John Knox, 1993), 32.

29 E. Bosshard-Nepustil, *Rezeptionen von Jesaia 1–39 im Zwölfprophetenbuch: Untersuchungen zur literarischen Verbindung von Prophetenbüchern in babylonischer und persischer Zeit* (OBO 154; Fribourg, Switzerland: Universitätsverlag; Göttingen: Vandenhoeck & Ruprecht, 1997), summary on p. 408.

R. E. Wolfe was the first to propose that thirteen redactional layers, which he differentiates, worked across the boundaries of the individual writings. This is why he labels his model a "strata hypothesis."[30] A notable layer, for example, is the "Day of Jahwe Editor," which contains the following passages: "in Amos 4:12b (from עקב); 5:13, 18c (from הוא), 20; Obad 15a (to הגוים); Joel 1:15; 2:1d (from כי)–2b (to וערפל), 10–11; 3:1– 5 (Eng., 2:28–32); 4:1–3, 12, 14–17 (Eng., 3:1–3, 12, 14–17); Zeph 1:7–8a (to יהוה), 14–16.18c (from ביום); 2:1–3; 3:8b–e (from חכו)" (103). Thus, almost every passage containing the phrase "Day of YHWH" belongs to this layer. Wolfe discerns four steps in the redaction. First, Amos and Hosea were combined. Second, Micah, Nahum, Habakkuk, and Zephaniah were added, yielding a collection of the six preexilic prophecies. Third, a "Book of the Nine" developed by the insertion of Joel, Jonah, and Obadiah. The book became complete with the addition of Haggai, Zechariah, and Malachi.

D. A. Schneider thinks along similar lines.[31] The basis, according to Schneider, was the collection of Hosea, Amos, and Micah in the time of Hezekiah. Under Josiah's rule, Nahum, Habakkuk, and Zephaniah were attached. During the exile, Joel, Obadiah, and Jonah entered the collection. Finally, Haggai, Zechariah, and Malachi were added in the time of Nehemiah.

Nogalski attributes the most extensive redactional activity to the "Joel-related layer." This redaction combined a preexisting "Deuteronomistic Corpus" (Hosea-Amos-Micah-Zephaniah) with Nahum, Habakkuk, Haggai, Zech 1–8, Joel, Obadiah, and Malachi. Subsequently, Jonah and Zech 9–14 entered the collection.[32]

Schart assumes more steps, in which the collection continually grew. First, Hosea and Amos were combined. For the next step he agrees with Nogalski that there must have been a corpus consisting of Hosea-Amos-Micah-Zephaniah. Then Nahum and Habakkuk were inserted. After that, Haggai and Zech 1–8 were attached. Subsequently, Joel, Obadiah, and Zech 9–14 were added. Finally, Jonah, as a satirical narrative, and Malachi completed the book.[33]

The main difficulty for all the different models is establishing controls about what is considered deliberate redactional shaping and what

---

[30] R. E. Wolfe, "The Editing of the Book of the Twelve," *ZAW* 53 (1935): 91.
[31] "Unity of the Book of the Twelve" (see n. 17).
[32] See his summaries: Nogalski, *Precursors*, 276–82; *Processes*, 274–80.
[33] See Schart's summary, *Entstehung des Zwölfprophetenbuchs*, 304–6.

is only accidentally connected. Which features should be construed as important goals of the final text, and which should be viewed as less significant? It seems wise to begin reconstruction of the redaction history with those passages which most obviously stem from editors: the superscriptions.[34] Given that starting point, it is most plausible that Hosea, Amos, Micah, and Zephaniah once existed as a separate collection. The superscriptions of these four writings follow the same patter, and, through the names of the kings mentioned, they convey the following scenario: First, Hosea and Amos prophesied simultaneously in the northern kingdom; thereafter, Hosea and Micah prophesied at the same time in Judah.[35] The writing of Hosea was deliberately placed in the first position, although the historical prophet Amos probably delivered his oracles earlier than Hosea. The redactors wanted the reader to perceive the writing of Amos in the light of Hosea, presumably because they were committed to Hosea's theological position. Some have used the concept "Deuteronomistic" to characterize these redactors.[36] This seems unwise, since typical Deuteronomistic language can only rarely be identified, for example, in Amos 3:7 ("his servants the prophets").[37] To be more cautious, one may speak of a redaction that inserted passages in addition to the superscriptions, passages which come close to Deuteronomistic thoughts.[38] Schart, especially, has pulled together numerous observations which have already been made concerning this redaction.[39] The central point is that all transgressions were conceived as conducted directly against God. The root of all evil is the distortion of the personal relationship to YHWH that was es-

---

[34] See already G. M. Tucker: "It is all but self-evident that the superscriptions were not created by the prophets themselves. They refer in the third person, and retrospectively, to the activity of the prophet, and to the books which contain the prophetic words" ("Prophetic Superscriptions and the Growth of a Canon," in *Canon and Authority: Essays in OT Religion and Theology* [ed. G. W. Coats and B. O. Long; Philadelphia: Fortress, 1977], 65).

[35] D. N. Freedman, "Headings in the Books of the Eighth-Century Prophets," *AUSS* 25 (1987): 16–20; Collins, *Mantle of Elijah*, 62; Nogalski, *Precursors*, 84–89; Schart, *Entstehung des Zwölfprophetenbuchs*, 41–46.

[36] W. H. Schmidt, "Die deuteronomistische Redaktion des Amosbuches: Zu den theologischen Unterschieden zwischen dem Prophetenwort und seinem Sammler," *ZAW* 77 (1965): 171; Nogalski, *Precursors*, 86–88.

[37] See the critique of Schmidt by N. Lohfink, "Gab es eine deuteronomistische Bewegung?" in *Studien zum Deuteronomium und zur deuteronomistischen Literatur III* (Stuttgart: Katholisches Bibelwerk, 1995), 65–142.

[38] Collins, *Mantle of Elijah*, 62; Schart, *Entstehung des Zwölfprophetenbuchs*, 46.

[39] See, for example, Schmidt, "Deuteronomistische Redaktion," 191–92; Schart, *Entstehung des Zwölfprophetenbuchs*, 218–33.

tablished through the exodus. In order to underscore the last point, the redactors, at crucial points of the composition, inserted passages referring to the exodus (Amos 2:10; 3:2; 9:7; Mic 6:4–5). Social, cultic, or juridical degeneration is seen as the result of the fundamental corruption of the identity of Israel, which is determined by the exodus. It is remarkable that the redaction also reflected on the role of the prophets within God's history with Israel and Judah (Amos 2:11–12; 3:7).

If one asks for precursors to this corpus, it can be argued convincingly that the writings of Hosea and Amos once formed a single composition. J. Jeremias in particular has proposed this hypothesis.[40] On the one hand, there are additions in the writing of Hosea that pick up language from Amos. The second half of Hos 4:15 uses words from Amos 4:4; 5:5; and 8:14. Hosea 8:14 is closely related to Amos 3:9–11 and 6:8. The passages appear at positions at which a reader from Judah possibly could perceive the transgressions of northern Israel as something that would never happen in Judah. However, the aim of the redactional additions is to counteract those reactions. On the other hand, there are verses like Amos 3:2; 7:9; 2:8; 5:25; 6:8; and 1:5, which are heavily loaded with vocabulary and topics from the writing of Hosea. Almost all of these redactional passages are located at important points in the composition of Amos. This implies that Amos, even at an early stage, must already have been designed with the ideas of Hosea in mind. Schart has further pursued this insight.[41] In his view, the same redactors edited both writings as a single composition. The overall structure was governed by the summons to hear (Hos 4:1; 5:1; Amos 3:1; 4:1; 5:1). In both writings the prophet first addresses "the Israelites" (Hos 4:1; Amos 3:1) and secondly the "House of Israel" (Hos 5:1; Amos 5:1). The writings were combined in order to convince the reader that these prophecies of doom are truly the word of God. Schart points toward the letters from Mari, which show that the authority of oracle, especially unfavorable oracles, could be strengthened if a second oracle, independently uttered by a different speaker, confirmed the message of the first one.

---

[40] J. Jeremias, "Die Anfänge des Dodekapropheton: Hosea und Amos," *Hosea und Amos: Studien zu den Anfängen des Dodekapropheton* (Tübingen: Mohr, 1996), 34–54. Compare already Wolfe, "Editing of the Book of the Twelve," 91–93; Schneider, "Unity of the Book of the Twelve," 23; Schmidt, "Deuteronomistische Redaktion," 173.

[41] Schart, *Entstehung des Zwölfprophetenbuchs*, 101–55.

As a redactional stage later than the corpus which comprised Hosea, Amos, Micah, and Zephaniah, there must have been something like a "Joel-related layer," which formed a corpus at the core of which stood the Day of YHWH passages. After some forerunners, it was Nogalski who put together strong and fascinating arguments for this stage in the formation of the book.[42] Besides large parts of Joel, this layer probably contained a version of Obadiah. According to Nogalski, little glosses dealing with locusts and the fertility of the land were also inserted in older writings to recall the vivid picture of Joel 1–2, for example, Nah 3:15a?, 16b, and Hab 3:16b–17. However, it seems difficult to find out exactly how many writings and passages this Joel-related layer comprised. Although Wolfe, Nogalski, Bosshard-Nepustil, and Schart agree that there was something like a "Day-of-YHWH layer," which contained a large part of Joel, these authors differ considerably. This problem is closely related to problems in the last phase of the redaction history of the Book of the Twelve. Did the collection of the Joel-related layer end with an earlier version of Malachi, which was attached to Zech 8, as Nogalski proposes?[43] Or did it conclude with Zech (9–)14, with Malachi entering later, as Schart prefers? In any case, Jonah was likely the last independent writing to be added. In this respect Nogalski and Schart agree with Jones, who argues from the manuscript evidence that because Jonah's position within the sequence of the Twelve is different in all three variants, it was probably added last. Over the last decades a strong consensus has emerged that Mal 3:22–24 was added to the Book of the Twelve as a conclusion to the second part of the Hebrew canon, the "Nebiim."[44]

---

[42] Nogalski, *Processes*, 275–78. See, for example, Wolfe, with his proposed "Day-of-YHWH editor," and E. Bosshard-Nepustil, "Beobachtungen zum Zwölfprophetenbuch," *BN* 40 (1987): 30–62.

[43] Bosshard-Nepustil, Kratz, and Steck suggest an even more complex connection between Zechariah and Malachi (E. Bosshard-Nepustil and R. G. Kratz, "Maleachi im Zwölfprophetenbuch," *BN* 52 [1990]: 27–46; O. H. Steck, *Der Abschluß der Prophetie im Alten Testament: Ein Versuch zur Frage der Vorgeschichte des Kanons* [Biblisch-Theologische Studien 17; Neukirchen-Vluyn: Neukirchener, 1991]). They argue that prior versions of Malachi originally were designed as extensions of former versions of Zech 9–14. The superscription, Mal 1:1, came later, and the original cohesion was interrupted.

[44] W. Rudolph, *Haggai, Sacharja, Maleachi* (KAT 13/4; Gütersloh: Gütersloher, 1976), 291; Nogalski, *Processes*, 185; Steck, *Abschluß*, 134–36; Schart, *Entstehung des Zwölfprophetenbuchs*, 302–3.

Hermeneutical Implications

These new insights into the redaction history of the Book of the Twelve change the way in which the meaning of the whole and its parts can be construed.[45]

First, the well-known fact should again be emphasized that the original words of the historical prophets underwent a deep transformation within the literary transmission. Without the different redactors, the first written records would have been left in an archive. With their adaptation, these records became an unparalleled body of literature, which played an important role in the interaction between Israel and its God. The ongoing rewriting of the prophetic heritage certifies that the prophetic collections were successful in mediating the word of God into different historical situations. In this respect, the prophetic books pursued the function of the original prophets.

A second well-known fact may also be stressed. The literary remains of the preexilic prophets were mostly shaped under the impression that the original oracles had been fulfilled. The exiles of northern Israel and Judah functioned as the basic proof for a precursor of the Book of the Twelve, which presumably contained at least Hosea, Amos, Micah, and Zephaniah. However, the prophecies of doom also provoked the confident hope that God would once again bring peace and well-being to Israel within a renewed creation.

Third, from an early stage in the transmission process onward, prophetic oracles were perceived in light of the history of prophecy. One may already compare Jer 28:8, in which Jeremiah uses the conformity of his message with the prophetic tradition as an argument against his opponent. More important, the redactors sought to present the prophets as a coherent whole. New prophecy had to demonstrate how it was related to the literary prophetic tradition. This does not mean that the prophetic messages remained unchanged, but every new prophecy had to be conceived as picking up and expanding aspects of the tradition under the pressure of new experiences of God.

Fourth, the prophetic writings were transmitted as parts of collections. It is very likely that the redactors did expand and rewrite so that preexisting prophetic writings would articulate what the historical prophet, under whose name the redactors worked, would have said,

---

[45] Steck deals extensively with the hermeneutical implications of the latest redaction-critical enterprises (*Prophetenbuecher*, 127–204). See also B. S. Childs, "Retrospective Reading of the Old Testament Prophets," *ZAW* 108 (1996): 362–77.

if the prophet had been confronted with the problems of their own time. Whenever redactors were confronted with a new prophecy that could not be harmoniously integrated within the existing collection, a new writing was designed under a new author's name. In many cases, presumably, this writing circulated independently for a while before it was added to the existing group. Inclusion became possible when redactors could develop a theological position in which the differences between the older corpus and the new writings could either be integrated or became insignificant.[46] Within a given collection, the writings were combined in such a way that the meaning of the whole overruled the meaning that a certain text had in its original historical setting. The theological position held by the last redactors was inferred into every part of the collection. For example, within the Joel-related layer, all passages dealing with the Day of YHWH were interpreted as references to the scenario described in Joel, no matter what the original meaning of those passages would have been. Therefore, it is imperative that the interpreter not isolate one prophetic writing against others; rather, the interpreter should read the prophetic writing as part of a collection and see that it contributes to a consistent meaning. It is particularly important to look for redactional passages concerned with developing complex scenarios, in which different concepts can be reconciled.

As a fifth point, it is important that the redactors did not produce a flat coherence without deviations, tensions, and even contradictions. It must be borne in mind that the final text of the Book of the Twelve does not support the idea of one prophet overlooking the history of Israel from one point in time as, for example, occurs in Isaiah. Instead, the corpus presents twelve different prophets from different times. The overarching unity of this book is much more unsettled than in Isaiah. Whereas former exegetes hesitated to conceive the individual messages as part of a higher unity, postmodern thought is intrigued by that idea. The Book of the Twelve postulates that messages from different times, from persons with special insights, speaking from different backgrounds, when read together form a complex unity. The reader is forced to proceed from one prophecy to the next, each time imagining the hidden theme of the whole, the judging and restoring presence of God in history, from a different perspective. For the postmodern reader, it is not important to obtain a final coherent vision of what the book is about. Much more important is the arrangement of the prophecies in a way

---

[46] See Schart, *Entstehung des Zwölfprophetenbuchs,* 309–14.

that the single units present a distinct but memorable perspective, which at the same time needs to be balanced by the next unit. None of the prophecies needs to be criticized as long as the reader has delight in moving on. The trajectory of this complex process forms the canonical guidance with which the reader can achieve his or her own vision of the God of Israel.

4

Sequence and Interpretation
in the Book of the Twelve

Marvin A. Sweeney

Sequence: A Clue for Conceptualizing
the Book of the Twelve

Recent years have seen a major shift in discussion concerning the Twelve Prophets, in that scholars are now beginning to move beyond the older literary-critical paradigm, which treats the Twelve Prophets as individual prophetic books, to a newer literary-critical paradigm, which examines the Book of the Twelve as a coherent literary whole.[1] Whereas the older paradigm examines the distinctive literary forms, perspectives, and compositional histories of each of the twelve prophetic books, the newer paradigm treats the Twelve as a single book and thereby raises

---

[1] For discussion of the issue, see Karl Budde, "Eine folgenschwere Redaktion des Zwölfprophetenbuchs," *ZAW* 39 (1921): 218–29; Roland Emerson Wolfe, "The Editing of the Book of the Twelve," *ZAW* 53 (1935): 90–129; Peter Weimar, "Obadja: Eine redaktionskritische Analyse," *BN* 27 (1985): 35–99; Erich Bosshard-Nepustil, "Beobachtungen zum Zwölfprophetenbuch," *BN* 40 (1987): 30–62; Paul R. House, *The Unity of the Twelve* (Bible and Literature Series 27; JSOTSup 97; Sheffield: Almond Press, 1990); Erich Bosshard-Nepustil and Reinhold Gregor Kratz, "Maleachi im Zwölfprophetenbuch," *BN* 52 (1990): 27–46; Odil Hannes Steck, *Der Abschluss der Prophetie im alten Testament: Ein Versuch zur Frage der Vorgeschichte des Kanons* (Biblisch-theologische Studien 17; Neukirchen-Vluyn: Neukirchener, 1991); Terence Collins, *The Mantle of Elijah: The Redaction Criticism of the Prophetical Books* (Biblical Seminar 20; Sheffield: JSOT Press, 1993): 59–87; James D. Nogalski, *Literary Precursors to the Book of the Twelve* (BZAW 217; Berlin and New York: de Gruyter, 1993); idem, *Redactional Processes in the Book of the Twelve* (BZAW 218; Berlin and New York: de Gruyter, 1993); R. J. Coggins, "The Minor Prophets — One Book or Twelve?" in *Crossing the Boundaries: Essays in Biblical Interpretation in Honour of Michael D. Goulder* (ed. S. E. Porter, P. Joyce, and D. E. Orton; Biblical Interpretation Series 8; Leiden: Brill, 1994), 57–68; Barry Alan Jones, *The Formation of the Book of the Twelve: A Study of Text and Canon* (SBLDS 149; Atlanta: Scholars Press, 1995); John Barton, "The Canonical Meaning of the Book of the Twelve," in *After the Exile* (ed. J. Barton and D. J. Reimer; Macon, Ga.: Mercer University Press, 1996), 59–73; James W. Watts and Paul R. House, eds., *Forming Prophetic Literature: Essays on Isaiah and the Twelve in Honor of John D. W. Watts* (JSOTSup 235; Sheffield: Sheffield Academic Press, 1996).

questions concerning its literary form, theological or ideological perspective, and the history of its composition. This is not to say that the newer paradigm supplants the older paradigm; studies of the individual books of the Twelve Prophets continue to produce significant and innovative results. Nevertheless, the new paradigm introduces an important dimension into the study of the Twelve Prophets in that it considers the presentation of the Twelve Prophets as a single prophetic book — one of the major forms in which the Twelve is encountered by its audience — to be a constitutive element in interpretation.

This new paradigm, of course, introduces tension into the discussion in that the interpretation of the Twelve as individual prophetic books is not entirely or even necessarily compatible or consistent with the interpretation of the Twelve as a single work of literature. Ben Zvi treats this issue in a recent study in which he challenges "writer/redactor-" or "production-centered" interpretative approaches that posit the "Book of the Twelve" as a deliberate composition, and calls for an "audience-" or "reception-centered" approach that points to the emergence of the "Book of the Twelve" by default.[2] Ben Zvi points first to the variety of forms in which the Book of the Twelve appears and the absence of a superscription for the book as a whole, and he asks whether it is appropriate to speak of the book as an intentional composition or simply as a fluid collection of individual prophetic writings that crystallized into its various forms. He employs Obadiah to raise questions concerning the lexical associations between the various books. Must they be considered deliberate attempts by the "authors" of the Twelve to create a single literary work, or examples of a "default model" in which textual links are the result of their secondary juxtaposition and association within the literary context of the Book of the Twelve?

Overall, Ben Zvi finds little evidence that the Book of the Twelve was deliberately composed as such by writers or redactors, and opts instead for a reader-centered strategy, which focuses on the educated writers and readers who ascribed meaning to the individual books in relation to their own social and intellectual matrices by reading and rereading them in relation to each other. Ben Zvi is certainly correct to emphasize the role of the ancient readers or implied audience in the interpretation of the so-called Book of the Twelve, but his proposal raises a methodological question that requires further examination, that is, the extent to

---

[2] E. Ben Zvi, "Twelve Prophetic Books or 'The Twelve': Some Preliminary Considerations," in Watts and House, *Forming Prophetic Literature*, 125–56.

which one can distinguish between the writer/redactor/producer and the reader/recipient in such a scenario.[3] The anonymous readers act as recipients of the text and interpret it accordingly, but in the act of interpreting the texts of the Twelve Prophets and defining their places within the larger Book of the Twelve, these readers become authors and redactors as well. This is implied in Ben Zvi's designation of these readers as "writers," but in his reluctance to ascribe to them any demonstrable role in the composition of the individual prophetic books that comprise the "Book of the Twelve" he provides little guidance as to their "authorial" or "productive" activities or to their interpretation of the Twelve Prophets.

There are various criteria by which such guidance may be found, such as the intertextual allusions within the Twelve that constitute instances of inner-biblical exegesis and composition,[4] the commentaries on the Twelve Prophets and citations that appear among the writings from Qumran and other Second Temple–period literature, and the ancient translations of the Twelve Prophets[5] that provide the basis for discerning the hermeneutical perspectives of the translators. Nevertheless, these criteria must be qualified in relation to the overall conception of the Book of the Twelve. Intertextual allusions have loomed large in the current discussion, but they do not always provide reliable criteria by which to establish the conception and composition of the Book of the Twelve.[6] The commentaries, citations, and translations may well provide valuable hermeneutical perspectives with regard to this issue, but they generally presuppose an already fixed composition.

A fourth criterion that has not been sufficiently examined, however, is the arrangement of the twelve prophetic books within the larger Book of the Twelve. This criterion is especially important in that it points to

---

[3] For discussion of the methodological issue, see Rolf Knierim, "Criticism of Literary Features, Form, Tradition, and Redaction," in *The Hebrew Bible and Its Modern Interpreters* (ed. D. A. Knight and G. A. Tucker; Chico, Calif.: Scholars Press, 1985), 123–65, esp. 150–58; Marvin A. Sweeney, *Isaiah 1–39, with an Introduction to Prophetic Literature* (FOTL 16; Grand Rapids and Cambridge, England: Eerdmans, 1996), 10–15.

[4] See esp. Nogalski, *Literary Precursors;* idem, *Redactional Processes;* and idem, "Intertextuality in the Twelve," in Watts and House, *Forming Prophetic Literature,* 102–24, for discussion of intertextual factors in the formation of the Book of the Twelve.

[5] For discussion of the formation of the Twelve in relation to the Septuagint and versions extant among the scrolls from the Judean wilderness, see Jones, *Formation of the Book of the Twelve.*

[6] See Ben Zvi, "Twelve Prophetic Books," 140–42 for a critique of Nogalski on this point.

the overall conception and composition of the Book of the Twelve as an autonomous literary work. Sirach 49:10 demonstrates that there was a conception of the "Twelve Prophets" as early as the mid–second century B.C.E., although it provides no clue as to its arrangement. Other ancient sources indicate at least five different sequences for the Book of the Twelve, which demonstrates that the arrangement was quite fluid but that the concept of the book as a whole was secure.[7] Two of these sequences, that of the Septuagint (Hosea; Amos; Micah; Joel; Obadiah; Jonah; Nahum; Habakkuk; Zephaniah; Haggai; Zechariah; Malachi) and that of the Masoretic Text (Hosea; Joel; Amos; Obadiah; Jonah; Micah; Nahum; Habakkuk; Zephaniah; Haggai; Zechariah; Malachi) have dominated conceptions of the Book of the Twelve within Judaism, Western Christianity, and modern critical scholarship.

Attempts to explain the rationale for these sequences have emphasized chronological principles, even when lexical associations or analogies with other works, such as the book of Isaiah, are taken into account.[8] Scholars have observed that some synchronically based chronological principle is clearly discernible in the arrangement of both versions of the Book of the Twelve, in that each begins generally with prophets that are explicitly placed by their contents in the eighth century B.C.E. and then proceeds to prophets of the seventh and sixth centuries B.C.E. There are problems with the chronological sequence of both versions, particularly in relation to Joel, Obadiah, and Malachi, the

---

[7] See Ben Zvi, "Twelve Prophetic Books," 134, n. 24. The sequences include the (1) MT, 8HevXIIgr, and MurXII (Hosea; Joel; Amos; Obadiah; Jonah; Micah; Nahum; Habakkuk; Zephaniah; Haggai; Zechariah; Malachi);(2) LXX, *4 Ezra* 1:39–40 (Hosea; Amos; Micah; Joel; Obadiah; Jonah; Nahum; Habakkuk; Zephaniah; Haggai; Zechariah; Malachi);(3) *Martyrdom and Ascension of Isaiah* 4:22 (Amos; Hosea; Micah; Joel; Nahum; Jonah; Obadiah; Habakkuk; Haggai; Zephaniah; Zechariah; Malachi); (4) *Lives of the Prophets* (Hosea; Micah; Amos; Joel; Obadiah; Jonah; Nahum; Habakkuk; Zephaniah; Haggai; Zechariah; Malachi); and (5) 4QXII, which contains fragments of nine books (Joel; Obadiah; Jonah; Nahum; Habakkuk; Zephaniah; Haggai; Zechariah; Malachi), some of which show books in sequence: 4QXII[a] contains fragments of Zechariah and a sequence of Malachi–Jonah; 4QXII[b] contains a sequence Zephaniah–Haggai; 4QXII[g] contains sequences for Amos–Obadiah and Nahum–Habakkuk. For discussion of 4QXII[a] and the other manuscripts of the Twelve from Cave 4 at Qumran and elsewhere in the Judean desert, see Russell Earl Fuller, "The Minor Prophets Manuscripts from Qumran, Cave IV" (Ph.D. diss., Harvard University, 1988); idem, "The Form and Formation of the Book of the Twelve: The Evidence from the Judean Desert," in Watts and House, *Forming Prophetic Literature*, 86–101.

[8] See Nogalski, *Literary Precursors*, 3–4; Paul Redditt, "Zechariah 9–14, Malachi, and the Redaction of the Book of the Twelve," in Watts and House, *Forming Prophetic Literature*, 245–68, esp. 261–63, for discussion and critique of this view.

contents of which make them difficult to place chronologically. Obadiah would have to be the first of the prophets in that the book presupposes a ninth-century setting, insofar as traditional sources identify Obadiah with Elijah's associate, who announced the presence of the prophet to the Israelite king Ahab (1 Kgs 18).[9] The reference to the Valley of Jehoshaphat indicates that Joel alludes to the same general period in the ninth century, even though its own historical setting must remain uncertain.[10] Of the eighth-century prophets, Jonah and Amos would have to come first in that they are placed only in the reigns of Jeroboam ben Joash and Uzziah,[11] followed by Hosea, whose setting ranges from the

---

[9] See Paul R. Raabe, *Obadiah* (AB 24D; New York: Doubleday, 1996), 49. The superscription of the book of Obadiah provides little basis for establishing its historical setting, identifying it simply as "the vision of Obadiah." The book calls for the downfall of Edom at the Day of YHWH, and charges Edom with having gloated over the defeat of Jerusalem by foreigners. It looks to the reestablishment of Zion and Israelite/Judean control over all the land of Israel, the Phoenician coast, the Negev, the Shephelah, and the Transjordan. Based on analogies with exilic and postexilic texts such as Ps 137; Lam 4; Isa 34; 63:1–6; and Ezek 25:12–14, many argue that the portrayal of Jerusalem's defeat must be understood in relation to the Babylonian exile. Although the Babylonian exile clearly influences the reading of the book, the figure of Obadiah has traditionally been identified with the ninth-century prophet Elijah's associate, who announced the presence of the prophet to the Israelite king Ahab (869–850 B.C.E.; see 1 Kgs 18), a contemporary of Jehoshaphat. In the aftermath of the reigns of these kings, 2 Kings reports that Jerusalem was threatened and perhaps taken by Hazael of Aram (2 Kgs 12:17–18); it was later taken by Jehoash of northern Israel (2 Kgs 14:8–14). Insofar as Edom was expected to be a vassal and ally of Judah during this period (2 Kgs 8:20–22; 14:7), the charges against Edom detailed in Obadiah could well be read in relation to events from the ninth and early eighth centuries B.C.E. Even if they must be read in relation to the Babylonian exile, the identification of Obadiah with Elijah's associate establishes that the book presupposes a ninth-century setting, which would present Obadiah as the earliest of the Twelve Prophets.

[10] The superscription of Joel provides no basis for establishing the historical setting of the book, identifying it simply as "the word of YHWH that came to Joel ben Pethuel." The prophet is otherwise unknown. The book presents a scenario in which the land is devastated by locusts and an unidentified nation that has come against it, and the people are lamenting at the altar of the temple (Joel 1). It anticipates the Day of YHWH, in which YHWH will act to restore the fertility of the land (Joel 2) and to conduct holy war against the nations in the Valley of Jehoshaphat, thereby restoring the security of Judah, Jerusalem, Israel, and all creation (Joel 3–4 [MT]). The reference to the Valley of Jehoshaphat apparently recalls the Judean king Jehoshaphat's defeat of Moab, Ammon, and the men of Mount Seir (Edom) in the Valley of Berachah near Teqoa, which is recorded in 2 Chron 20. Jehoshaphat ruled 873–849 B.C.E., but this does not define the historical setting envisioned in the book. The mention of the Greeks (Joel 4:6 [Eng., 3:6]) and the Sabaeans (Joel 4:8 [Eng., 3:8]) suggests settings ranging from the late eighth century through the Persian period and beyond, but the precise setting must remain uncertain.

[11] The contents of the book of Jonah clearly presuppose the period of Assyrian

time of Jeroboam ben Joash through Hezekiah,[12] and then Micah, who
is placed in the reigns of Jotham, Ahaz, and Hezekiah.[13] Of the seventh-
century prophets, Zephaniah would have to be the first, although some
would argue that Nahum must precede.[14] In any case, Habakkuk would
have to be the last in that the book presupposes the period following the
reign of Josiah.[15] Of the sixth-century prophets, the setting of Haggai
in the second year of Darius requires that he precede Zechariah, who is

---

ascendancy as its historical setting, and the identification of Jonah ben Amittai with
the prophet mentioned in 2 Kgs 14:25 likewise establishes the reign of Jeroboam ben
Joash (786–746 B.C.E.) as the setting presupposed by the book. This would portray
Jonah as a contemporary of Amos. The superscription of Amos clearly identifies
the historical setting as the reigns of the Judean king Uzziah (783–742 B.C.E.) and
the Israelite king Jeroboam ben Joash (786–746 B.C.E.). The book thereby presents
Amos as an eighth-century prophet, but chronologically he must be considered prior
to Hosea.

[12] The superscription of the book of Hosea identifies its historical setting in the
reigns of the Judean kings Uzziah (782–742 B.C.E.), Jotham (742–735 B.C.E.), Ahaz
(735–715 B.C.E.), and Hezekiah (715–687/6 B.C.E.) and the Israelite king Jeroboam
ben Joash (786–746 B.C.E.), which establishes a historical range from 786 B.C.E.
through 687/6 B.C.E. Basically, it presents Hosea as a prophet from the eighth and
perhaps the early seventh century B.C.E.

[13] The superscription of Micah identifies the historical setting of the book as the
reigns of the Judean kings Jotham (742–735 B.C.E.), Ahaz (735–715 B.C.E.), and
Hezekiah (715–687/6 B.C.E.), which would make him a younger contemporary of
Hosea. It looks forward to the Babylonian exile, in that it argues that ultimately
Israel will return together with the nations to Zion to acknowledge YHWH's sovereignty in the aftermath of Babylonian captivity (Mic 4–5; N.B. 4:10). Nevertheless, it
presents Micah as an eighth-century prophet.

[14] The superscription of Zephaniah identifies the reign of King Josiah (640–609
B.C.E.) as the setting of the book, which places the prophet prior to the time of
Habakkuk and potentially prior to the time of Nahum. The date of Zephaniah's
composition is disputed, and many see the book as an eschatological portrayal of
world judgment. Nevertheless, the book is formulated as an exhortation to seek
YHWH. The contents of the book, which call for the purification of Jerusalem and
judgment against Judah's enemies on the Day of YHWH, fit well with the early years
of Josiah's reform. Chronologically, Zephaniah must be placed prior to Habakkuk.
For discussion of Zephaniah, see Marvin A. Sweeney, "A Form-Critical Reassessment
of the Book of Zephaniah," *CBQ* 53 (1991): 388–408. The superscription of Nahum
provides no overt historical setting for the book, but the prophet's vision concerning
Nineveh clearly presupposes the downfall of the city, whether realized or impending.
Although Nineveh fell in 612 B.C.E., many argue that the book may be dated earlier in
the seventh century because of the reference to the fall of Thebes in 664 B.C.E. (Nah
3:8–9), so that the announcement of Nineveh's downfall must be read as anticipation
of the event. In either case, the book presents Nahum as a seventh-century prophet.
For discussion of Nahum, see Marvin A. Sweeney, "Concerning the Structure and
Generic Character of the Book of Nahum," *ZAW* 104 (1992): 364–77.

[15] The two superscriptions of the book of Habakkuk (Hab 1:1; 3:1) provide no
overt reference to the historical setting. The reference to the rise of the Neo-
Babylonian Empire in Hab 1:5–11 and the threat that it poses to Judah clearly places

placed in Darius's second through fourth years.[16] The setting of Malachi is uncertain.[17]

A chronological principle does not provide the full rationale for the sequence of the Twelve Prophets in either the LXX or the MT. Nevertheless, the work of previous scholars on both versions suggests not a random, but a deliberate sequence of prophets within the whole. Much of this work, however, has been based in redaction-critical questions or other diachronic presuppositions that have unduly influenced the interpretation of the book. In an effort to identify the principle or principles that help determine the sequence of each version, it is necessary to examine the sequence of prophets within both the LXX and MT versions of the Book of the Twelve from an exclusively synchronic perspective. In this regard, the sequence of books within both the LXX and MT versions may well address diachronic questions concerning the formation of the Book of the Twelve, in that the sequence points to hermeneutics by which the individual prophetic books are both received and presented as constitutive components of the "Book of the Twelve" as a whole.

---

the setting in the late seventh or early sixth centuries B.C.E., in the aftermath of the reign of Josiah, when the Babylonians ultimately established hegemony over Judah.

[16] The date formulas of the book of Haggai clearly identify the second year of the Achaemenid king Darius (521–485 B.C.E.), i.e., 520 B.C.E., as the historical setting of the book, which places it at the beginning of temple construction carried out by Zerubbabel and Joshua ben Jehozadak in 520–515 B.C.E. Hence, the book presents Haggai as a late-sixth-century prophet. The date formulas of Zechariah identify the second through fourth years of Darius (520–518 B.C.E.) as the historical setting. Although scholars agree that Zech 9–14 must date to a period much later than the late sixth century, the lack of overt indicators that these chapters constitute a separate book subsumes them to the message and setting of Zech 1–8. The entire book thereby presents Zechariah as a late-sixth-century prophet, who must be viewed as contemporary with Haggai but who continued speaking after Haggai had ceased.

[17] Finally, Malachi provides no overt indication of its historical setting, and many have questioned whether "Malachi" constitutes a proper name or merely the designation "my messenger," perhaps in reference to the prophet Elijah who is to return (Mal 3:1; 4:5–6). Some have argued that its identification as a maśśā᾽ (מַשָּׂא) indicates that it is to be read in sequence with the maśśā᾽ôt defined in Zech 9–11 and 12–14, so that it might not even constitute a distinct prophetic book. Despite its compositional prehistory, the present expanded form of the superscription in Mal 1:1 identifies it as a distinct book in the present form of the Twelve. Many see the concern with the priests as evidence of a postexilic setting, but, indeed, Malachi provides no overt evidence for such claims. The concern with the purity and proper functioning of the temple could be placed in many different periods of Judah's existence. For an overview of discussion concerning Malachi, see R. J. Coggins, *Haggai, Zechariah, Malachi* (OTG; Sheffield: JSOT Press, 1987).

Reading the Sequences of the LXX and MT

Although it seems evident that chronological considerations may at some point have influenced the sequence in both versions of the Book of the Twelve, other criteria must be identified. In order to establish the rationale for the sequence of both the LXX and the MT versions of the Book of the Twelve, it is necessary to examine the twelve individual prophetic compositions that constitute the book. The Book of the Twelve, apart from its presentation as a single assemblage, lacks overt indicators that the twelve individual prophetic works are to be read as a coherent whole. Each of the twelve individual works therefore constitutes a potentially self-standing composition that can be read independently of the current literary context of the Book of the Twelve. Each conveys its own unique contents, literary structure, generic characteristics, sociohistorical setting, and theological or ideological outlook, so that each of the component prophetic works of the Book of the Twelve potentially constitutes a distinctive and autonomous literary communication. This helps to account for the variety of versions in which the book appears. Nevertheless, the placement of the individual books within the Book of the Twelve necessarily compromises their communicative autonomy and subsumes them to the overall communicative outlook of the book as a whole; that is, when the individual books are read in relation to each other, their communicative functions and outlooks change. In this respect, it is noteworthy that both the LXX and MT versions of the Twelve each begin with Hosea and end with Malachi; indeed, the sequence of the last six books, Nahum, Habakkuk, Zephaniah, Haggai, Zechariah, and Malachi, is identical in both versions.

Hosea seems particularly well suited to its introductory role. It begins by raising the question of the disrupted relationship between YHWH and Israel by comparing it to the disrupted marriage of the prophet to his wife Gomer. The nature of the analogy is spelled out throughout the book, which charges Israel with having abandoned its covenant relationship with YHWH throughout its history. It is noteworthy, however, that the book calls for a reconciliation, both between Hosea and his wife and between YHWH and Israel. The book ends with an appeal by the prophet for Israel to return to YHWH so that the relationship might be restored. The book thereby stands as a programmatic introduction to a major issue posed by the Twelve, the restoration of Israel and its relationship with YHWH following punishment at the hands of various nations. The statements in Malachi concerning YHWH's distaste for divorce take on new meaning when read in relation to Hosea, especially since Malachi also calls for the restoration of the covenant between YHWH and Israel.

The LXX sequence of the Twelve then continues with Amos and Micah.[18] They are not presented in chronological order, but according to thematic concerns. Amos is designed as a polemical discourse that ultimately calls for the destruction of the royal sanctuary of the northern kingdom of Israel at Beth-El and the restoration of Davidic rule over all Israel.[19] Amos is clearly Judean and employs a Judean perspective as he attacks the northern kingdom and its rulers throughout the book. Ultimately, Amos must be recognized as a book that calls for the downfall of the northern monarchy and the reunification of the people of Israel around the house of David and the Jerusalem temple. Micah follows naturally in this sequence. It begins by establishing that Samaria's and Israel's punishment would provide the model for the anticipated punishment of Judah and Jerusalem. But once the punishment of Jerusalem and Judah is complete, the people of Israel would be returned from their exile and reunited at Zion under the rule of YHWH. The nations are also included in the scenario; they recognize YHWH and come to Zion as the exiles are gathered from their midst. Likewise, a (Davidic) ruler will arise from Bethlehem and defeat the Assyrian enemy as part of the general restoration. The book concludes with statements of YHWH's expectations of the people for the future and a liturgical composition that expresses confidence in YHWH's mercy and capacity to forgive.

The initial LXX sequence of Hosea, Amos, and Micah expresses concern with the disruption and ultimate restoration of Israel's relationship with YHWH, as well as with restoring the unity of the people of Israel and Judah around the house of David and the Jerusalem temple. The next four books in the LXX sequence, Joel, Obadiah, Jonah, and Nahum, shift their concern to the nations. Joel is especially well suited to begin this section in that it presents people mourning at the temple over an unidentified nation and a locust plague that threaten the land — whether the land is Israel or Judah or both is uncertain. The book en-

---

[18] For studies of the interrelationship of Hosea and Amos, see Jörg Jeremias, "Die Anfänge des Dodekapropheton: Hosea und Amos," in *Congress Volume: Paris, 1992* (ed. J. A. Emerton; VTSup 61; Leiden: Brill, 1992), 87–106; idem, "The Interrelationship between Amos and Hosea," in Watts and House, *Forming Prophetic Literature*, 171–86.

[19] See Marvin A. Sweeney, "Formation and Form in Prophetic Literature," in *Old Testament Interpretation: Past, Present, and Future* (ed. J. L. Mays, D. L. Petersen, and K. H. Richards; Nashville: Abingdon, 1995), 113–26.

visions a response to this threat on the Day of YHWH, in which YHWH brings a heavenly host to turn back the threats, defeats the nations that have attacked Jerusalem and Judah, and restores the natural vitality and fertility of the land. The lack of historical specificity enables the book of Joel and its presentation of the Day of YHWH to take on a programmatic character much as Hosea does; the enemy is not identified, and the threat is expressed against creation as well as against Judah and Jerusalem. Joel can therefore speak to any period in Judah's and Israel's history in which an enemy threatened the existence of YHWH's people and in which that threat was removed.

The book of Obadiah, by contrast, is quite specific about the identity of the nation that threatens Jerusalem. The book is a diatribe against Edom for standing by, gloating, and rendering assistance as foreigners ravage Jerusalem. Obadiah is generally read in relation to the Babylonian exile, but nothing in the book requires this context. It employs the motif of the Day of YHWH and makes it clear that the judgment is directed against all of the nations, not just Edom, so that Edom easily stands as a symbol for all nations that threaten Jerusalem. This becomes especially important within the overall context of the Book of the Twelve as Joel defines a programmatic understanding of the Day of YHWH in relation to the nations at large,[20] and Malachi begins with a notice of Edom's destruction. The book envisions the restoration of Zion and calls for the subjugation of surrounding nations in much the same pattern as Zephaniah or Zechariah.

The book of Jonah reverses course in relation to Obadiah in that it presents a scenario in which even Nineveh can be forgiven and granted mercy by YHWH. The LXX sequence has already made clear that Israel can be forgiven and restored if it repents; the same possibility is envisioned for Assyria. By analogy with the model of Edom in Obadiah, such forgiveness perhaps can be extended to the other nations as well. The following book of Nahum, however, makes clear that no such forgiveness will be granted in the absence of repentance. Nahum argues that YHWH has been in control of events from the beginning, including the

---

[20] Note also that Joel cites extensively from Obadiah, indicating that it was composed to stand in relation to Obadiah. See Siegfried Bergler, *Joel als Schriftinterpret* (BEATAJ 16; Frankfurt/Main: Peter Lang, 1988). Joel quotes extensively from other books as well, indicating the late date of its composition. Particularly noteworthy in the present instance is the reversed citation of Mic 4:1–5/Isa 2:1–4 in Joel 4:10 (Eng., 3:10), which suggests that Joel was designed to follow Micah, as in the LXX sequence. The citation would make little sense unless the reader had already encountered Mic 4:1–5.

punishment of Judah by Assyria, and is now taking action against Assyria for its arrogance in abusing the people of Judah and Israel. Insofar as Nahum also looks forward to the restoration of Israel, it prepares for the books that follow.

Whereas the LXX version of the Twelve is organized first to address concerns with Israel and Judah and then with the nations, the MT version appears to adopt a different principle of organization, in which these concerns are mixed. The MT places both of the programmatic books at the beginning. Hosea again raises the question of the disrupted relationship between Israel and YHWH and calls for Israel's repentance and return. Likewise, the book of Joel outlines the threat posed against Israel by the unspecified enemy nation, and envisions the defeat of the threatening nation and the restoration of the people in Jerusalem at the Day of YHWH. The portrayal of cosmic upheaval and restoration feeds on the imagery of Hosea, which portrays natural upheaval of the land as a correlate to the disruption of Israel's relationship with YHWH (Hos 4) and thereby expresses the cosmic dimensions of the scenario that will come to the forefront again in Zechariah.

The book of Amos follows and begins to spell out the implementation or realization of the scenarios set down in the programmatic books of Hosea and Joel. It charges abuse against the northern kingdom of Israel, again calling for the destruction of the Beth-El temple, the death of Jeroboam ben Joash, and the reestablishment of Davidic rule over Israel. Although these specific proposals were never realized, the book does point to the destruction of the northern kingdom of Israel in the late eighth century. The concluding call for possession of Edom may well speak to eighth-century Judean concerns with dominating its neighbor, but in the context of the Book of the Twelve, it provides a suitable transition to the book of Obadiah. Although Obadiah, when read in isolation from the other books of the Twelve, appears to be set in the ninth century, its placement may indicate Edom's seizure of Eilat and other attacks against Judah during the Syro-Ephraimitic War (2 Kgs 16:5–6; 2 Chron 28:16–17) and perhaps Edom's failure to join Hezekiah's revolt or to support Jerusalem during Sennacherib's siege. Again, the condemnation of Edom and restoration of Zion presages YHWH's defeat of enemy nations later in the Twelve (e.g., Nahum; Zeph 2:4–15; Zech 9–14), and serves as the premise in Malachi for the call to observe YHWH's covenant.

That Jonah precedes Micah in the MT version of the Book of the Twelve is noteworthy in that Micah speaks clearly about Jerusalem's demise. When viewed within the sequence of the Book of the Twelve, Jonah's articulation of YHWH's potential forgiveness for Assyria may suggest an offer of mercy to Nineveh prior to its assaults against Jerusalem and Judah during the reign of Hezekiah. Insofar as Micah points to Israel as a model for the fate of Judah and Jerusalem, it may presuppose Sennacherib's invasion of Judah as the beginning of YHWH's punishment of Jerusalem. Israel's restoration to Zion presupposes return from the Babylonian exile, but it points to the defeat of the Assyrians as the first stage of the restoration in which a new king from Bethlehem will arise to defeat Israel's enemies. In the present MT form of the Book of the Twelve, Micah clearly looks toward the Babylonian exile, but it does so from the perspective of the Assyrian period.

Indeed, Micah's concern with the defeat of Assyria provides a suitable introduction for the book of Nahum in the MT sequence of the Twelve.[21] Nahum argues that YHWH has been in control of events from the beginning and was responsible for Assyria's punishment of Judah, but Nahum also argues that YHWH is punishing Nineveh for its arrogant treatment of Judah. Although there is little evidence that Nineveh was deliberately portrayed as a symbol for the nations in Nahum, its placement in the Book of the Twelve suggests this role, especially when Nahum is read in the aftermath of books like Joel, Obadiah, and Micah, which speak in nonspecific terms about the nations or mix their references so that Edom and Assyria appear as models for enemy nations in general. As noted above, Nahum also occupies a similar position in the LXX version, although it is directly preceded by Joel, Obadiah, and Jonah so that the symbolic character of the book is even more clearly emphasized. Indeed, the actual downfall of Nineveh would help to validate the following prophetic books in both versions.

Beginning with Nahum, the sequence of the LXX and MT versions of the Book of the Twelve is identical. Habakkuk immediately follows Nahum's presentation of Nineveh's demise with its own portrayal of the threat posed to Judah by the rise of the Neo-Babylonian Empire. The book portrays a dialogue between the prophet and YHWH in which Habakkuk protests the evil done to Judah by the Babylonians.[22] As in

---

[21] Note also the intertextual relationship defined by Nogalski, "The Redactional Shaping of Nahum 1 for the Book of the Twelve," in *Among the Prophets: Language, Image, and Structure in the Prophetic Writings* (ed. P. R. Davies and D. J. A. Clines; JSOTSup 144; Sheffield: Sheffield Academic Press, 1993), 193–202.

[22] See Marvin A. Sweeney, "Structure, Genre, and Intent in the Book of Habakkuk," *VT* 41 (1991): 63–83.

Nahum, YHWH claims responsibility for bringing the Babylonians and then argues that they, too, will be brought down on account of their greed and arrogance in treating their subjects. The book calls for patience in waiting for YHWH to act, outlines the atrocities of the evil, and concludes with a liturgical psalm that expresses confidence in YHWH's defeat of the enemy.

The book of Zephaniah may well be set historically during the reign of Josiah, but its placement in the Book of the Twelve indicates a somewhat different conception of the chronology and role of the book.[23] It calls for the purge of evil from Jerusalem and Judah, and looks forward to the defeat of Philistia, Ammon and Moab, Ethiopia, and Assyria prior to Jerusalem's restoration. Insofar as Zephaniah follows Habakkuk, which is concerned with the threat posed to Judah by Babylonia, and precedes Haggai, which is concerned with temple reconstruction, the book apparently represents the defeat of Jerusalem, Judah, and the other nations by the Babylonian Empire as an expression of the Day of YHWH. It thereby presents that defeat as YHWH's means of purging the city from evil and of preparing it for the role outlined in Mic 4. The placement of Zephaniah within the Twelve helps prompt the many eschatological understandings of the book in the history of interpretation.

The book of Haggai presupposes temple reconstruction in the early postexilic or Persian period. It argues that the reconstruction will bring recognition of YHWH by the nations and the return of exiles, events previously articulated in various books of the Twelve Prophets. Likewise, its portrayal of Zerubbabel as the "signet ring" of YHWH builds on the portrayals of the rise of righteous Davidic rule that appear throughout the Twelve. The book of Zechariah continues this theme, although it does not envision the rise of a Davidic monarch until the eschatological manifestation of YHWH in the world. It employs the visions of the prophet to portray the reconstruction of the temple in cosmic terms, as a sign of YHWH's universal sovereignty, and argues that the priests will rule until the new Davidic king and YHWH appear. It recaps the vision, in Mic 4, of the nations streaming to Zion with Israel, and then describes the eschatological scenario whereby the new king appears, the cosmos is transformed, and the nations defeated as YHWH establishes sovereignty at Zion.

Finally, Malachi, in its call for the renewed observance of the covenant, rehearses various themes from the Twelve, such as the destruction

---

[23] See also Collins, *Mantle of Elijah*, 76–77.

of Edom/Esau, the disrupted covenant between YHWH and Israel, the polluted state of the temple and the priesthood, and the Day of YHWH. In projecting YHWH's appearance, Malachi calls for observance of Mosaic Torah, and thereby recalls the instruction in YHWH's Torah that will be given in Zion (Mic 4); it looks forward to the appearance of Elijah, who is perhaps associated with the allusions to Jehoshaphat in Joel and Obadiah, when Israel turns its heart back to YHWH. Insofar as Malachi expresses YHWH's distaste for divorce and calls for the return of Israel to YHWH, it rounds out the themes introduced in the book of Hosea.

Conclusions

On the basis of the preceding discussion, several observations and conclusions can be made. First, it is clear that a chronological principle does not fully explain the sequence of books in either the LXX or the MT versions of the Book of the Twelve. Chronology is influential in that the books are grouped roughly by the eighth, seventh, and sixth centuries, but various problems appear. Joel and Malachi present no chronological setting. Obadiah may relate to the ninth century, but it does not begin either the LXX or MT sequence. Within the various centuries, the sequence does not appear to be chronological; Jonah and Amos should be the earliest of the eighth-century books, and Habakkuk should be the last of the seventh-century books. The placement of the books in each sequence may reflect a different concept of chronology from that presented in the individual book. Within the MT sequence, Obadiah may presuppose Edom's actions against Jerusalem and Judah during the late eighth century, and in both sequences, Zephaniah apparently expresses the purging of Jerusalem during the Babylonian exile. Nevertheless, chronological principles provide some basis for the organization of both LXX and MT versions insofar as they follow a general sequence of centuries, but such principles are skewed in placing individual books within each century.

Second, thematic factors appear to play a role in the organization of the Book of the Twelve, but these factors differ in the LXX and MT versions. The LXX presents a sequence that, in Hosea, Amos, and Micah, first emphasizes YHWH's judgment against the northern kingdom (Israel), the implications of judgment for Jerusalem and Judah, and the potential for Israel's restoration in Zion. The LXX in Joel, Obadiah, Jonah, and Nahum then turns to the nations; it points to the Day of YHWH as a programmatic day of judgment against the nations and of restoration for Zion. It then lays out the specifics of YHWH's plans by portraying Edom's punishment as a model for the other nations, by articulating the principle that repentance will result in mercy and forgiveness, and by demonstrating that punishment will ensue if nations continue to abuse the roles to which YHWH assigns them. The LXX then turns in Habakkuk, Zephaniah, Haggai, and Zechariah to Jerusalem and the Babylonian exile. It first points to Babylon as a power established by YHWH that will fall when it abuses its position, and then outlines the process by which Jerusalem and various nations will be purged by the Babylonians prior to restoration. Restoration involves rebuilding the temple as a sign of YHWH's sovereignty over the nations, the restoration of Davidic rule, and the nations' submission to YHWH as indicative of the restoration's cosmic significance. Finally, the book of Malachi rehearses the themes of the Twelve and presents a renewed call for Israel's repentance and observance of the covenant, thereby recapping the themes introduced by Hosea.

Although for the last six books the MT employs the same sequence as the LXX, the first six are arranged according to a different principle. Instead of first presenting the books concerned with Israel and then those concerned with the nations, the MT mixes books together. The result is the placement of two programmatic books at the beginning — Hosea outlines the disrupted relationship between YHWH and Israel and calls for Israel's repentance; Joel outlines YHWH's defense of Jerusalem and Israel on the Day of YHWH, emphasizing the transformation of the cosmos as YHWH manifests sovereignty over the nations. Following books then lay out the details of these two programmatic books. Amos, as expressions of the Day of YHWH, takes up the punishment of northern Israel, the destruction of Beth-El, and the reinstatement of the house of David, and Obadiah does the same for the punishment of Edom and other nations. Jonah expresses the principle — applied to Israel in Hosea — that the nations, exemplified by Assyria, might also repent and receive mercy from YHWH. Micah then portrays Israel's punishment as a means by which Jerusalem will be prepared for its role as the holy center, where all the nations of the earth will join Israel in acknowledging YHWH's sovereignty. Nahum outlines the consequences for Assyria when it refuses to repent, and the rest follows as in the LXX version with an outline of the punishment and restoration of Jerusalem during the course of the Babylonian exile and its aftermath. Whereas the LXX version distinguishes stages, focusing first on Israel and then the nations prior to presenting Jerusalem's punishment and restoration, the MT presents the process as a continuum, emphasizing Jerusalem from the outset. In calling for the return of Israel, Hosea makes clear that Israel must return to Jerusalem and David as well as to YHWH, and Joel emphasizes Jerusalem's defense as the primary concern of the Day of YHWH.

These differences point to different conceptions of the Book of the Twelve that may relate to the theological concerns of the circles in which each version was transmitted. The LXX organization of Israel, nations, and Jerusalem also appears in the LXX version of Jeremiah and in Ezekiel. Many have argued that the LXX originated in the Alexandrian Jewish Diaspora and reflects the concerns of an exiled Jewish community living among the nations.[24] Unfortunately, no manuscript evidence confirms this point; the earliest LXX manuscripts of the Twelve are Christian manuscripts that date to the third and fourth centuries C.E. Indeed, the concern with Israel, the nations, and the restoration of the nations in Jerusalem fits well with Christian theology and its understanding of the role of prophecy as a means to predict the fulfillment of Israel's destiny in the revelation of Christ to the nations. The MT sequence, on the other hand, focuses especially on the role of Jerusalem, including the punishment of Israel and the nations, and the implications these developments have for the purging of Jerusalem and its place as the center of YHWH's world sovereignty. Such concern would be particularly characteristic of an indigenous Jewish community centered around Jerusalem. It could easily derive from either the Persian or the Hellenistic periods, when Jerusalem was subject to foreign rule.[25] In this respect, it is noteworthy that the second-century B.C.E. Wadi Murabba'at manuscript and the mid–first century B.C.E. Nahal Hever Greek manuscript both derive from Judah, and present the same order of books that later appears in the MT.[26]

Further research and discussion is necessary in order to test the validity of the proposals outlined here. In any case, this essay points not only to the fluidity of conceptions of the Book of the Twelve in antiquity, but to the fluidity of interpretation of the individual books, once they became parts of the whole.

---

[24] For overviews, see H. B. Swete, *An Introduction to the Old Testament in Greek* (repr., New York: Ktav, 1968); Sidney Jellicoe, *The Septuagint and Modern Study* (Oxford: Oxford University Press, 1968); Emanuel Tov, *The Text-Critical Use of the Septuagint in Biblical Research* (Jerusalem: Simor, 1981); Melvin K. Peters, "Septuagint," *ABD* 5.1093–104.

[25] Cf. Steck, *Abschluss* (see n. 1 above), who argues that the Book of the Twelve derives from the period of the Diadochi wars.

[26] For discussion, see Fuller, "Form and Formation of the Book of the Twelve"; Jones, *Formation of the Book of the Twelve.*

5

The Book of the Twelve as a Witness
to Ancient Biblical Interpretation

Barry A. Jones

Recent Studies: Evaluating Models

The one who approaches the subject of the Book of the Twelve joins a conversation already in progress. One issue in this discussion is the question posed in the title of R. J. Coggins's essay, "The Minor Prophets: One Book or Twelve?"[1] During the 1980s and 1990s, studies of the Twelve by O. H. Steck and by his colleagues and students have argued for the answer "one book." According to this view, the Twelve is the result of an intentional redactional effort to unify the various traditions of the Minor Prophets into a single literary work.[2] The culmination of this approach is J. D. Nogalski's two-volume study.[3] Nogalski examines, patiently and in great detail, evidence for the use of redactional *Stichwörter* in the literary seams between adjoining books of the Twelve and argues from this evidence that the Twelve is a redactionally connected whole. Steck has focused his research on the concluding chapters of the Twelve, Zech 9–14 and Malachi, and parallels between them and the later chapters of the book of Isaiah. He has reconstructed what he considers to be the final stages in the redactional composition of this material. He sees in the final stage, particularly Mal 3:22–24, not only the completion of the Book of the Twelve, but also the redactional completion of the prophetic

---

[1] In *Crossing the Boundaries: Essays in Biblical Interpretation in Honour of Michael D. Goulder* (ed. S. E. Porter, P. Joyce, and D. E. Orton; Biblical Interpretation Series 8; Leiden: Brill, 1994), 57–68.

[2] See especially Steck's *Der Abschluß der Prophetie im alten Testament: Ein Versuch zur Frage der Vorgeschichte des Kanons* (Neukirchen-Vluyn: Neukirchener, 1991) and related articles by Steck cited therein. For works employing Steck's methodologies, see P. Weimar, "Obadja: Eine redaktionskritische Analyse," *BN* 27 (1985): 94–99; E. Bosshard-Nepustil, "Beobachtungen zum Zwölfprophetenbuch," *BN* 40 (1987): 30–62; and E. Bosshard-Nepustil and R. G. Kratz, "Maleachi im Zwölfprophetenbuch," *BN* 52 (1990): 27–46.

[3] *Literary Precursors to the Book of the Twelve* (BZAW 217; Berlin: de Gruyter, 1993), and *Redactional Processes in the Book of the Twelve* (BZAW 218; Berlin: de Gruyter, 1993).

section of the canon of Hebrew Scriptures, beginning with the book of Joshua and ending with Malachi.[4]

The arguments of Steck, Nogalski, and others have the appeal of employing a self-conscious and consistent methodology and, in the case of Nogalski, the sheer weight of argumentation. They attempt to carry the day. The field of biblical studies, however, appears to have an inherent resistance to open-and-shut cases. E. Ben Zvi has troubled the interpretive waters charted by redaction-historical studies and has also enlivened the discussion of the formation of the Book of the Twelve. In both his detailed *Historical-Critical Study of the Book of Obadiah*[5] and in a lengthy essay on the proposed unity of the Twelve,[6] Ben Zvi's response to the question of one book or twelve may be paraphrased as follows: "One long, self-contained scroll, yes; one grand, unified, literary corpus, no."

A deciding factor for Ben Zvi is the question, "How would the intended audience have read the contents of the Book of the Twelve?" According to Ben Zvi, internal textual markers directed the ancient reader to the immediate context of each thought-unit and to the broader context of the individual book, but no further. He takes issue, for example, with Nogalski's claim that the book of Obadiah was written primarily to occupy textual space within the macrostructure of the Twelve between Amos and Micah. Ben Zvi argues that a reference to a literary context beyond the boundaries of the individual book requires reading the material in Obadiah in a way that is often in competition with or contradictory to readings governed by the immediate context. Certainly one may read Obadiah in any literary context one chooses, including the context of world literature, but to do so is something quite different from saying that Obadiah has its primary meaning within a context beyond the boundaries of its internal demarcations. A far more convincing argument could be made for Obadiah as part of a unified Book of the Twelve, according to Ben Zvi, if it were not so clearly marked with an individual introduction, a conclusion, and an attributed source and title, "the vision of Obadiah" (Obad 1). Simplicity of logic dictates that ancient readers were more likely to pay attention to the clearly marked context of individual books than to broader literary relation-

---

[4] Steck, *Abschluß der Prophetie*, 127–36.

[5] BZAW 242; Berlin: de Gruyter, 1996.

[6] "Twelve Prophetic Books or 'The Twelve'? A Few Preliminary Considerations," in *Forming Prophetic Literature: Essays on Isaiah and the Twelve in Honor of John D. W. Watts* (ed. P. House and J. W. Watts; JSOTSup 229; Sheffield: Sheffield Academic Press, 1996), 124–35.

ships that can only be discerned by following uncommon patterns of reading. With regard to the question of one book or twelve, Ben Zvi concludes that the Book of the Twelve is "a collection or anthology of [twelve] separate, independent works" and is to be read as such.[7]

The views represented by Steck and Nogalski on the one hand and Ben Zvi on the other describe two directions in approaching the material in the Book of the Twelve. Surely there is wisdom in Coggins's response to his own question of "one book or twelve" with the answer "both one book and twelve."[8] Each approach has its strengths and weaknesses. Nogalski's work goes to great lengths to establish objectively what so many readers of the Twelve have sensed subjectively, namely, that these texts reverberate with common themes and voices found throughout the collection.[9] The sheer density of repetitions and textual allusions adds weight to Nogalski's thesis and confirms, although does not prove, the readerly intuition that "something must be behind all of these points of contact." Despite Nogalski's efforts, however, the simplicity of Ben Zvi's argument is also compelling. Surely clearer means of unifying these texts were available to ancient scribes had this been their ultimate aim. It is telling, as Ben Zvi observes, that nowhere in ancient manuscripts does one find an overarching superscription for "the Twelve," yet the individual books within the Twelve are clearly marked by their own internal superscriptions.[10]

In response to Ben Zvi's argument, Steck seems correct to search for unifying redactional materials in Zech 9–14 and Malachi. The material in Zech 9–14 is neither strongly connected with its preceding chapters in Zechariah nor is it clearly distinguished as a separate unit. Of the named books that comprise the Twelve, Malachi is least clearly marked as a separate unit, signaled as it is by the barest of attributions. The name mal'ākî (מלאכי), if it is a name, is barely such. Arguments for redactional unity seem strongest precisely in those places where internal

---

[7] Ibid., 131.

[8] Coggins, "Minor Prophets," 67–68.

[9] For a sophisticated discussion of the Twelve as an interplay between "one" text and "many" voices, see Herbert Marks, "The Twelve," in *The Literary Guide to the Bible* (ed. R. Alter and F. Kermode; Cambridge: Harvard University Press, 1987), 207–33.

[10] A rejoinder is possible to Ben Zvi's invocation of Occam's Razor, namely, that explaining Obadiah by reference to a wider composition of the Twelve unnecessarily complicates explanation of its contents. It is equally parsimonious to observe that a separate book of Obadiah is nowhere attested in ancient manuscripts and that to invent such a self-standing circulation again is to complicate unnecessarily the explanation of its location in the scroll of the Twelve. Arguments from logic are not self-validating.

attributions are weakest, namely Zech 9–14, Malachi, Joel, and Obadiah. Still, redactional analysis is unavoidably hypothetical in nature. It must work backward in time from existing texts to earlier forms that, if they ever existed, exist no longer. Therefore, the best that this approach can hope to achieve is to demonstrate a high degree of probability that the texts were produced in just such a way for just such a purpose. Although consensus is possible, the likelihood of dissent, such as that shown by Ben Zvi and others, is inherent within redactional approaches.[11]

The Contribution of Manuscript Evidence

In surveying this state of affairs, I am reminded of the prophet Elijah's words in 1 Kgs 18:21: "How long halt ye between two opinions?" My intention for weighing in on this question is to offer a contribution from a different perspective. I wish to introduce ancient manuscript evidence for the Book of the Twelve and the postbiblical interpretive traditions about these texts.

The conclusion of my research into the manuscript evidence has been that the surviving textual witnesses preserve a diversity of arrangements of the Twelve that were in circulation during the last two centuries before the common era.[12] This conclusion is based on evidence for an alternative Hebrew arrangement of the Twelve preserved in Greek manuscripts of the Minor Prophets and on the arrangement preserved in the fragmentary Qumran manuscript 4QXII[a]. In 4QXII[a], Malachi is definitely not the last book of the scroll, and the fragments of Jonah are best explained as following directly the ending of Malachi.[13]

The placement of Malachi and Jonah preserved in 4QXII[a] helps illustrate the differing approaches of Steck and Ben Zvi. Steck has argued that the sequence Malachi-Jonah is secondary to the MT sequence for two primary reasons. First, 4QXII[a] preserves the text of Mal 3:22–24, demonstrating that this text was composed when that scroll

---

[11] The possibility of consensus on redactional reconstructions is undermined, in my opinion, by Steck's attempt to date isolated redactional layers to rather specific times in the third and second centuries B.C.E. For example, Steck dates the final redaction of the Twelve between 220–201 B.C.E. or 198–190 B.C.E. See Steck, *Abschluß der Prophetie,* 156.

[12] Barry A. Jones, *The Formation of the Book of the Twelve: A Study in Text and Canon* (SBLDS 149; Atlanta: Scholars Press, 1995).

[13] This manuscript is published in R. Fuller, "The Minor Prophets," in *The Prophets* (ed. E. Ulrich; vol. 10 of *Qumran Cave IV;* DJD 15; Oxford: Clarendon Press, 1997), 221–28. See also the discussion in Jones, *Formation,* 6; and O. H. Steck, "Zur Abfolge Maleachi-Jona in 4Q76 (4QXII[a])," *ZAW* 108 (1996): 250.

was copied.[14] Second, Steck has reconstructed the original meaning of Mal 3:22–24 within the redactional history of the Twelve as part of a macrostructural *inclusio* encompassing the entire prophetic corpus, from Joshua to Malachi. For Steck, Mal 3:22–24 originated as the epilogue to this corpus. The sequence of 4QXII[a], therefore, is necessarily secondary. Although Ben Zvi has not to my knowledge written about Mal 3:22–24 specifically, following his approach elsewhere would imply that Mal 3:22–24 should be read as the clearly marked conclusion to a separate literary unit with a clear introduction and an attributed, if not clearly identified, source. It is quite possible, following Ben Zvi's logic, that the persons responsible for the sequence of 4QXII[a] read Mal 3:22–24 as the conclusion to the book of Malachi rather than the final words of the Book of the Twelve or the prophetic corpus.[15]

I have argued elsewhere that 4QXII[a] preserves the original placement of Jonah within the Book of the Twelve.[16] Although 4QXII[a] certainly supports the position that Jonah was the last book among the Twelve to be written, the originality of one sequence of the books over another is impossible to establish. Perhaps it is better to speak not so much of any "original" arrangement of the Twelve, but rather of an original *diversity* of arrangements in circulation among Jewish communities of the final centuries before the common era. One arrangement, reflected in manuscripts of the LXX, has survived only in translation. Yet another, seen in 4QXII[a], survived only as an archaeological discovery. Finally, only one arrangement, that of the MT, has survived as a continuing textual tradition in Hebrew. This understanding of the various witnesses to the Book of the Twelve is consistent with the textual diversity of other books within the Hebrew Bible. It also fits well with the dynamics of the process of canonization, which moves from diversity and multiplicity to definiteness and uniformity.

What of the question "One book or twelve?" The diversity of ancient arrangements of the Twelve appears to support Ben Zvi's argument that the Twelve is a collection of individual books of varied arrangement rather than a single unified work of definitive shape.[17] The unique con-

---

[14] Steck, "Zur Abfolge," 250. Fuller dates 4QXII[a] to ca. 150 B.C.E. ("Minor Prophets," 221).

[15] Malachi 3:22–24 is read this way by B. Glazier-McDonald, *Malachi: The Divine Messenger* (SBLDS 98; Atlanta: Scholars Press, 1987), 244–45.

[16] Jones, *Formation,* 130–32.

[17] Ben Zvi himself makes use of this evidence in his argument (see "Twelve Prophetic Books," 130).

tent of the book of Jonah is certainly the weakest link in any theory of the Twelve as an intentional literary unity. The movement of Jonah within the manuscript witnesses confirms the evidence of its form and content. In spite of this conclusion, however, the manuscript evidence still provides substantial evidence for an ancient perception of the "oneness" of these twelve writings. The consistency with which the Twelve was written and reckoned as a single volume in antiquity and the general stability of its arrangement, the attested variations notwithstanding, indicate that the scroll of the Twelve represents something more than a means of gathering items in one place that might otherwise be lost if stored separately. Redactional theories of the Book of the Twelve as a literary unity suggest that the editorial shaping of the book (in the MT version) was an attempt to govern its interpretation. Comparisons of the varying arrangements of the Twelve suggest that the compilation is itself the result of ancient interpretations of the individual books within the collection. These interpretations distinguished between the individual books, but nevertheless recognized a sense of oneness that makes the compilation coherent and meaningful. Seen in this light, the Book of the Twelve may be said to be a witness to some of the earliest stages in the interpretive history of the Minor Prophets. It provides significant evidence, therefore, for possible ancient interpretations of individual books that influenced their placement within the Twelve. The arrangement of certain books may provide interpretive clues for how these texts were read by the compilers of the Twelve, clues which may in fact have been inscribed within the books themselves. In order to test this hypothesis, the remainder of this essay examines ancient interpretations of the Minor Prophets, with attention given to the books of Obadiah and Jonah.

Evidence from Postbiblical Interpretation

Readers who seek to identify a historical context for the book of Obadiah receive very little help from the text itself other than the references to the "day of [Judah's] calamity." Ancient readers, including the traditions preserved within the *Lives of the Prophets,* the Talmud, and Jerome, sought to fill this information gap by identifying the source of Obadiah with King Ahab's steward of the same name mentioned in 1 Kgs 18. Ben Zvi has argued that it is reasonable to conclude that the authors of Obadiah had an identifiable person in mind in attributing the book to its namesake, and that the Obadiah mentioned in 1 Kgs 18 was the most

easily identified figure of that name for readers aware of Israel's literary traditions.[18] Attribution to this literary figure would suggest, if not
an accurate historical background, then at least an intended historical
background for the book of Obadiah in the monarchic period. A putative origin for Obadiah in the monarchic period, although generally
ruled out by historical-critical judgments, is a possible intended reading
of the book that is consistent with the title in v. 1, חזון עבדיה, "vision of
Obadiah." Ancient readers presumably would not have questioned the
possibility of interpreting the contents of Obadiah as a prophetic vision
from a named figure of Israel's literary past. The ancient readers cited
above certainly did not object to such a reading.

The placement of Obadiah in the first half of the Twelve, and particularly adjoining the book of Jonah in both the LXX and the MT
arrangements, is consistent with both the observations of the ancient
interpreters and the clues offered within the book. To be sure, critical
scholarship overwhelmingly assigns Obadiah to the exilic or postexilic
period. If one is interested in the intended understanding of the background of the book rather than the actual historical context, however,
then the placement of Obadiah within the Twelve reflects the interpretation that its author(s) likely intended. That in Obadiah and Jonah
we have two late prophetic books with putative contexts in the monarchic period raises questions about possible archaizing tendencies within
the latest books among the Twelve. What was there about the late,
postmonarchic period of biblical composition that produced works attributed to figures from monarchic times? Although this question has
no immediately clear answer, it would not be perceived as a question at
all if not for the latent interpretations preserved within the arrangement
of the Twelve and parallel interpretations from postbiblical sources.

Although the book of Obadiah adjoins the book of Jonah in the MT
and LXX manuscript traditions of the Twelve, this is not the case in
4QXII[a]. There Jonah appears to follow Malachi, presumably at the end
of the scroll of the Twelve. This sequence should come as little surprise,
since almost all commentators on Jonah immediately remark about its
incongruity with the other Minor Prophets. Jonah's placement at the
end of the scroll may reflect ancient readers' awareness of this fundamental difference as well. A midrashic tradition preserved in *Numbers
Rabbah* 18:21 separates Jonah from the Twelve as "a book by itself." Although this late haggadic tradition cannot be read as direct evidence for

---

[18] Ben Zvi, *Historical-Critical Study*, 16–18.

the circulation of the book of Jonah separate from the rest of the Twelve, it does show that Jonah's distinctiveness with regard to the other Minor Prophets was apparent to ancient readers, including perhaps those who appended it to the end of the Minor Prophets scroll.

Differences in genre between Jonah and the rest of the Twelve may not be the only explanation for the sequence of 4QXII[a]. Steck has offered another explanation for the placement of Jonah in 4QXII[a] that also has parallels in ancient exegetical traditions. He suggests that the placement of Jonah after Malachi may be based on the theme of an anticipated repentance of the non-Jewish peoples that would be analogous to the repentance of Israel called for in Mal 3:22–24.[19] The combined themes of Gentile conversion following a general repentance among the people of Israel is found already in Tob 14:6–7. Steck's explanation of 4QXII[a] provides an excellent example of an ancient interpretation of prophetic traditions preserved within one of the arrangements of the Twelve.

The theme of Gentile repentance so clearly emphasized in Jonah nevertheless created a problem for the reputation of the prophet himself. That Nineveh's reprieve allowed Jonah's prophecy of judgment to fall to the ground empty is acknowledged in the report of the *Lives of the Prophets* concerning Jonah. There Jonah is reported to have moved to a land of foreigners out of shame, "for I spoke falsely in prophesying against the great city of Nineveh." Far from being a mere exegetical flight of fancy, Sasson has identified divine freedom to annul announced actions, and the hardships that such freedom caused for Israel's prophets, as key themes of the book of Jonah itself.[20] In this light, the book of Jonah is a defense of Israel's prophets, who were compelled to deliver messages for which even they had no firm promise of fulfillment, and at the same time a defense of Israel's God, whose treatment of these prophets is required by an overarching drive toward mercy. This interpretation presents Jonah as something of an epilogue to Israel's prophetic literature, seeking to explain the ways of God with the humans portrayed therein. Such a view of the book is most consistent with the sequence attested in 4QXII[a], where Jonah does indeed stand as an epilogue to the Twelve, perhaps displacing or serving as an alternative

---

[19] Steck, "Zur Abfolge," 252. Steck's treatment of 4QXII[a] is based on his assumption that the MT arrangement of the Twelve is original and that other arrangements are secondary. For an argument that 4QXII[a] could be the original placement of Jonah within the Twelve, see Jones, *Formation*, ch. 4.

[20] J. Sasson, *The Book of Jonah* (AB 24B; New York: Doubleday, 1990), 283–86.

to the retrospective epilogue in Mal 3:22–24 and its variant ending in LXX Mal 3:22–24.

The theme of repentance is certainly prominent in Jonah. Nevertheless, the book has lent itself to a variety of interpretations throughout its history.[21] Although the theme of Gentile repentance is seen in the actions of the sailors and the Ninevites, this theme is nevertheless undermined by known historical events concerning the city of Nineveh. Ancient readers knew that Nineveh had long ago been destroyed. Nahum celebrates this destruction in an exuberant oracle of judgment. Tobit assumes wide knowledge of this fact when it reports in 14:15 that Tobit's son, Tobias, lived to see the destruction of Nineveh as predicted in Scripture. Such knowledge made it possible for interpreters to discount the repentance of Nineveh as short-lived. According to such an interpretation, the Ninevites soon reverted to their former ways and were destroyed. This interpretation is reflected in the *Targum of Jonah* 4:5, in which Jonah sits outside the city of Nineveh to see "what would *ultimately* happen to the city."[22] One Greek manuscript tradition for Tob 14:4 attributes the prophecy of Nineveh's destruction not to the prophet Nahum but rather to the preaching of Jonah. According to this reading of Jonah, his was not a false prophecy, merely a proleptic one. The well-known tendency of early biblical exegesis to telescope events in the distant past made such an interpretation of Jonah even more acceptable. Seen in the light of this interpretation, therefore, the juxtaposition of Jonah with the book of Nahum in the LXX sequence of the Twelve may be the product of the same reading tradition. Jonah and Nahum both deal with the city of Nineveh, and, as has often been pointed out, both end with a rhetorical question.[23] These similarities of theme and form may have led interpreters to harmonize their message as well, thereby saving Jonah's reputation as a prophet at the expense of the dominant message of the book. T. Collins, in his thematic analysis of the Book of the Twelve, traces the theme of "The Nations as Enemies and Allies" across the span of the collection.[24] The book of Jonah appears to have presented both perspectives to ancient readers, depending on

---

[21] A useful survey of the history of interpretation of Jonah is found in the appendix to J. Limburg, *Jonah: A Commentary* (OTL; Louisville: Westminster/John Knox, 1993), 99–123.

[22] See the comments on this translation by Sasson (*Book of Jonah*, 279).

[23] See the comments in Coggins, "Minor Prophets," 66.

[24] T. Collins, *The Mantle of Elijah: The Redaction Criticism of the Prophetical Books* (The Biblical Seminar 20; Sheffield: JSOT Press, 1993), 66–83.

one's line of interpretation, and perhaps also on the sequence of the Minor Prophets one was reading. The nation of Nineveh appears as a potential ally if it provides Israel with a positive example of the power of repentance. Such a reading seems close to the original intent of the book and may be best seen if the book stands apart from the rest of the Twelve as it does in 4QXII[a]. The view of Nineveh as an enemy to Israel that receives its just deserts, although not present in the text of Jonah itself, is an interpretation that becomes possible if its reading is colored by its context in the Twelve, under the influence of oracles against foreign nations such as those found in Nahum, which adjoins Jonah in the LXX, and Obadiah, which adjoins Jonah in both the LXX and the MT.

The positions of Obadiah and Jonah in the various arrangements of the Twelve attested by ancient manuscripts resonate with ancient readings of these books present in postbiblical exegetical traditions. It seems reasonable to trace a line of continuity, therefore, between the interpretations that lay behind the arrangements of the Twelve and the parallel interpretations found in subsequent literature. Whatever may be said about the composition history of the Minor Prophets, the compilation of the Book of the Twelve seems clearly to reflect the early interpretive history of these prophetic texts. The variations within the extant arrangements of the Twelve perhaps demonstrate only a sampling of the numerous possible interpretations of the Minor Prophets circulating in ancient times. My concern for contemporary study is that this variety not be lost to attempts to identify a single editorial aim belonging to the compilers of the Book of the Twelve. Whatever the consensus that emerges concerning various redactional approaches to the Twelve, my preference is that the variety of possible interpretations reflected in manuscript remains of the Minor Prophets be preserved from the tendencies of the canonical process, both ancient and modern, toward fixity and uniformity.

6

How to Read the Book of the Twelve
as a Theological Unity

Rolf Rendtorff

I am glad to be invited to participate in the Formation of the Book of the Twelve Seminar. It is the third time that I have had the opportunity to participate in an SBL seminar on the formation of a complex part of the canon of the Hebrew Bible: first on the Pentateuch, then on the book of Isaiah, and now on the Book of the Twelve. In addition, at the 1994 SBL International Meeting I was involved in discussion on the formation of the book of Psalms.[1] In my view it is a very important and promising development in biblical studies, not to be satisfied with more sophisticated analyses of biblical texts but to try to understand the texts in their given form and to find out what intention and message they would have had.

It has often been noted that the Book of the Twelve has been taken as one book from the formation of the canon of the Hebrew Bible.[2] But only recently have scholars begun to study the formation of this book.[3] Most are concerned with the development of the book in its different

---

[1] My involvement in this topic is also demonstrated by the doctoral thesis of my student Matthias Millard, *Die Komposition des Psalters: Ein formgeschichtlicher Ansatz* (FAT 9; Tübingen: Mohr, 1994).

[2] See in particular Sir 48:10; *B. Bat.* 14b/15a.

[3] See Paul R. House, *The Unity of the Book of the Twelve* (JSOTSup 97; Sheffield: JSOT Press, 1990); Terence Collins, *The Mantle of Elijah: The Redaction Criticism of the Prophetical Books* (The Biblical Seminar 20; Sheffield: JSOT Press, 1993), 59–87; Raymond C. van Leeuwen, "Scribal Wisdom and Theodicy in the Book of the Twelve," in *In Search of Wisdom: Essays in Memory of John G. Gammie* (ed. L. G. Perdue et al.; Louisville: Westminster/John Knox, 1993), 31–49; James D. Nogalski, *Literary Precursors to the Book of the Twelve* (BZAW 217; Berlin, et al: de Gruyter 1993); James D. Nogalski, *Redactional Processes in the Book of the Twelve* (BZAW 218; Berlin: de Gruyter, 1993); Richard J. Coggins, "The Minor Prophets — One Book or Twelve," in *Crossing the Boundaries: Essays in Biblical Interpretation in Honour of Michael D. Goulder* (ed. S. E. Porter, P. Joyce, and D. E. Orton; Biblical Interpretation Series 8; Leiden: Brill, 1994), 57–68; Aaron Schart, *Die Entstehung des Zwölfprophetenbuchs: Neubearbeitungen von Amos im Rahmen schriftenübergreifender Redaktionsprozesse* (BZAW 260; Berlin: de Gruyter, 1998).

stages up to the final shape. In this essay I shall try to take the next step, namely to read the Book of the Twelve as a unity, taking such development for granted.[4]

Individuality, Chronology, and Themes

At the beginning we have to look at some obvious shaping elements that give the reader access to the book. The superscriptions of the different parts of the book, or "writings,"[5] serve particular functions. First, they preserve a certain identity for every individual writing. This is, by the way, one of the basic differences between the Book of the Twelve and the book of Isaiah. In the latter, no other name of a prophet except that of Isaiah is mentioned. Even in Isaiah the reader is confronted with a number of hints to differences in time and circumstances, but these are not linked to different prophetic personae.

Second, the superscriptions give the Book of the Twelve an explicit chronological framework. A number of writings are precisely dated, and by that dating they are closely linked to certain historical and political periods. The dating begins in the period when the kingdom of Israel still exists, and two of the prophets, Hosea and Amos, act in this framework. The author of the third dated writing, Micah, is active at the same time in the kingdom of Judah. Thus, the three cover one period, more or less the same period as Isaiah. The next prophet with a dated superscription, Zephaniah, acted during the last decades of the kingdom of Judah. In this case, the dating is of particular relevance because, immediately after Zephaniah, a great chasm occurs between the end of independent Israelite or Judean political existence and life under Persian rule, including the Babylonian exile. Nothing of that chasm is mentioned in the texts, but the reader understands it when the next two prophets, Haggai and Zechariah, are dated according to the Persian king Darius. The reader will be confronted with new problems.

But what about the writings that are not dated? It would be too simple to say that those who put the individual writings together had no information about the time of the activity of these prophets. From that point

---

[4] This is also the explicit approach of Edgar W. Conrad, "The End of Prophecy and the Appearance of Angels/Messengers in the Book of the Twelve," *JSOT* 73 (1997): 65–79.

[5] In this essay I use the word "book" only for the Book of the Twelve, while calling the individual parts "writings." When necessary to refer to the prophet, as opposed to the literary product, I will indicate this specifically (e.g., the prophet Hosea, the prophet Joel, etc.).

of view, the question why the undated writings have been put where they now stand would be even more urgent. Seemingly, in most cases, there were no particular chronological reasons. But what other reasons could there have been?

Only recently have scholars begun to ask these kinds of questions. Some of the writings deal centrally with topics that do not appear at all in other writings. One of these topics is the "Day of the LORD." This day is mentioned once in Amos (5:18–20), where the reader gets the impression that such a day *is* well-known to Amos's audience. But from what source do they know? The present reader of the Book of the Twelve knows from the writing that precedes Amos, from Joel, where the Day of the LORD is the central topic. It is again the central topic in the writing that follows Amos: Obadiah. That means that these three, Joel, Amos and Obadiah, form a group of writings in which the Day of the LORD is of central importance. Joel as well as Obadiah are undated; they could have been placed for other than chronological reasons. Therefore it would make sense if their position were based on the common topic of the Day of the LORD. Since Amos's position is given by its dating, Joel and Obadiah might have been incorporated to surround, or even to frame, Amos.[6] As a result, from this group of writings almost at the beginning of the Book of the Twelve, the theme of the Day of the LORD has a strong impact on the book up to its end (Mal 3:23 [Eng., 4:5]). Below I discuss this question in detail.

Let us continue to ask about the position of the other undated writings within the Book of the Twelve. Why does Jonah follow Obadiah? Some scholars see the placement from a chronological point of view because of the assumed identification of the Jonah of the Twelve with the one of 2 Kgs 14:25. But if the authors (or "redactors," or whoever) of the final text wanted to emphasize this identification and to use it as an argument for Jonah's placement, why did they not say it explicitly? The reader on his own cannot find any relationship between the actions and the message of the two Jonahs. But are there any relationships between Jonah and Obadiah? The main topic of Jonah is whether rescue from divine judgment is possible. This is also one of the central questions of Joel with regard to the Day of the LORD. But for Obadiah this is not a problem; for him, only Judah will be saved. In opposition, Jonah's message says: On the contrary, even Nineveh can be saved if it really will repent.

---

6 This idea is found in Schart, *Entstehung des Zwölfprophetenbuchs*, 261–82.

Related to this question is the position of Nahum. How is the relation between Jonah and Nahum to be understood? Their common theme is the fate of Nineveh, of which the reader might ask, Did Nineveh repent or not? These questions will also have to be discussed below. Together with this inquiry, we have to ask about the position of Habakkuk. In this case a clear chronological reason seems obvious. Habakkuk speaks about the enemy that only appeared in the last period of Israel's or Judah's preexilic history: the Chaldeans, that is, Babylon. This brings Habakkuk close to Zephaniah, who is dated into that period. Finally, Malachi quite obviously belongs in the postexilic era and could not have been put anywhere else.

The Day of the LORD in Joel

Before following certain threads that run through the Book of the Twelve, some remarks of caution are in order. Even if we hope to understand something of the internal coherence of the different writings assembled in this book, we have to be aware that the individual writings have preserved their specific profiles. We might find quotations or references shared explicitly between different writings, but the coherence will be recognizable mainly by interrelations in themes and terminology. We have to imagine that those responsible for the composition of the Book of the Twelve assumed that the reader would read the preceding writings and relate them to what he or she read later.

In this respect, let us follow the first thread that runs through almost the whole Book of the Twelve: the Day of the LORD.[7] Joel, where this topic appears first, is something of a collection of different views of that day. At first, the Day of the LORD befalls Israel (chs. 1–2); at the end, it is a divine judgment against Israel's enemies (ch. 4 [Eng., ch. 3]) in which Israel is just a bystander; and in between, it is a great cosmic event that affects "all flesh" (ch. 3 [2:28–32]). Of particular importance is the question of how Israel, or any human being, might escape the threatening danger of this day. At the peak of events in the first description of the coming of the LORD's day, God's voice is heard: "Yet even now, turn back to me (שׁוּבוּ עָדַי) with all your hearts" (2:12). There is a chance to turn, to repent — even now! The prophet adds, quoting one of the

---

[7] See also my article "Alas for the Day! The 'Day of the LORD' in the Book of the Twelve," in *God in the Fray: A Tribute to Walter Brueggemann* (ed. Tod Linafelt and Timothy K. Beal; Minneapolis: Fortress, 1998), 186–97.

most fundamental confessions of God's grace and mercy: "For he is gracious and merciful, slow to anger and abounding in kindness" (2:13; cf. Exod 34:6). But the prophet knows that there will be no guarantee that God will turn away (יָשׁוּב) from these plans; there can only be a fearful hope: מִי יוֹדֵעַ, "Who knows?" (2:14). But when the people assemble and the priests pray, "Spare your people, O LORD!" (2:16–17), God hears the prayer. God gives the people back what they had lost, makes the country fruitful, and assures them of peace and joy (2:19–26). For the people this is not only the end of the disaster, but more: "You shall know that I am in the midst of Israel, and that I am the LORD, your God, and there is no other" (2:27).

In the following chapter the appearance of the Day of the LORD is quite different. It is an eschatological event in a rather strict sense. It will happen "after that" (3:1 [2:28]), which obviously means "at the end of the days" or the like.[8] Neither Israel nor its enemies are mentioned, but the events will affect "all flesh." Portents of different kinds will occur, which will also have dangerous sides, like blood and darkness, and the Day of the LORD is called "the great and terrible" day (3:3–4 [2:30–31]). Therefore, again, the question arises, "Who will be saved?" This time the prophet answers: "Everyone who calls on the name of the LORD shall be saved" (3:5 [2:32]). This is not too far from the first answer that there must be return, or repentance, to be saved. At this point it becomes clear that all this will not happen in a vacuum, far from reality, "for on Mount Zion and in Jerusalem there shall be the assembly of those who escape (פְּלֵיטָה)." These events are indissolubly connected with God's relation to all humankind, which has its center in Zion. Further, God will call those who survive.[9] This statement provides an important interrelation, between "to call on (קרא) the name of the LORD" and the LORD's "calling (קרא)" the survivors, the latter statement appearing as a kind of divine reaction to the first. If I understand this passage correctly, it announces the existence of a very limited group of survivors after the Day of the LORD, a group not comprised exclusively of Israelites, but of all those who, under the impact of the divine spirit (3:1–2 [2:28–29]), will call on God's name in the days of need. They are also the ones whom God will call into the group of survivors.

The last chapter of Joel (ch. 4 [3]) again shows a different view of the

---

[8] In Acts 2:17 this text is quoted: Καὶ ἔσται ἐν ταῖς ἐσχάταις ἡμέραις.

[9] Some commentators have difficulties with the last words of 3:5 (2:32); the JPS Bible says, "Meaning of Heb. uncertain."

Day of the LORD. Israel's (or Judah's) enemies are punished by God. Israel is not affected. And even when "the sun and the moon are darkened and the stars withdraw their shining" (4:15 [3:15]) and "the LORD roars from Zion" (4:16 [3:16]), God will be a "refuge" and a "stronghold" for the people. They shall know that God dwells in Zion and that Jerusalem shall be holy (4:17). This depiction of the Day of the LORD seems to be incompatible with the two foregoing views in several respects. In particular the question "Who will be saved?" does not arise, because "God's people" (4:16) seem to remain untouched. But this is not the message of Joel as a whole. At the beginning of the first appearance of the LORD's day (chs. 1–2), Israel was far from being saved and had to repent deeply to escape the threatening events.

Joel shows that the Day of the LORD can be experienced under quite different circumstances. In some cases Israel itself feels threatened, and therefore the question of escape and survival takes the center. In other cases Israel is looking at events that happen to other people, without being affected itself. Finally, Israel is involved in the events of that day as part of humankind ("all flesh"), in which case only individuals can survive, whether Israelites or not. Therefore, we have to read Joel not as one consistent message of one prophet but as a collection of different and in certain respects divergent views of what could be meant by the phrase "the Day of the LORD." When studying the Book of the Twelve in sequence we have to keep in mind that the potential reader is aware of these different aspects of the Day of the LORD.

The Day of the LORD in Amos, Obadiah, and Jonah

Entering Amos, the reader is confronted again and again with descriptions of disastrous events in which the LORD is acting. When told that "the LORD roars from Zion" (Amos 1:2), the reader will be reminded of the last chapter in Joel, in which this threatening sound does not endanger Israel but only its enemies (Joel 4:16 [3:16]). In Amos, words of divine judgment against Israel's neighbors follow immediately, and the LORD's action is described as a "day of battle" (Amos 1:14). But then it becomes clear that Israel will be included in the divine judgment as well (2:4–5, 6–16). At the last moment of the disaster, when even the most courageous of the warriors runs away naked, it is said that this will happen "on that day" (2:16). This is not too far from the expression "the Day of the LORD." Later, the LORD's punitive action is announced by "on the day of my punishing Israel" (3:14). In these cases the reader coming from Joel, cannot hear the word "day" as a simple indication of time. It is the day when the LORD acts.

When it comes to explicit use of the "Day of the LORD" (5:18–20), the reader is fully aware of the context of this expression. The people whom Amos is addressing prefer Joel's explanation of this important future day in the last chapter (ch. 4 [3]), that it is God's punishment of Israel's enemies. They might even have understood — or rather misunderstood — Amos's repetition of the words from Joel (Amos 1:2 = Joel 4:16 [3:16]) in that sense. But Amos warns them of the other side of the Day of the LORD that is also explained in Joel: that it is darkness and not light. In Joel, particular danger arrives when the Day of the LORD affects Israel itself (Joel 2:2). This is the difference between Amos's audience and Amos himself in their respective expectations of the Day of the LORD. Amos expects this day to come as a judgment over Israel.

Immediately before, Amos had sharply criticized the social and legal behavior of his audience (5:7–12) and had named the present an "evil time" (5:13). He called his audience to turn around, to do the opposite of what they had done before: "Seek good and not evil.... Hate evil and love good, and establish justice in the gate," and he added: "Perhaps (אולי) the LORD, the God of hosts, will be gracious to the remnant of Joseph" (5:14–15). This again recalls Joel, in which, at the peak of dangerous events on the Day of the LORD, God called the people to return, and the prophet added: "Who knows but he may turn and relent" (Joel 2:12–14). Amos's אולי comes quite close to Joel's מי יודע. Amos then begins to describe wailing and mourning, culminating in the words: "Then I pass through your midst, says the LORD" (5:16–17). All these are signs of a God coming to judge and punish the people. Therefore, if this really were the Day of the LORD, it would be directed against Israel; the only chance to escape would be to turn away from evil and repent.

Reading Amos in this way, the passage about the Day of the LORD is not as isolated as some commentators see it. The preceding description of God's coming to judge Israel, as well as the call to "seek good and not evil," that is, to turn and repent, belong to the context of the Day of the LORD in Joel, which establishes the wider context for Amos. One could add other texts. In the long poem in Amos 4, the prophet describes several ways by which God punished the people, always ending with "yet you did not return to me, says the LORD" (4:6, 8, 9, 10, 11). One of God's punishments is the locusts (4:9). The reader will remember that, when faced with a locust plague in Joel, the people *did* return and were saved and restored (Joel 2:1–27). So the Joel text can serve as a contrast to the bad situation that Amos describes. When God is "forming locusts" (Amos 7:1), it again reminds the reader of Joel. Another text is the mention of Zion in Amos 6:1. Are those "who are at ease in Zion" those who drew the wrong conclusions from Joel, in which, at the end, it is said that God dwells on Zion (Joel 4:17, 21 [3:17, 21]), and already earlier that on Zion "there shall be those who escape (פליטה)" (3:5 [2:32])?

When read sequentially with Joel, the features of the Day of the LORD are present throughout Amos.[10] But then the reader continues to Obadiah. Again the Day of the LORD is the central topic. But this time this day is expected only to come over Israel's (or Judah's) closest enemy: Edom/Esau. This reminds one of Joel 4 (3), where Israel's enemies on that day are also the only target of divine punishment. The extension of the day to "all nations" (Obad 15) is also in accordance with Joel. Finally, the expectation that on Mount Zion "there shall be those who escape (פליטה)" (Obad 17) sounds like a quotation from Joel 3:5 (2:32). But there is one remarkable difference: In Joel the remnant will consist of the believers from all nations who called the name of the LORD, and whom the LORD calls. In Obadiah it is only the house of Jacob (or house of Joseph) that shall rule over their enemies from Mount Zion, and there will be no survivor of the house of Esau (Obad 18). But the reader still remembers Amos's words: "Why do you want the day of the LORD? It is darkness, not light" (5:18). The reader, therefore, has to read Obadiah with this critical question in mind. When finally it is said, "The kingdom shall be the LORD's" (Obad 21), it makes clear that ultimate rulership is with God and not with humans, be it Israel or anyone else. Obadiah is best read in the critical light of Amos.

Continuing to Jonah with these questions in mind, the reader will be confronted with an almost contradictory message. Obadiah seems to say that only Judah will be saved. Jonah explains that, on the contrary, the Gentiles also have a chance to be saved when they turn back and repent. Read in this way, Jonah offers another critical reference toward the position of Obadiah — and, of course, not only toward Obadiah but also toward this kind of thinking among people in Judah and among potential readers of the Book of the Twelve. There is always, for

---

[10] It would be worthwhile to study the use of the term "day" in this wider sense, because the studies on the Day of the LORD, using "form-critical" methods, tend to be too technical. In this context it would be interesting to study the term "on that day" (ביום ההוא); cf., e.g., Amos 2:16; 8:3, 9, 13. This formula can also express a positive expectation, as in Amos 9:11. But how is that related to the complexity of the idea of the "Day of the LORD"?

every human, a chance to be saved — if they turn back. The people in
Nineveh did, and God reacted to their behavior (Jonah 3). They did
what, according to Amos, the Israelites did not (Amos 4). At the decisive point, the king of Nineveh speaks like the prophet did in Joel
2:14: "Who knows (מי יודע) but God may turn and relent." I compared
this statement above with Amos's "perhaps (אולי)." It can be seen again
that the different aspects of turning back, of repentance, are among elements running through the Book of the Twelve and providing different
views on prophetic preaching.

The Day of the LORD in Nahum, Habakkuk, and Zephaniah

Before following up on this additional development regarding the
Day of the LORD, we meet another use in the Book of the Twelve. In
Nahum, Nineveh appears again (Nah 1:1, etc.), but this time not as a
repentant city as in Jonah but as one punished terribly by God. The
city or its representatives are said to do (or to be) בליעל (wickedness,
or "a wicked one," 1:11; 2:1), and nothing is heard about willingness
or a chance to repent. The end of Nineveh will be a cause for joy for
Nahum's audience (2:1 [1:15]). How can this be related to the message
of Jonah?

In my view, Jonah does not portray Nineveh as a real political power.
Nineveh is not seen primarily as a danger for Israel and Judah but as
the prime example of a Gentile city that is sinful thus deserving divine
judgment). In spite of its sinful nature, it has the chance to repent and
to survive. Neither Israel nor Judah appears in Jonah. There is just the
prophet Jonah, who has to explain in narrative form a theological problem, namely whether God's grace will also embrace repentant Gentiles.[11]
The message is that even an extraordinary sinful Gentile city like Nineveh can repent and be saved. Nahum, however, is much closer to the
experience that Judah had with the real Nineveh. Judah felt it to be
dangerous and not God-fearing, lacking signs of repentance. Reading
Nahum after Jonah the message can only be that Nineveh as the representative of Gentile powers had a chance to repent and to be saved, yet
the real Nineveh did not seize this chance; on the contrary, it acted like
a "city of bloodshed" (Nah 3:1). Therefore it will be punished by God.

---

[11] There is an additional problem, that of the "false prophet" whose predictions
will not be fulfilled; but this does not touch our present discussion.

The divergence or even contradiction between Jonah and Nahum is in a sense comparable with the relation between Joel and Obadiah. Nahum and Obadiah show a one-sided view, seemingly untroubled by any idea of Israel's or Judah's sins. As shown with Obadiah, the reader of the Book of the Twelve encounters several other views that can help him to correct Obadiah's by putting it into a wider framework.

Habakkuk, concerned basically with the lack of justice within his own people, follows Nahum. The Chaldeans appear as the successors of the Assyrians (i.e., of Nineveh) as the leading power of the world surrounding Israel. They come to punish Israel, and only later does the tide turn so that the Chaldeans are judged by God as well. In Zephaniah, Nineveh is mentioned again as destroyed by God (2:13), but after that Jerusalem is punished as well (3:1–8). Judah's and Jerusalem's sins are one of the main themes of Zephaniah. Thus both Habakkuk and Zephaniah offer a framework to counteract Nahum's one-sidedness.

In Zephaniah, the Day of the LORD is again the dominant theme. The day is coming over the whole world and humankind, but first over Judah (1:4–6). Yet there is one characteristic difference between Zephaniah and all the former writings that deal with the Day of the LORD. Zephaniah at the beginning names the reason why this disaster is coming: because of Judah's sins, in particular in the cultic field, but also in the exploitation of its neighbors (1:11–13). Such a statement is not only another counterbalance to Nahum, but its effect is tied to Obadiah. It adds a specific element to the theme of the Day of the LORD. When the day comes upon Israel, it is the divine reaction to Israel's sins. Even Joel did not say this explicitly. But now, looking back from the end of the prophetic writings about the Day of the LORD, it is evident that judgment for Israel's sins is one of the decisive reasons for the coming of disaster.[12]

Another important point is the prophet's call to gather and "seek the LORD ..., seek righteousness, seek humility ...!" with its continuation: "Perhaps you will find shelter on the day of the LORD's wrath" (2:1–3). These phrases are close to Amos 5:14–15: "Seek" (בקשו; Amos: דרשו), and then the hopeful אולי looking forward to a gracious divine reaction.

---

[12] Zephaniah has his own terminology. Alongside the term יום יהוה (1:7, 14; 2:2, 3), he uses the expanded terms יום עברת יהוה (1:18) and יום אף יהוה (2:2, 3); he calls the day גדול and מר; and he uses the following expressions: יום שופר ותרועה, ענם וערפל, יום חשך ואפלה, יום שאה ומשואה, יום צרה ומצוקה (1:15–16). These expressions should be included in a broader study of the terminology of the Day of the LORD (see n. 10).

As mentioned above, these words of Amos again are close to those of Joel, in which God calls the people to return (שובו עדי), and the prophet adds: "Who knows (מי יודע) whether he may turn and relent" (Joel 2:12–14). When reading the Book of the Twelve in its entirety the reader will realize that these three prophets — Joel, Amos, and Zephaniah — are very close to each other in relating the Day of the LORD to the call to repent or to "seek," and in expressing a reticent and even fearful hope that God might listen and react to a change in the behavior of the people. This is important for understanding the Book of the Twelve as a whole, because these three prophets represent the span within which the topic of the Day of the LORD appears, except for Malachi (see below). Thus, in a certain way, they provide the message of the whole book.

The Day of the LORD in Malachi 3

The last chapter of the Book of the Twelve[13] speaks again of the Day of the LORD. The full title יום יהוה is only mentioned at the very end (Mal 3:23 [4:5]), where the day is again called "the great and terrible day of the LORD." But that day had been announced already at the beginning of the chapter. God will send a messenger, "but who can endure the day of his coming?" (3:1–2) This recalls the first appearance of the Day of the LORD in the Book of the Twelve, where the same question was asked (Joel 2:11). The term's first and last appearance seem to form a kind of *inclusio:* The question "who can endure?" is always (presumed?) present when the Day of the LORD is near.

This time the Day of the LORD will first be a time of scrutiny within Israel, a refinement and judgment with regard to cultic and social behavior (Mal 3:2b–5). But then God will write in a book those who fear God and value God's name, and "on the day that I am preparing" they will be God's special possession (סגלה) (1:16–17). Again the reverence for the name of the LORD plays an important role, as previously in Joel 3:5 (2:23) and Zeph 3:9, 12. Finally, the day will come "like an oven" and burn all the evildoers like straw (Mal 3:19 [4:1]). In Obad 18, the house of Esau was the straw and the house of Jacob the flame, but, in Malachi, the judgment is based on an internal distinction: "The evildoers will burn like straw, while for those who revere the name of the LORD, the sun of righteousness shall rise; and they shall tread down the wicked under their feet" (3:20–21 [4:2–3]).

---

13 In the Hebrew Bible, Mal 3 is the last chapter, but 3:19–25 corresponds to chapter 4 in the English Bible.

The last verses of Malachi (3:22–24 [4:4–6]) are simultaneously the last paragraph of the נביאים (Nebiim). Here the Day of the LORD appears in a remarkable context. The naming of Moses alongside Elijah at the end of the collection of prophetical writings connects the first two main parts of the Hebrew Bible, Torah and Nebiim.[14] The second coming of Elijah will happen "before the day of the LORD comes." This wording recalls Joel 3:4–5 (2:31–32). But what is the meaning of the last verse, Mal 3:24 [4:6]? God "will turn the hearts of parents to their children and the hearts of children to their parents." That means that God will bring reconciliation among those split according to the discussions previously recounted in Malachi. This reconciliation will be necessary in order to avoid the eschatological judgment. Again, this recalls Joel, where it is said that those who call on the name of the LORD shall escape. The parallelism is obvious: Certain fundamental behaviors before God are essential to be blessed with eschatological salvation.

Summary

I tried in this essay to find out whether definable lines run through the Book of the Twelve, indicating common themes or conceptions. Obviously, the Day of the LORD is one of the dominating themes. The question is whether there are deliberate interrelations among the different writings that deal with this theme. Observing the compositional relationships among Joel, Amos, and Obadiah has proven very fruitful.[15] In following the insights gained by study of the highly complex interrelationships, many more common elements appeared. I mention in particular the complex of repentance and salvation in the face of the Day of the LORD. Those observations should not be limited to certain terms but should pay attention to similar ideas expressed by different words, for example, שוב, בקש, דרש, and so on, and, of course, אולי and מי יודע. The same is true with regard to the term "Day of the LORD" itself. In many cases where the term "day" appears, be it alone or in certain combinations, the reader of the Book of the Twelve should associate it with something like the Day of the LORD. The outcome is far from unified; on the contrary, in the Book of the Twelve we find a number of controversies, and even contradictions, that are characteristic of the Hebrew Bible in general.

---

[14] See J. Blenkinsopp, *Prophecy and Canon: A Contribution to the Study of Jewish Origins* (Notre Dame, Ind.: University of Notre Dame Press, 1977), 120–23.

[15] See nn. 10, 12.

Finally, I point out that in studying the Book of the Twelve as a whole there is no simple alternative between "diachronic" and "synchronic" reading. The diachronic features are not only obvious but are marked explicitly by the different datings of a number of writings. On the other hand, those who gave the writings their shape (whatever we call them) obviously wanted the reader to read the writings as a connected whole and to reflect on their different messages. I think it is a challenging and fascinating exegetical task to follow their advice.

Part Two

HEARING THE BOOK OF THE TWELVE

J

7

Joel as "Literary Anchor"
for the Book of the Twelve

James D. Nogalski

Introduction

A strong consensus appears to be developing regarding two aspects of the shape of the Twelve. First, the chronological framework created by the dated superscriptions provides one element unifying the corpus. The six writings with dated superscriptions/incipits provide the framework that moves deliberately from the eighth-century Assyrian period into the postexilic Persian period.[1] Second, recurring words, images, and phrases also play a role in linking the writings of the Twelve, leaving one with the impression that more must be said than that the Twelve progresses chronologically. After these statements, however, the consensus breaks down quickly. Are these unifying elements created redactionally or simply decisions of positioning? How, if at all, does the chronological framework relate to the recurring words? Do these recurring words overlook, ignore, presume, or transcend the chronological frame? This essay, from the perspective of Joel's pivotal function, seeks to open a dialogue on the literary aim(s) of the larger corpus.

To understand the discussion, it will be necessary to note in advance that two basic models for reading prophetic literature — the synchronic and the diachronic — operate in the various approaches to the Twelve. Synchronic models have the advantage of keeping questions of literary shape in the foreground without hypothesizing about the date(s) and order in which the writings were incorporated. Conversely, in order to treat the literary nature of the whole, they have the disadvantage of having to treat the *entire* corpus as a single entity. In other words, synchronic

---

[1] See the following discussions: James D. Nogalski, *Literary Precursors to the Book of the Twelve* (BZAW 217; Berlin: de Gruyter, 1993), 85; Aaron Schart, *Die Entstehung des Zwölfprophetenbuchs: Neubarbeitungen von Amos im Rahmen schriftübergreifender Redaktionsprozesse* (BZAW 260; Berlin: de Gruyter, 1998), 36–46.

models do not provide a means by which one may determine which aspect(s) should be more important than others for reading the Twelve. Diachronic models have the advantage of being able to account for multiple theological perspectives by seeing divergent opinions as part of a writing's transmission, whose formulation originated before, during, or after it entered the larger corpus. Diachronic models have difficulty, however, talking about the literary aims of the larger corpus, because they get bogged down in issues of development. This essay addresses one aspect of this last problem for diachronic models by building on my previous suggestion that Joel serves as the "literary anchor" for the Book of the Twelve.

In so doing, I argue that Joel forms a necessary (but not the only) interpretive key for unifying major literary threads in the Twelve, as seen in at least three ways: dovetailing genres, recurring vocabulary, and the presumption of a "historical paradigm" that "transcends" the chronological framework of the dated superscriptions. Joel deliberately creates a transition between Hosea and Amos by dovetailing genres. Hosea ends with an extended call to repentance, while Joel begins with the same genre. Joel ends with an extended pronouncement of eschatological judgment against the nations, while Amos begins with an extended group of oracles against the nations. Recurring vocabulary takes place in Joel's reinterpretation of images and phrases from neighboring writings, and in the use of Joel's reinterpreted images in subsequent writings. This use of Joel in other contexts provides the clues for determining the transcended "historical" paradigm which shapes the Twelve. I have elsewhere labeled this formative literary development as "the Joel-Related Layer."[2]

What Kind of "Book" Is the Twelve?

In the last century, scholarly research into the prophets and prophetic literature has focused on numerous issues, including biographies of the prophets, historical settings of the various units, the theology of a given prophet, prophetic forms, and the development of the book. Only relatively recently has serious attention turned to the message conveyed by prophetic books rather than the individual oracles.[3] When the question

---

[2] See the summary in James D. Nogalski, *Redactional Processes in the Book of the Twelve* (BZAW 218; Berlin: de Gruyter, 1993), 275–78.

[3] For examples, see Odil Hannes Steck, *Die Prophetenbücher und ihr theologisches Zeugnis: Wege zur Nachfrage und Fährten zur Antwort* (Tübingen: Mohr, 1996), 2–14

of message is asked of the Book of the Twelve, however, the difficulties of
the task increase dramatically, for this collection is composed of twelve
books (or writings). To what degree should the meaning of the individual writings determine the message of the Twelve as a whole? How does
one find passages which have more direct bearing on the meaning of
the Twelve than on the meaning of the writing? One must make some
basic (yet also preliminary) decisions about the character of a particular
prophetic book before one can proceed in the task of reading it. To do
so, one should note how the Book of the Twelve differs from the other
three prophetic books in how it presents itself.

First, the other three prophetic books mention only a single prophet
explicitly. Whether one works diachronically or synchronically, this
simple observation creates a significantly different perception for a
reader of the Twelve. The Book of the Twelve presents itself as YHWH's
word to twelve different persons. Second, the Book of the Twelve, like
Isaiah, covers a lengthy period, from the time of Uzziah/Jeroboam to
the Persian period (and beyond). This observation differentiates the
purpose of the Book of the Twelve from the more limited time frames
of Jeremiah, which concerns the time leading up to Jerusalem's destruction, and Ezekiel, which concerns the time from the first exile
onward.

The combination of the first two differences leads to a third distinction: the presumed setting of the text. Isaiah mentions only one prophet,
which creates its own difficulties for conceptualizing how the prophet
"speaks" in contexts which obviously presume a Persian setting.[4] In the
end, one is forced to hear the prophet as anticipating the events of later
generations from an eighth-century prophetic "persona," or one must
presume different prophetic voices.[5] Thus Isaiah, in some sense, anticipates the events from the eighth century into the postexilic period.
By contrast, the Book of the Twelve "walks the reader through" this
same period with prophetic voices more clearly delineated. The twelve
prophetic writings alternate between documenting YHWH's message to
various groups and anticipating the outcome of the people's failure to
respond appropriately.

(ET: *The Prophetic Books and Their Theological Witness* [trans. James D. Nogalski; St.
Louis: Chalice Press, 2000], 3–13).

[4] See discussions in Christopher R. Seitz, "How Is the Prophet Isaiah Present in
the Latter Half of the Book? The Logic of Chapters 40–66 within the Book of Isaiah,"
JBL 115 (1996): 219–40; Steck, *Prophetenbücher,* 45–61.

[5] See the discussion in Seitz, "How Is the Prophet Isaiah Present," 224–28.

How does this change of prophetic voices affect the reader of the Twelve? The reader must pay careful attention to the change of the *Sitz im Buch.* The texts within these writings sometimes address different groups, which vary according to chronological, geographical, literary, and attitudinal considerations. When reading the Twelve, whether synchronically or diachronically, one must take these differences seriously. References to Israel, Samaria, Bethel, or Ephraim in Hosea, Amos, and Micah should not evoke the same images as references to Judah, Jerusalem, and Zion.[6] Even though the prophets are roughly contemporary, the geographical distinctions (along with the theological message) require different messages from YHWH. Similarly, the group from Bethel in Zech 7:1ff. does not represent the same group in Amos, because the chronological situation has changed. Nevertheless, one must also ask whether the reader should presume knowledge of YHWH's message to Bethel in Amos.[7] Documenting the ways in which the writings in the Twelve presume the message of other works presents a monumental task, which has only recently begun to be explored.[8] This task is generally easier to conceptualize for writings containing the dated superscriptions, but the undated writings should be given careful consideration from this perspective as well. The remainder of this essay looks at some of the ways that Joel presumes its location in the Book of the Twelve, and ways in which Joel is cited by other writings in that corpus.

Dovetailing Genres from Hosea to Joel to Amos

Studies of Joel over the last several years correctly portray it as a highly integrated work, but they have generally not asked how Joel relates to the Book of the Twelve. When this question is raised, the sophisticated nature of the Joel's integration becomes all the more astounding.

---

[6] Note also the complicated task of determining the identities of groups given such names as "Jacob," "Joseph," "House of Jacob." See the discussion, for example, in Schart, *Entstehung des Zwölfprophetenbuchs,* 139.

[7] Several commentators have noted Zech 1:2–6 as evidence that Zechariah is presuming knowledge from outside that writing. For example, see the discussion in David L. Petersen, *Haggai and Zechariah 1–8* (OTL; Philadelphia: Westminster, 1984), 132.

[8] For example, Schart, *Entstehung des Zwölfprophetenbuchs;* Erich Bosshard-Nepustil, *Rezeptionen von Jesaja 1–39 im Zwölfprophetenbuch: Untersuchungen zur literarischen Verbindung von Prophetenbüchern in babylonischer und persischer Zeit* (OBO 154; Fribourg, Switzerland: Universitätsverlag, 1997); Helmut Utzschneider, *Künder oder Schreiber? Eine These zum Problem der Schriftprophetie auf Grund von Maleachi 1,6–2,9* (BEATAJ 19; Frankfurt: Peter Lang, 1989); Siegfried Bergler, *Joel als Schriftinterpret* (BEATAJ 16; Frankfurt: Peter Lang, 1988); Nogalski, *Redactional Processes.*

One important dimension of Joel's relationship to the larger literary context arises when one notes the way in which the genres of Joel coincide with those of the writings on either side. Hosea ends with an extended call for Israel's repentance, the outcome of which is not narrated.[9] In prophetic literature, only Joel begins with a call to repentance. But, as well as the dovetailing with Hosea, the end of Joel, an eschatological oracle against the nations, dovetails genres with Amos. Other prophetic writings close with pronouncements against the nations, but the way in which Joel and Amos are related through quotations indicates an intentional association.[10] These overlapping genres deserve closer analysis.

Hosea 14:2–9 comprises a two-part call to repentance. Hosea 14:2–4 advances the call proper, culminating in a specific prayer of repentance that presupposes Israel's sins involving (1) political dependence on nations rather than YHWH and (2) idolatry. These accusations do not appear for the first time in chapter 14.[11] In that prayer, the people are told to say:

> Assyria will not save us. We will not ride on horses. Nor will we again say, "our god," to the works of our hands, for in you the orphan finds mercy. (14:3)

Hosea 14:5–9 (Eng., 14:4–8) then changes to divine speech and offers words of promise.

> I will heal their apostasy, I will love them freely, for my anger has turned away from them. I will be like the dew to Israel; he will blossom like the lily, and he will take root like Lebanon. His roots will sprout, and his beauty will be like the olive tree, and his fragrance like Lebanon. Those who live in his shadow will again raise grain, and they will blossom like the vine. His renown will be like the wine of Lebanon. O Ephraim, what more do I have to do with idols? It is I who look after you. I am a luxuriant cypress. From me comes your fruit.

---

[9] Jörg Jeremias, *Der Prophet Hosea* (ATD 24/1; Göttingen: Vandenhoeck & Ruprecht, 1983), 169–70. By contrast, Douglas Stuart, *Hosea–Jonah* (WBC 31; Waco, Tex.: Word, 1987), 211–18. Stuart treats this passage as a promise to the future Israel.

[10] See discussions in James D. Nogalski, "Intertextuality and the Twelve," in *Forming Prophetic Literature: Essays on Isaiah and the Twelve in Honor of John D. W. Watts* (ed. Paul R. House and James W. Watts; Sheffield: Sheffield Academic Press, 1996), 105–8; Schart, *Entstehung des Zwölfprophetenbuchs,* 219; Raymond C. van Leeuwen, "Scribal Wisdom and Theodicy in the Book of the Twelve," in *In Search of Wisdom: Essays in Memory of John G. Gammie* (ed. Leo G. Perdue, Bernard Scott, and William Wiseman; Louisville: Westminster/John Knox, 1993), 41.

[11] For the theme of depending on Assyria and Egypt rather than YHWH, cf. 5:13; 7:11, 16; 8:9; 9:3; 10:6; 11:5, 11; 12:1; 13:4. The anti-idolatry theme appears in virtually every chapter.

These verses have often been interpreted as the divine "response" to the prayer of 14:3. However, Jeremias convincingly demonstrates that, in fact, one should *not* presuppose that the prayer of 14:3 has been expressed.[12] Instead, 14:5–9 offers the foundational promise of YHWH's salvific intention, on which the call to repentance is built. This promise is not offered *because* Israel has repented; it offers the reason *why* Israel should repent. The significance of the call to Israel and its position at the end of the writing lies in the open-ended nature of the invitation. It becomes a type of divinely initiated RSVP to which Israel is called to respond, but no response is narrated. In fact, the final verse indicates that the open-ended nature of the call is transferred to the reader:

> Whoever is wise, let him understand these things; whoever is discerning, let him know them, for the ways of YHWH are right, and the righteous will walk in them, but transgressors will stumble in them.

In short, the promise of 14:5–9 becomes part of the invitation to repent, but the reader is "left hanging" with respect to the response.

If one wishes to determine how Israel responded to this invitation, one must broaden the literary horizon beyond Hosea. In a very real sense, the "story" must continue. But how does it continue? Interpreters in bringing resolution to Hosea often mention Samaria's destruction, noting the tragedy of Israel's failure to respond. However, one should note that reference to the events of 722 requires knowledge that goes beyond Hosea alone. One must assume a reader's knowledge of the history of the northern kingdom in order to make this association. But how does a reader gain this knowledge? Generally, knowledge of the events of 722 is assumed by interpreters, but the *literary* continuation of this open-ended invitation is not addressed. By enlarging the literary horizon beyond Hosea, the multivolume prophetic work that came to be known as the Book of the Twelve provides the literary resolution, albeit after following more than one interpretive avenue.

Following the chronological framework of the Twelve that orders the eighth-century prophetic writings, Amos demonstrates conclusively that Israel (the northern kingdom) does not respond positively to the invi-

---

[12] Jeremias, *Hosea,* 169. Jeremias notes three ways that the text itself argues against the presumption that the prayer has already been expressed. First, the divine speech of 14:5–9 speaks of Israel in the third person. YHWH does not address Israel directly, as one would assume if YHWH were responding to the prayer. Second, the healing of Israel's disloyalty (מְשׁוּבָה) would require repentance from Israel, but such is not the case here. Third and most significant, Hos 14:9 presupposes a time prior to the repentance.

tation in Hosea. These associations have begun to be explored, but it is
not my purpose to explore the ways in which this literary thread continues in Hosea and Amos.[13] Instead, in this section of the paper and
the next, I investigate what happens when Hosea's call to repentance is
read along with the extended call to repentance in Joel.

Joel's call to repentance differs from Hos 14:2–9 in several pivotal
respects, including its addressees, the presumption of guilt, the threat
of punishment, and the eschatological dimension. Hosea 14:2–9 should
be read as addressing the people of the northern kingdom of the eighth
century. By contrast, Joel lacks specific chronological markers, and addresses "all the people of the land" (1:2) in a way that, as it becomes
increasingly clear, focuses on Judah and Jerusalem (see especially 1:13–
16; 2:1ff.). While Hos 14:2ff. treats the people as a single entity, Joel
challenges several specific groups throughout the first chapter (1:2, 5,
11, 13). Moreover, while Hosea delineates specific accusations against
Israel within the prayer of 14:3, no such accusations appear *explicitly* in
Joel. The threatened punishment in Hosea, as with the promise, appears
to lie in the future. By contrast, the punishment in Joel is both current
and future. The land is (and/or will be) devastated from a composite
series of threats: a series of locust plagues, drought, and enemy attack.
This element leads to one of the most obvious differences between
Hos 14:2–9 and Joel 1–2. The threat in Joel contains an eschatological dimension that is not matched in Hosea. Hosea 14:2–9 presumes
YHWH will punish Israel, but does not describe that punishment in detail. Joel anticipates on the Day of YHWH an enemy attack (2:1–11) that
causes the devastations of the locusts and the drought imagery to pale
in comparison.

Hosea 14:2–9 and Joel 1–2 certainly differ. However, two similarities
between the calls to repentance in Hos 14:2–9 and in Joel 1–2 deserve
attention as well. First, as with Hosea, Joel contains a critical passage in
which the call to repent is grounded with a promise of bounty, without ever stating explicitly that the prayer of repentance was executed.
Joel 2:12–27 contains a series of admonitions to gather the people to
repent in an attempt to avoid the coming day of destruction (2:12–16),
including the prayer which was to be spoken by the priests (2:17). Sub-

---

[13] For the growing evidence that the Hosea/Amos connections have a long, common redactional history that presupposes a reader's knowledge of both writings,
see the discussions in Jörg Jeremias, "The Interrelationship between Amos and
Hosea," in House and Watts, *Forming Prophetic Literature,* 171–86; Schart, *Entstehung
des Zwölfprophetenbuchs,* 101–55.

sequently, the promise of YHWH's positive actions appears in 2:18–27, but, as with Hos 14:5ff., the restoration still lies in the future and the reader is never told explicitly whether the people repent.[14] These promised actions include (1) the return of the agricultural bounty (2:19, 21, 24); (2) the removal of the army (2:20); (3) the restoration of the rains (2:22); (4) recompense for the years of the "locusts" (2:25); and (5) removal of the famine (2:26f.). These actions reverse the punishments and threats of 1:2–2:11 in much the same way that Hosea's promissory section resolves the problems mentioned earlier in Hosea.

Second, between the two calls to repentance vocabulary recurs in quotes and strong allusions to agricultural fertility images, whereby Joel adapts a major motif of Hosea. In Hosea's call to repentance, the fertility images appear in the promise and offer resolution to the anti-Baal/anti-idolatry polemic, which admonishes Israel for failing to recognize YHWH as the source of its abundance (e.g., 2:10, 15; 9:10; 11:2; 13:1). In Joel's call to repentance, the fertility imagery refers to things that have been devastated. In Joel 1:2–2:11, these fertile elements have been removed or destroyed by locusts, drought, and enemy attack; they will only be restored following repentance of all the inhabitants (2:12ff.). Even the introductory verse of Joel 1:2 takes on a larger perspective as a transitional element than as an independent summons to attention.[15]

---

[14] Note especially the formulation in 2:19, with the quote from YHWH cited using *vav*-consecutive constructions, followed by the statements of what YHWH is about to do (participle + הנה).

[15] Joel 1:2 is typically treated as a teacher's "call to attention," because commentators presume an independent existence for Joel. This interpretation creates at least three difficulties that can be resolved if one sees the verse as a deliberate reference to Hos 14. First, this call to attention appears more frequently in prophetic literature than in Wisdom literature. More important, in prophetic literature the phrase generally plays a *connecting* role. Second, when Joel 1:2 is treated as an independent introduction, "this" has no antecedent, requiring the presumption of two *different, proleptic antecedents* ("Hear this *word* ... has this *locust plague* happened in your days or the days of your fathers?"). Third, the rhetorical question makes no sense literally. When the question is asked — "Has this happened in your days, or in the days of your fathers?" — the implied answer is no. Yet when "this" is interpreted as a reference to the locust plague(s), a comparative preposition must be presumed (Has *anything like* this happened in your days?). If one asks what happens if Joel 1:2 is read in conjunction with Hosea, all three problems disappear. First, "hear this" plays a connecting function that is typical for prophetic examples of this phrase. Second, "this" has one (not two) concrete (not proleptic) antecedent in Hosea's call to repentance (and foundational promise): "has this *repentance* occurred?" Third, the rhetorical question makes sense because the expected negative answer is consistent with the subsequent description. No, this *repentance* has not happened, and, as a result, the land is devastated.

Most convincingly, Joel 2:24 specifically alters Hos 9:2 by changing it from a description of punishment to a promise of fertility. It will be necessary to treat the recurring vocabulary in the next section, but first it will be helpful to look briefly at the transition between Joel and Amos created by overlapping genres.

Joel 4:1–21 (Heb.) presents a message of eschatological judgment on the nations. Thematic structure holds the chapter together as a composite unit.[16] It is formulated to serve a dual function as the conclusion to Joel (especially in 4:18–21) and as an eschatological transition to Amos (hence the quote of Amos 1:2 in Joel 4:16 and the use of Joel 4:18 in Amos 9:13 to bracket the beginning and end of Amos).[17] I will not explore the manner in which Joel 4 shapes the reading of Amos, since Schart has already done this at considerable length.[18] I simply make several observations on how Joel causes the reader to hear Amos differently.

First, unlike Amos, Joel's message to the nations does not utilize a refrain to address individual nations in succession. Joel does highlight particular nations for specific crimes (Tyre, Sidon, and the regions of Philistia in 4:4 for their enslavement of Judeans and Jerusalemites, and Edom and Egypt in 4:19), but the majority of the chapter focuses on YHWH's retribution against "all surrounding nations" (4:11, 12), a phrase that takes on greater significance when seen as a transition to Amos 1–2. Second, in keeping with Joel's overall message, Joel 4:1–21 presents a judgment that, with its emphasis on the Day of YHWH, creates an eschatological framework. Schart even suggests that Joel's concentration on the "Day of YHWH" provides a concrete antecedent for the suffix "it" in the refrain of Amos (I will not take "it" back).[19] Third, the link from Joel 4:16 to Amos 1:2 accents the Zion tradition, meaning that these nations represent those that will attack Jerusalem. Fourth,

---

[16] See my discussion in *Redactional Processes*, 26–41. Some of the unifying elements of this chapter include the thematic chiastic structure, and the reversal of the destruction of chapters 1–2 (through citation of verses and catchwords from those passages).

[17] See particularly the discussions in Schart, *Entstehung des Zwölfprophetenbuchs*, 81; Nogalski, *Redactional Processes*, 36–37; and idem, *Literary Precursors*, 104–5, 116–22.

[18] Schart, *Entstehung des Zwölfprophetenbuchs*, 220–23. See also my discussion of the "eschatologization" of Amos 1:2 in "Intertextuality," 105–8.

[19] Schart, *Entstehung des Zwölfprophetenbuchs*, 222. Note also the similar technique created by the introduction of Joel 1:2, in which "this" can be read as a reference to Hosea's promise of 14:5ff. See above, n. 15. See also van Leeuwen, "Scribal Wisdom," 41–42. Van Leeuwen argues that Joel 4:21 "has no real function other than to link Joel and Amos in a manner that contrasts Judah (4:16–20) and Israel, the primary topic of Amos."

this enlarged perspective carries over into the remainder of Amos (see especially 1:2; 4:6–11; 7:1–4; 9:13).

To summarize, Joel at the beginning dovetails genres with Hosea and with Amos at the end. In so doing, Joel adds two dimensions to both pre-existing contexts. First, Joel emphasizes the Zion context as compared with the northern contexts of Hosea and Amos. This Zion emphasis occurs both in the call to repentance of Joel 1–2 (cf. Joel's temple imagery and 2:1) and in Joel's pronouncement to the nations (Joel 4:1, 16, 17, 21). Second, in both instances Joel adds a transcendent eschatological dimension not present in the preexisting forms of Hosea and Amos. The enemy attack in Joel 1–2 not only lacks the concrete references to political entities present in Hosea (cf. Hos 14:3 with Joel 1:6), it also portrays the enemy in cosmic terms (2:1–11). This cosmic dimension also characterizes the judgment against the nations in Joel 4:1ff. (see 4:9–17, and the adapted citation of Amos 1:2 in Joel 4:16). In short, the overlapping genres allow Joel to shape the reader's perspective by providing a transition from Hosea to Joel to Amos that transcends the eighth-century chronological framework, and that emphasizes Zion as the central geographical (and theological) lens.

The Recurring Fertility Language of Joel

As mentioned previously, the recurring vocabulary of Joel can be noted in (1) Joel's use (and often adaptation) of images and phrases from earlier writings; and in (2) the redactional implantation of Joel's vocabulary into other contexts. Both of these elements require exploration, but it is also important to note that this recurring vocabulary centers around four interrelated motifs held together by their relationships to the historical paradigm introduced in Joel and played out in the remaining writings of the Twelve: agricultural fertility (or the lack thereof), the centrality of Judah and Jerusalem, the Day of YHWH, and theodicy. Cooper and van Leeuwen have explored the theodicy language of Joel.[20] The Day-of-YHWH language will only be mentioned briefly by way of illustration. The centrality of Judah and Jerusalem pervades almost every writing in the Twelve.

I want to focus on the fertility motif and its relationship to Joel's

---

[20] Alan Cooper, "In Praise of Divine Caprice: The Significance of the Book of Jonah," in *Among the Prophets: Language, Image, and Structure in the Prophetic Writings* (ed. Philip R. Davies and David J. A. Clines; JSOTSup 144; Sheffield: JSOT Press, 1993), 144–63; van Leeuwen, "Scribal Wisdom," 31–49.

transcendent historical paradigm. This motif is not selected randomly, but extends observations on ideas that recur in redactionally significant passages detailed in my previous work.

The fertility imagery of Joel entered the above discussion of the overlapping genres. Joel's call to repentance adapts the agricultural imagery promised in the call to repentance of Hos 14:2–9. More can be said, however, since the fertility images begin already with the anti-Baal polemic of Hos 2:10–25. In Hos 2:10ff., the wife (Israel) takes her agricultural bounty and gives it to her lovers (other gods). Since she does not recognize that the grain, wine (תירוש), and oil come from YHWH, YHWH determines to remove these elements and others from the land to shame her as punishment for the days she worshiped Baal (2:10–15 [Eng., 2:8–13]). YHWH will then take her to the wilderness so that he might win her back to a faithful relationship (2:16–22 [Eng., 2:14–20]). Once the fidelity is restored, YHWH will restore the grain, wine (תירוש), and oil (2:24 [Eng., 2:22]). When this imagery reappears in Hosea, it becomes clear that the people are not capable of the fidelity demanded by YHWH. In the woe oracle of Hos 7:13–14, Ephraim only laments to receive the grain and wine, not because of a change of heart.

> Woe to them, for they have strayed from me! Destruction is theirs, for they have rebelled against me. I would redeem them, but they speak lies against me. And they do not cry to me from their heart when they wail on their beds. They assemble themselves for the sake of grain and wine (תירוש). They turn away from me.

In other words, there has been no change on the part of Ephraim. As a result, the vats and the threshing floor will no longer feed them (9:1–2). Against this background the promise of 14:5–8 takes on added dimensions. If the people speak honestly (14:3–4 [Eng., 14:2–3]), YHWH will heal their apostasy and fertility will return to the land so that "the inhabitants will return in his shade. They will grow grain and they will blossom like the vine ... " (14:8a [Eng., 14:7a]).

When one follows this fertility imagery beyond Hosea, one cannot escape the sense that Joel presumes knowledge of this motif, juxtaposing the current situation with the promise of Hos 14:5ff. Joel 1:2 asks whether "this" has happened in a construction that implies it has not, and then describes the present, in which the fertile land lies in ruins because the people have not repented (cf. the imperatives for repentance).[21] The ruin of the land stems from locusts, drought, and enemy

---

[21] Note how the fertility motif is tied to the promises of the exodus in Bergler, *Joel als Schriftinterpret*, 247–94.

invasion. The specific combination of "grain, wine, and oil" occurs in Joel 1:10; 2:19; 2:24, but Joel 1–2 is rife with agricultural images, in which the land has ceased to produce until the people return to YHWH. This combination of "grain, wine, and oil" also appears in a logical sequence that forces one to see Joel and Hosea together. First, "grain, wine, and oil" appear in the description of the devastated situation (1:10): "For the grain is ruined. The wine has dried up. The oil has failed." Second, these same three elements appear in the promise of their restoration (2:19): "And YHWH *will answer,* and will say to *his people* [cf. Hos 2:23–25], 'Behold, I am about to send you the grain, the wine, and the oil, and you will be satisfied.'" Finally, "wine" and "oil" appear with a synonym for grain in the affirmation of Joel 2:24, which explicitly reverses the judgment of Hos 9:1–2: "And the threshing floors will be full of wheat (בר), and the vats will overflow with wine (תירוש) and oil." Use of Joel language to express images of fertility is not limited to this combination of grain, wine (תירוש), and oil, but this combination illustrates how Joel extends and reinterprets the paradigm of Hosea.

Other texts in the Twelve use Joel's fertility language. Haggai 1:11 and 2:19 show how Joel's fertility imagery has been "harvested" redactionally as part of the continuing message of the Twelve. In Haggai, the first writing set in the postexilic section of the Twelve, 1:10–11 states:

> [10]Therefore, because of you the sky has withheld its dew and the earth has with-held its produce. [11]And I called for a drought on the land, on the mountains, on the *grain, on the wine* (תירוש), *on the oil,* on what the ground produces, on men, on cattle, and on all the labor of your hands.

Haggai 1:11 extends the description of the punishment with a litany of items which the drought has affected, including the grain, wine (תירוש), and oil.

Haggai 2:19 includes related images from Joel, which are also com-bined to help develop the fertility motif. The verse contains a rhetorical question that has been expanded by references to Joel that make no sense in Haggai.[22]

> Is the seed still in the granary? *Or has even the vine, or the fig tree, or the pomegranate, or the olive tree not borne fruit?*

This combination also evokes the devastated elements of Joel 1–2 in much the same manner as the grain, wine, and oil (note also that Hag

---

[22] See my discussion in *Literary Precursors,* 228–29. Not only does this expansion create syntactical difficulties, it also provides a strange picture of placing a vine, a fig tree, a pomegranate, and an olive tree in an underground storehouse.

2:17 quotes Amos 4:9 in a way that touches on this same imagery). One should probably differentiate the fertility idioms that ultimately have their "roots" in the fertility traditions of the promised land (as, e.g., in Deut 8:8), and the specific literary references to the repentance paradigm of Hosea/Joel. Joel demonstrates awareness of Hosea in other ways than the use of fertility imagery, and other combinations of images could be named, but time and space do not permit full explorations. The subject does require that we look at another important aspect of Joel's fertility motif, namely, the locusts.[23]

Joel's locust imagery functions in two ways: to depict the destruction of fertility and to anticipate enemy attacks. Elsewhere I have stated in detail my reasons for arguing that Joel's locusts are not literal references to actual locust plagues but are metaphors for natural disasters and the hordes of attacking armies that invade the land in succession.[24] Not only does Joel itself make this association, but locust images in Amos, Nahum, Habakkuk, and Malachi are interpreted in this way, often through explicit allusions to Joel. Schart argues that Amos 4:9* includes at least one phrase that cites Joel.[25] The drought language of Joel is thus taken up as another example of Israel's failure to heed YHWH's warning and call to repentance. Amos 4:9 presumes the drought of Joel has been sent, but that the people have *not* returned/repented. Nahum 3:15aγ ("It will

---

[23] As an example of other links in imagery, reference to the "virgin" (Israel) in Joel 1:8 takes up the language of Hos 2:1ff. See my discussion in *Redactional Processes*, 18–22. Multiple combinations of these terms appear in at least the following passages within the Twelve:" grain," "wine," and "oil" (Hos 2:10; 2:24; Joel 1:10; 2:19; 2:24; Hag 1:11); "grain" and "wine" (Hos 2:11; 7:14; 9:1–2; 14:8; Zech 9:17); other combinations (Hos 4:11; 14:7–8; Joel 1:12; 2:22; Amos 4:9; Mic 4:4; 6:15; Hab 3:17; Hag 2:19). Undoubtedly, not all of these passages were created for the Book of the Twelve, but when read carefully, some exhibit other criteria that suggest the allusions were created intentionally as part of the book's unification (see esp. Hos 2:10, 24; Amos 4:9; Hab 3:17; Hag 2:19).

[24] See my discussion in *Redactional Processes*, 2–6, 23.

[25] See the discussion in Schart, *Entstehung des Zwölfprophetenbuchs*, 61. Schart argues that ותאניכם וזיתיכם יכל הגזם alludes to Joel 1:6–7, based on the references to the fig tree and olive tree, as well as on the use of גזם for locust. However, since גזם appears in 1:4, and since the earlier portion of the verse refers both to scorching (east wind) and mildew, it is also plausible that the entire verse summarizes the drought imagery from Joel. Amos 4:9 is a self-contained verse that fits the context, making precise determination of the genetic relationship difficult. The relationship is complicated further by the fact that Hag 2:17 cites Amos 4:9 without the phrase in question. The missing reference to the locust could have been the intention of the redactor (in most other redactional insertions, the locust language refers to attacking nations), or could be explained by Schart's contention that Haggai entered the multivolume corpus prior to Joel, but after Amos.

devour you like the locust") and 3:16b ("The creeping locust [ילק] strips
and flies away") incorporate Joel's vocabulary and interpret Assyria and
Babylon as locusts of great numerical strength and power.[26] Habakkuk
1:9, using a different word than Joel, elicits images of Babylon as a locust
"horde"; nevertheless, the passage is also associated with the redaction
of the developing corpus.[27] The passage forms part of a description of
Babylon that takes many of the images that Nah 3 uses for Assyria, but
makes them more threatening by applying them to Babylon. In addition,
one can hardly ignore the way in which Habakkuk's description of Babylon's destructive force (1:6–11) coincides with images of the attacking
enemy in Joel 2:1–11. Malachi 3:10–11 also employs images from Joel,
thereby offering a final promise of "agricultural fertility" (this time to
the righteous remnant) if the people will use the fruits of the land for
true worship of YHWH:

> [10]Bring the whole tithe into the *storehouse*, so that there may be food in my house,
> and test me now in this, says the LORD of hosts, if I will not open the windows
> of heaven for you, and pour out a blessing for you until there is no more need.
> [11]Then I will rebuke *the devourer* for you, so that it may not destroy the fruits of
> the ground; nor will your vine cast [its grapes] in the field, says the LORD of Hosts.

The reference to the devourer is generally interpreted as a locust, even
by those not reading the Twelve as a unit. One sees the convergence of
Joel's fertility promises (Joel 1:17; 2:24), YHWH's blessing of rain (2:23),
and the removal of the locusts (2:25).

The Day of YHWH and Theodicy in Joel

Before moving to the paradigm of history presented by Joel, it is necessary to mention briefly three additional threads that run through Joel
and the Twelve: the Day-of-YHWH sayings, theodicy, and repentance.
The centrality of the Day-of-YHWH language in Joel adds to the impression of Joel's function as literary anchor for the Book of the Twelve. This
language deserves a more detailed treatment than I can give here; that
treatment will have to wait for another study. I mention only one aspect
of Joel's Day-of-YHWH language in this context. This motif can be recognized by the phrase "the Day of YHWH," or by the related phrases,
"in that day" and "in those days." When one isolates the Day-of-YHWH

---

26 Nogalski, *Redactional Processes*, 120–21.
27 Ibid., 146–50. Schart argues the inclusion of Nahum and Habakkuk predates
the addition of Joel (and Obadiah). Details of this argument cannot be treated here.
See Schart, *Entstehung des Zwölfprophetenbuchs*, 204ff.

references in Joel, virtually every one has a close (if not verbatim) parallel in the Book of the Twelve. The chart on the following page will demonstrate this relationship more clearly than a narrative description. Interpreting the significance of these parallel formulations is no simple task, but their presence further solidifies the impression that Joel is the writing through which all major themes of the Twelve must travel. One must also mention Joel's discussion of theodicy, which plays out across the Book of the Twelve.

Cooper and van Leeuwen have documented the presence of a series of texts in the Twelve that delves into the theodicy language of Exod 34:6–7, regarding the fate of Israel and Judah.[28] Their works, together, demonstrate that at least two fundamentally different responses to the question are deliberately incorporated in the Book of the Twelve. Neither author attempts to explain how this motif was incorporated redaction-historically, but they demonstrate intentional interplay with the Exodus text and with other texts in the Twelve. More needs to be done to situate this motif within the development of the Twelve as a whole, since the motif is not isolated. Cooper, particularly, demonstrates how this motif is also associated with an ongoing discussion about God's response to repentance, as seen in the divine responses and the interplay between Jonah and Nahum. Van Leeuwen, on the other hand, also highlights the manner in which this theodicy language is associated with the Day of YHWH, and the sense in which Joel serves as the essential interpretive backdrop for this language in the Twelve. In this light, I suspect it is no accident that this particular theodicy language appears only within the first seven writings, while other images are used in the remaining writings.

Joel's Paradigm of History

Now it is time to return to one of the first questions raised in this study: How does one incorporate one or more of these recurring concepts into a comprehensive analysis of the literary intention(s) of the Twelve? While, in a very real sense, this task still seems daunting, I would nevertheless attempt to correlate several observations in the hopes of at least advancing the dialogue. First, one must cease thinking of Joel as a collection of unrelated postexilic messages, and investigate its role in the Book of the Twelve more closely. This statement does not argue that

---

[28] Cooper, "In Praise of Divine Caprice," 144–63; van Leeuwen, "Scribal Wisdom," 31–49.

Joel		Parallel	
1:15 (2x)	Alas for the day! For the Day of YHWH is near, and it will come as destruction from the Almighty.	Zeph 1:14	*Near is the* great *Day of YHWH,* near and coming very quickly; the sound of the Day of YHWH! In it the warrior cries out bitterly.
2:1	Blow the trumpet in Zion; sound the alarm on my holy mountain! Let all the inhabitants of the land tremble, for *the Day of YHWH is coming,* it is near.	Joel 3:4	See below. Cf. also the combination of "day(s)" + "come" in Hos 9:7; Zeph 2:2; Mal 3:23.
2:2 (2x)	a day of darkness and gloom, a day of clouds and thick darkness!	Zeph 1:15	A day of wrath is that day, a day of trouble and distress, a day of destruction and desolation, *a day of darkness and gloom, a day of clouds and thick darkness*
2:11	Truly the Day of YHWH is great; terrible indeed — who can endure it?	Mal 3:23	Behold, I am going to send you Elijah the prophet, before the coming of the *great and terrible Day of YHWH*
3:2	Even on the male and female slaves, in those days, I will pour out my spirit.		No parallel
3:4	The sun shall be turned to darkness, and the moon to blood, before the great and terrible Day of YHWH comes.	Joel 2:10b	The sun and the moon grow dark, and the stars lose their brightness. (cf. Joel 2:11)
4:1	For then, in those days and at that time, when I restore the fortunes of Judah and Jerusalem	Zeph 3:20	At that time I will bring you in, even at the time when I gather you together; indeed, I will give you renown and praise among all the peoples of the earth when I restore your fortunes before your eyes, says YHWH
4:14	Multitudes, multitudes, in the valley of decision! For the Day of YHWH is near in the valley of decision.	Joel 1:15	See Joel 1:15 above
4:18	In that day *the mountains shall drip sweet wine, the hills* shall flow with milk, and all the streambeds of Judah shall flow with water; a fountain shall come forth from the house of YHWH and water the Wadi Shittim.	Amos 9:13	Behold, the days are coming declares YHWH, when the plowman will overtake the reaper, and the treader of grapes him who sows seed; *when the mountains shall drip sweet wine and all the hills* will be dissolved.

Other Occurrences of "Day" in Joel

1:2 (2x)	Hear this, O elders, give ear, all inhabitants of the land! Has such a thing happened in your days, or in *the days of your fathers?*	Mal 3:7	From *the days of your fathers* you have turned aside from my statutes, and have not kept [them]. Return to me, and I will return to you says YHWH of hosts.... (cf. also Joel 2:13)

Joel is a preexilic creation. Rather, its literary cohesion, its deliberate overlapping of forms, and its use of images from Hosea and Amos all anchor Joel into *this literary context*, despite the fact that Joel is *almost* universally considered one of the Twelve's later writings.[29]

Second, Joel's presence between Hosea and Amos does not ignore the chronological context. It transcends it. It introduces or transforms many theological emphases of the Book of the Twelve. Subsequent allusions to Joel in the Twelve tend to regard him as having predicted events of that time. For example, Amos 4:9 presumes that YHWH has sent the drought and locust attack presumed in Joel 1, and that YHWH has now decided to bring an end to Israel. The locust imagery of Joel is taken up by redactional associations in Nah 3:15–17 to indicate that one "locust" (Assyria) who has invaded the land will be destroyed by another (Babylon); hence, the "horde" mentioned in Hab 1:9 is reminiscent of Joel 2:1–11.

Third, Joel offers a paradigm of history which "plays out" as one reads the Book of the Twelve, simultaneously providing the prophetic revelation and the clues necessary for a cohesive reading. As one encounters Joel's language across the Twelve, the realization is that one is not experiencing the unexpected. A cohesive reading which uses Joel as the anchor ultimately does two things. It explains why the history of YHWH's people occurred in the way it did, and it offers hope to readers that they will endure only by turning to YHWH. A few observations about some of the major themes will perhaps provide impetus for continued reflection.

Joel extends Hosea's call to repentance by juxtaposing the promissory images of fertility with the "current" situation, in which a series of "locust" plagues (1:4, 7), drought (1:5–20), and a locust/enemy attack of unparalleled proportions (2:1–11) will continue until and unless the people repent. *If* the people repent, YHWH will become zealous for his land again and restore what the drought has destroyed and what the "locusts" have eaten (2:12–25).[30] Afterward, the centrality of Zion will

---

[29] A few writers date Joel in the early postexilic period, between Haggai/Zechariah and Malachi (e.g., Paul L. Redditt, "The Book of Joel and Peripheral Prophecy," *CBQ* 48 (1986): 225–40). Most still date Joel well into the Persian period. See discussions in Leslie C. Allen, *The Books of Joel, Obadiah, Jonah, and Micah* (NICOT; Grand Rapids: Eerdmans, 1976), 19–25; James L. Crenshaw, *Joel: A New Translation with Introduction and Commentary* (AB 24C; New York: Doubleday, 1995), 21–29.

[30] This passage demands more attention since it contains considerable tensions about the extent to which the situation is reversed. Certain portions seem to imply that restoration of the fertility has begun (2:21–23), but the majority of the text still anticipates the need for restoration (e.g., 2:19, 25).

be restored (3:1–5; 4:1, 16, 17, 21). Throughout this period (note 4:1 has "in those days" and "at that time"), the nations will be judged for their actions against YHWH's people (4:1–21).

Note how Joel's language is then incorporated within this paradigm in other writings in the Twelve. Amos 4:9 uses Joel's fertility images to make the point that the people did not repent, even though they had been warned.[31] Israel is punished (Amos), although fertility and restoration are promised afterward (Amos 9:13, citing Joel 4:18). Micah offers the same choice to Judah and Jerusalem (Mic 1:5–9; 3:12), but the South continues in the path of the northern kingdom (6:1ff.). Micah reiterates promises to Judah that presume it will first experience punishments (4:1–4; 7:7f.). Nahum picks up Joel's threads again with the affirmation that YHWH punishes the guilty (Nah 1:3a) and in Nah 3:15–17, which interprets Assyria and Babylon as locusts, who themselves will soon be punished.[32] Habakkuk depicts the unprecedented nature of Babylon's attack by heightening the parallels between Assyria and Babylon,[33] and through subtle allusions to Joel 2:1–11.[34] Further, when discussing the fate of the people, Hab 3:17 returns to the fertility imagery of Joel to anticipate the coming destruction. Zephaniah draws upon the Day-of-YHWH sayings from Joel (Zeph 1:7, 14, 15) as well as, in Zeph 3:19–20, the eschatological promises of Joel and Micah.[35] Haggai returns to the fertility imagery, rooted in Joel, by confronting the returned exiles with the land's infertility. Haggai confronts this people and challenges them to rebuild the temple as a sign they are ready to return to YHWH, so that YHWH will himself begin to restore the blessings of the land. Note how this is accomplished in Hag 2:17, 19,* with the citation of Amos 4:9 and Joel 1, respectively. In Zech 1:2–6, this generation finally repents, leading to the statement that YHWH is now jealous for his land (Zech 1:15; cf. Joel 2:18–19 also with Hag 1:11; 2:17, 19). Zechariah 8:12 draws upon the fertility images of Joel, this time with reference to the rain as well (cf. Joel 2:23).[36] Thus, YHWH will save the remnant of this people

---

[31] Cf. also Joel 2:12, with the emphatic nature of the call to repentance: "Yet even now, return to me...."

[32] Note that both of these references are short redactional comments inserted into an existing context. See my discussions in *Redactional Processes*, 104–7 and 120–21.

[33] Ibid., 146–50.

[34] Note especially the similarities between Hab 1:7–10 and Joel 2:4–9.

[35] Nogalski, *Literary Precursors*, 181–215; idem, *Redactional Processes*, 47–48.

[36] Note also the way in which Zech 8:13, 15 takes up the comfort of the salvation oracle with the command "do not fear." This command appears only four times in the Book of the Twelve, in Joel 2:22; Hag 2:5; Zech 8:13, 15.

(or, the house of Judah and the house of Israel) that they will be a blessing rather than a curse among the nations (Zech 8:12–13). With Malachi, however, the people return to the same idolatrous behavior that they exhibited at the beginning. Hence one finds "catchwords" in Zech 8 and Malachi that juxtapose promise and reality in precisely the same way as the catchwords in Hosea and Joel.[37] Interestingly, and I suspect not accidentally, the last chapter of Malachi presupposes that until the people repent (again), the devourer will remain (3:7, 10). In the end, only those who fear YHWH — not the entire nation — respond to this message (3:16–18).

Diachronic questions will continue to draw my attention, but the side sympathetic with synchronic approaches could not resist offering a reading of the Twelve that, to me, reflects plausible reading strategies of the editors who brought these writings together. These authors/redactors, by using recurring language related to the fertility and infertility of the land, the repentance of the people, and God's punishment of the guilty (within and outside Israel), compiled and shaped Joel as the literary anchor for a historical paradigm.

---

[37] See my discussion in *Redactional Processes*, 197–200.

8

Superscriptions and Incipits
in the Book of the Twelve

John D. W. Watts

The study of prophetic superscriptions has to this point been done with varying understanding of their roles and the insights that can be gained. An important article by Gene Tucker views the superscriptions as part of the process in producing the canon and is the most comprehensive work on prophetic superscriptions available.[1] He is interested in the evidence provided by superscriptions as it relates to the understanding of canon. Tucker distinguished between "Scripture," which is in some sense authoritative, and "canon," which is fixed and cannot be changed. Canonical divisions belong to the very last stage of the shaping of the canon. Canonical divisions are Torah, Former Prophets, Latter Prophets, and Writings. Superscriptions were not shaped at this stage nor do they speak to these divisions. Tucker's point that superscriptions recognize the literature as "the word of God" is significant.

Other studies view superscriptions as parallel to and deriving from colophons. Colophons, written by copyists,[2] record at the end of the manuscript the name of the previous copyist, the date of the work, and any other data related to the copying process. The reader is not involved or interested. Superscriptions are not colophons, nor are they like colophons in content or purpose.

Sometimes superscriptions are not clearly differentiated from formulas which introduce and close oracles, but prophetic formulas are the subject for another study. Two formulas (Obad 1 and Zech 12:1) appear in the headings over books in the Twelve. But generally the elements used in such formulas differ from those in superscriptions.

---

[1] Gene M. Tucker, "Prophetic Superscriptions and the Growth of the Canon," in *Canon and Authority* (ed. George W. Coats and Burke O. Long; Philadelphia: Fortress, 1977), 70.

[2] H. M. I. Gevaryahu suggests that superscriptions derive from colophons ("Biblical Colophons: A Source for the Biography of Authors, Texts, and Books," in *Congress Volume: Edinburgh, 1974* [VTSup 28; Leiden: Brill, 1975], 42–59).

David Noel Freedman has written about headings over Isaiah, Hosea, Amos, and Micah as evidence of the purpose and process of scriptural redaction and publication.[3]

Superscriptions in Composition and Redaction

This study of superscriptions and incipits in the Prophets (especially the Twelve) views them as parts of the composition and redaction of the books from which valuable evidence concerning these processes may be gleaned. Narrative does not usually have a superscription. The opening sentence (an incipit) of the narrative serves the purpose and provides the information which the reader requires to understand what follows.

Superscriptions appear regularly over psalms and Wisdom collections. They are titles composed of nouns, not sentences, and may be elaborated by adding phrases and relative clauses. The superscriptions and incipits of the prophetic books are similar enough and use enough of the same terms to think of them as products of the same composers and editors as the poetic books, although perhaps several generations of editors.

Superscriptions and incipits in the Twelve, like those in Jeremiah and Ezekiel, structure the book and give it unity. The divergence in use of terms suggests a complex process of composition.[4] This complexity should be traced further in the genres used in the book.

The issue comes down to stages of composition and redaction. When and where does the development of superscriptions fit? Introductory and closing formulas such as "thus says Yahweh" and "expression of Yahweh" belong to the earliest history of the oracles and to their smallest units. They are inherent parts of the texts as transmitted. Even when such formulas are literary devices (as in Amos 1–2), they belong with the smaller textual units. Some prophetic literature uses formulas extensively, but superscriptions are different.

An *incipit* is a sentence which begins a narrative or a narrative book. A *superscription* is a title, sometimes expanded, over a book, a portion of a book, or a poem.[5] Incipits and superscriptions share similar func-

---

[3] David Noel Freedman, "Headings in the Books of the Eighth-Century Prophets," *AUSS* 25 (1987): 9–26. See also the general discussion of the content and structure of the headings of the Latter Prophets in F. I. Anderson and D. N. Freedman, *Hosea* (AB 24; Garden City, N.Y.: Doubleday, 1980), 143–49.

[4] Note that Isaiah also uses various terms, while both Jeremiah and Ezekiel are more consistent.

[5] Tucker, "Prophetic Superscriptions," 57.

tions and literary elements. Incipits begin narrative units and are a part of the narrative. Superscriptions properly belong over poetic units or collections of poetic units and are not part of the poems themselves. Together, incipits and superscriptions shape the compositional stage of prophetic literature.[6] The composition of books belongs to the stage of becoming "Scripture."

Use of superscriptions and incipits occurs throughout books, but also within books.[7] In 1:1, 2:1, and 13:1, Isaiah uses superscriptions that include the prophet's name and three different terms for genre. It is also clear in Isaiah that the use of superscriptions is optional. No superscription or incipit appears after chapter 13. Occasional overlapping and redundancy within the superscriptions, as well as in the incipits, should also be noted.[8]

Superscriptions and Incipits in the Book of the Twelve

A superscription appears over every Book of the Twelve except three. The narrative books, Jonah, Haggai, and Zechariah, begin with incipits. Superscriptions appear in several places inside the books. Some books have more than one superscription, and some have an incipit or formula to introduce the following book. Some superscriptions and incipits contain several layers.[9]

Several books have as many as three separate superscriptions piled

---

[6] This is the stage in which the books are being made up and shaped. *Redaction* takes place at various stages in the handling, preservation, and transmission of materials. *Composition* is the work of actually putting the books together.

[7] Jeremiah consistently uses superscriptions that contain the term דבר (word). Jeremiah 1:1 and 51:64 refer to "the words of Jeremiah." Jer 7:1; 11:11; 18:1; 21:11; 25:1; 30:1; 32:1; 34:1, 8; 35:1; 40:1; 44:1; 45:1 use "the word which was to Jeremiah." The formula changes to "which word of Yahweh was to Jeremiah in 46:1; 47:1; 50:1. Incipits using these elements occur frequently in Jeremiah but do not have a role in structuring.

Ezekiel uses incipit sentences in the same way and with the same elements as the superscriptions in Jeremiah. "The word of Yahweh was to me [Ezekiel]" occurs in 1:3; 3:16; 6:1; 7:1; 11:4; 12:1, 17, 23; 23:1; 24:1, 15, 20; 25:1; 26:1; 27:1; 28:1, 11, 20; 29:1, 17; 30:1, 17; 31:1; 32:1, 17; 33:1, 23; 34:1; 35:1; 36:16; 37:15; 38:1. These incipits mark new units in the book. The use of dates before some of them, and a variation in 40:1, mark the larger units. Ezekiel does not use superscriptions, perhaps in keeping with the narrative nature of the book.

[8] See the double incipit in Ezek 1:1 and 1:2–3, with one in first person and the other in third person.

[9] James Nogalski's study of *Stichwörter*, which "stitch" the books together, usually avoids the superscriptions. Exceptions are the word "Samaria" in Mic 1:1 and Obad 19 and "hand" in Mal 1:1 and Zech 8:13 (*Literary Precursors to the Book of the Twelve*

on top of each other. Each is an adequate superscription on its own (see below for Hos 1:1–2), not simply an element added to an existing superscription. If superscriptions are editorial headings used in organizing the material, what do these multiple superscriptions reveal about the history of the collection and the editing process?

My thesis is that some of the multiple superscriptions belong to the final stage of shaping the Book of the Twelve. I have called this the "top level," or, in the case of Hosea and other books with three layers of superscriptions or incipits, the "third level." Other superscriptions belong to an earlier stage of the process, in which smaller groups of text were gathered and treated together. I call these superscriptions the "middle" or "second" stage. Other superscriptions and incipits belong specifically to still-smaller units and were not part of the succeeding collating and editorial processes. I call these the "bottom" or "first" level. The terms "top," "middle," and "bottom" refer to the layers in an individual superscription. The terms "third," "second," and "first" refer to the superscriptions' relation to the process that gathered and shaped the smaller units into larger collections. I have also used the term "primary" for the first (or bottom) stage, or when only one stage is involved. I have used "secondary" when two or three stages are involved, and "tertiary" for the last stage when three stages are involved.

I also propose that the superscriptions or incipits of some books give no evidence of being a part of this gathering and shaping process. These are designated with an asterisk (*) and include Amos, Jonah, Haggai, and Zech 1–8.

Levels

Hosea 1:1, a superscription in two parts.
3   "The word of Yahweh (דבר יהוה)
       which was to Hosea, son of Beeri (אשר היה ל).
       In the days of Uzziah, Jotham, Ahaz, Hezekiah kings of Judah
       and in the days of Jeroboam son of Joash, king of Israel."
Hosea 1:2a, a second superscription.
2   "the beginning of the word of Yahweh by Hosea
       (תחלת דבר יהוה בהושע)"
Hosea 1:2b, an incipit beginning with *vav* consecutive.

[BZAW 217; Berlin: de Gruyter, 1993], 31 and 53–54). Nogalski usually thinks of the superscriptions as outside and not syntactically related to the text below.

2   "And then Yahweh said to Hosea (ויאמר יהוה אל)"
           All three elements use Hosea's name.

Joel 1:1, a single superscription.
3   "The word of Yahweh which was to Joel, son of Pethuel."

Amos 1:1, a layered superscription connected to the text by an incipit
                beginning with *vav* consecutive.
*   "The words of Amos who was among the shepherd of Tekoa,
*   which he envisioned
3   concerning Israel
3   in the days of Uzziah king of Judah and in the days of Jeroboam
                son of Joash king of Israel
*   two years before the earthquake."

Obadiah 1, a superscription followed by an expanded formula with
                information that usually is found in the superscription.
2   "The vision of Obadiah.
1   Thus says the Lord Yahweh
1   "to Edom (לאדום)."

Jonah 1:1 uses incipits because it is narrative.
*   "Then the word of Yahweh was to Jonah (ויהי דבר יהוה אל יונה)."
                The recipient of his message is named in v. 2
*   "to Nineveh (אל נינוה)"
Jonah 2:2 is an incipit introducing Jonah's prayer.
*   "Then Jonah prayed to Yahweh his God from the belly of the
                whale."
Jonah 3:1, a third incipit beginning this chapter.
*   "Then the word of Yahweh was to Jonah a second time."

Micah 1:1 has a multilayered superscription.
3   "The word of Yahweh which was to Micah the Morashtite
3   in the days of Jotham, Ahaz, Hezekiah, kings of Judah,
3   which he envisioned
3   against Samaria and Jerusalem."

Nahum 1:1a is the first of two superscriptions.
3   "a burden
3   of Nineveh"
Nahum 1:2b, a second superscription.
2   "the book of the vision of Nahum the Elkoshite"

Habakkuk 1:1 has a superscription in two layers.
3   "The burden
3   which Habakkuk the prophet saw."
         The subject of the prophecy, "the Chaldeans," is not mentioned
              until 1:6.
Habakkuk 3:1 has a superscription for the prayer.
*   "A prayer
3   belonging to Habakkuk the prophet
         on a Shigionoth"

Zephaniah 1:1 has a superscription in two layers.
3   "The word of Yahweh which was to Zephaniah the son of Cushi,
              son of Gedaliah, son of Amariah, son of Hezekiah,
3   in the days of Josiah son of Amon king of Judah."

Haggai uses incipits to open prophetic narratives in
*   1:1, 3; 2:1, 10, 20.
         These incipits use "the word of Yahweh was to Haggai
         the prophet." Three use exact dates
         from the reign of the Persian king Darius.

Zechariah 1–8 uses incipits to open narrative prophecy in
*   1:1, 7, like incipits in Haggai. Each of the visions opens with
              an incipit, "he showed me," or, "I saw."
*   Incipits reading "the word of the Lord was to me" occur in 6:9;
              7:1, 8; 8:1, with formulas of "thus says Yahweh" opening
              each of the prophecies.

Zechariah 9:1 has two superscriptions and an incipit, but does not use a
prophet's name.
3   "a burden"
A second:
2   "the word of Yahweh
         against (ב) Hadrach, its resting place Damascus
         for all the cities of Aram[10] and all the tribes of Israel belong
              to Yahweh.
         And also Hamath borders on it,
1   Tyre and Sidon, although they are very wise [skillful] and Tyre

---

[10] The כי clause modifies " its resting place Damascus." ליהוה ("to YHWH") in a
verbless clause usually indicates possession: "belongs to YHWH," "is YHWH's." The

built a stronghold for herself and heaped up silver like dust and gold[11] like the mud of the streets."

Zechariah 12:1 has two superscriptions and a formula but no prophet's name.

3   "a burden"

The second superscription has two layers:

2   "the word of Yahweh
against (על) Israel"

A formula:

1   נאום יהוה "expression of Yahweh, one stretching out the heavens and founding the earth and forming the spirit of humanity in itself."

Malachi 1:1 has two superscriptions.

3   "a burden"

The second superscription has two layers.

2   "the word of God by the hand of Malachi
to (אל) Israel"

Some superscriptions or incipits do not evidence having been part of this shaping process. These include the narrative books of Jonah, Haggai, and Zech 1–8. Only secondary elements in the superscription of Amos seem to be involved in the composition of the Twelve.

Amos 1:1–2a

The basic element of the title is דברי עמוס, "words of Amos." This formulation is unique in the Twelve; its only parallel in the Latter Prophets is Jer 1:1.

---

following parallel words ("and all the tribes of Israel") make one expect population units or places. The dominant words in 9:1–7 are places or peoples (Hadrach, Damascus, tribes of Israel, Hamath, Tyre and Sidon, and the Philistine cities). This list suggests that a place or people belongs to YHWH. *BHK* recommended emending the ד in אדם to ר (Aram). *BHS* expands this emendation to include changing עין (eye) to עוו (ruins). I accept the reading of "Aram," but suggest another emended form: ערי (cities of) in place of "ruins." The resulting "cities of Aram" brings the words into good parallel with what follows and into conformity with 9:1–7. The entire clause thus reads, "For the cities of Aram and the tribes of Israel belong to YHWH."

[11] חרוץ has a primary meaning of something dug out or engraved. It may refer to diligence.

It continues, "who was among the breeders of sheep from Tekoa (אשר היה בנקדים מתקוע)" and "which he envisioned two years before the earthquake."

The superscription shows multiple layers, which may indicate that it was originally a composite from two superscriptions: one over a book of "words" and the other over a book of "visions."[12] The second layer is the clause אשר חזה, which also becomes a link in the superscriptions of the Twelve.

This seems to have been the superscription over Amos before it became part of the Twelve. It also had an incipit, ויאמר, "then he said," to begin the book.

But the superscription played a role in the structure of other superscriptions in the Twelve. "Which he envisioned" is repeated in Mic 1:1 and Hab 1:1. The phrase על־ישראל, "over or against Israel," is inserted along with other similar phrases in other superscriptions. Royal names that date the prophecy are inserted to relate Amos to other prophecies with such dates.

Incipits

The narrative books of Jonah, Haggai, and Zech 1–8 make frequent use of incipits of a standard form: ויהי דבר יהוה אל, "then the word of Yahweh was to ... " This form was used in the Deuteronomic History, Jeremiah, and Ezekiel, but is missing in Isaiah. It shows no signs of having been influenced by other works in the Twelve and may have been composed before or outside the compositional and redactional work.

Note that major elements in the final stages of the redaction of the Twelve, "the word of Yahweh" and "which was to," are closely related to this incipit.

Incipits function on the top or third level in the Twelve. Hosea 1:2b ("Then Yahweh said to Hosea"), Amos 1:2a ("then he said"), and Obad 1b ("thus says Yahweh") belong to the books' authors and show no signs of having been involved with the processes that shaped the Twelve.

---

[12] See John D. W. Watts, "The Origin of the Book of Amos," *ExpTim* 66 (1955): 109–12; and idem, *Vision and Prophecy in Amos* (Leiden: Brill, 1958; Grand Rapids: Eerdmans, 1958), 27, 50 = *Vision and Prophecy in Amos: Expanded Anniversary Edition* (Macon, Ga.: Mercer University Press, 1997), 58, 85ff.

The Book of the Twelve
Titles (Substantives)

	Hosea	Joel	Amos	Obad	Jonah	Micah	Nahum	Hab	Zeph	Hag	Zech	9:1	12:1	Mal
Top Level														
Word of Y (which was)	1:1	1:1	*1:1						1:1					
Burden מַשָּׂא							1:1	1:1				9:1	12:1	1:1
Middle Level														
Word of Y	1:1										1:1	9:1	12:1	
Vision חָזוֹן				1			1:1							
Prayer תְּפִלָּה								3:1						
Basic Level														
Oracle נְאֻם													12:1	

Clauses in the Superscriptions

	Hosea	Joel	Amos	Obad	Jonah	Micah	Nahum	Hab	Zeph	Hag	Zech	9:1	12:1	Mal
Top Level														
which was to אֲשֶׁר הָיָה אֶל	1:1	1:1				1:1			1:1					
which he envisioned אֲשֶׁר חָזָה			1:1			1:1		1:1						

Phrases (on all levels)

	Hosea	Joel	Amos	Obad	Jonah	Micah	Nahum	Hab	Zeph	Hag	Zech	9:1	12:1	Mal
In the days of	1:1		1:1			1:1			1:1					
*In the month, year										*1:1+	*1:1+			
"Because" כִּי												9:1 (2x) כִּי לַיהוָה עֵין אָדָם / וְכֹל שִׁבְטֵי יִשְׂרָאֵל		
"to" לְ				1b לֶאֱדוֹם										
"on, against" עַל					1:1+ יוֹנָה	1:1 שֹׁמְרוֹן		3:1 שִׁגְיֹנוֹת					12:1 יִשְׂרָאֵל	
"to" אֶל			1:1 יִשְׂרָאֵל							1:1+ חַגַּי		9:1 אֶרֶץ חַדְרָךְ		1:1 יִשְׂרָאֵל
by" בְּ	1:2b הוֹשֵׁעַ									1:1+ חַגַּי				1:1 מַלְאָכִי
or "against"	1:2a הוֹשֵׁעַ													

*Incipit Sentences (all outside the development of "the Twelve")

Formula	Hosea	Joel	Amos	Obad	Jonah	Micah	Nahum	Hab	Zeph	Hag	Zech	Mal
"Then the word of Yahweh was to" ויהי דבר יהוה אל										1:1+	1:1+	
"Then Yahweh said to" ויאמר יהוה אל												
"Then he said" ויאמר	1:2b											
"Thus says Yahweh" כה אמר יהוה			1:2	1b							12:1 / 12:1 נאם יהוה	

(Zech 8 uses this repeatedly without a prophet's name.)

Use of Prophets' Names

	Hosea	Joel	Amos	Obad	Jonah	Micah	Nahum	Hab	Zeph	Hag	Zech	Mal
Top Level	1:1	1:1	*1:1	1		1:1	1:1	1:1	1:1		9–11	1:1
Middle Level	1:2a		7:10		1:1+			3:1	1:1+	1:1+	12–14	
Basic Level	1:2b					**************************						
No identification	1:2a,b		7:10,12,14	1	1						7:1,8	1:1
Place		1:1h				1:1						
Parent	1:1	1:1			1:1						1:1	
By guild		1:1								1:1		
"the prophet"								1:1		1:1	1:1+	
No name								1:1	1:1+	1:1+	6:9; 7:4, 8; 12:1; 8:1; 9:1	

At this basic level, five prophets are named: Hosea (Hos 1:2b), Amos (Amos 7:10), Jonah, Haggai, and Zechariah.

Zechariah 12:1 displays a superscription containing all three levels. The lowest, or basic one has a simple formula נאם יהוה "expression of Yahweh" followed by a hymnic participial phrase, "one stretching out heavens and establishing earth, one forming human spirit in his inward parts." The superscription is unique in the Twelve.

Zechariah 9:2b–3 is an apparent superscription to vv. 4ff. and is complex. But perhaps the words "Tyre and Sidon" are a title or superscription parallel to "Hadrach" in v. 1 and should be understood as "[Against] Tyre and Sidon." Then the prophecy against Tyre begins with כי, translated "although."[13]

Three Levels

This survey of superscriptions and incipits demonstrates three levels of composition or redaction in Hosea, Zech 9:1, and Zech 12:1. The second and third levels evidence common elements with other books in the Twelve. This suggests that they were part of the process which brought the books together.

The First (Bottom) Level

In Hosea 1:2b, "And then Yahweh said to Hosea" is an incipit which introduces the narrative frame for his first oracle.

In Zech 9:1, the sentences about Tyre and Sidon belong here and relate only to material internal to the chapter.

In Zech 12:1, "expression of Yahweh" is a simple nominal heading with its modifying participial phrases.

The headings in Amos 1:1* and Hab 3:1 and the incipits in Jonah, Haggai, and Zech 1–8 are of a similar elemental nature; they show no ties to the larger compiling process (except the added phrases in Amos).

---

[13] Then one should read:
    [Against] Tyre and Sidon.
    Although they are very wise,
    so that Tyre built a rampart for herself
        and then heaped up silver like dust
        and gold like street-mud,
    Behold Yahweh will dispossess her...

The Second (Middle) Level

Two major complexes are developed at the middle level. Hosea's middle level (1:2) reads: "the beginning[14] of the word of God by Hosea." If this phrase is read as "the word of Yahweh," it forms a group with the last three superscriptions in the Twelve, which have similar superscriptions at the middle level.

But there is ambiguity when דבר יהוה, "word of Yahweh," begins the sentence. It may be read "the word of Yahweh is," as a sentence. Or it may be read "the word of Yahweh," as nouns with no verb, and thus as a title. Zechariah 9:1 seems better as a sentence, because no message against Hadrach follows for this verse to introduce. Zechariah 12:1 can be read as a sentence: "The word of Yahweh [is] against Israel." But it is probably better treated as a title. Malachi 1:1 cannot be read as a sentence. It is a title or superscription. Hosea has its own ambiguity as we have seen.

Yet one cannot escape the recognition that the four uses of דבר יהוה are related. They are intentional ties between the first and last superscriptions in the Twelve, that is, between Hos 1:1 and Mal 1:1.

"Vision" (חזון) seems to enter at this middle level in Nahum's "the book of the vision" and in Obadiah, which has no higher level.

Names of prophets appear in superscriptions of the middle level in Hos 1:2a, Obadiah, Nahum, Hab 3:1, and Malachi.

The Third (Top) Level

The most intensive work to shape the Book of the Twelve took place at this level. New superscriptions were placed on top of others to relate books to one another. Phrases were added to give chronological direction and clauses are used to identify relationships.

A full title and clause are built from the incipit "then the word of Yahweh was to . . . ," which reads, "The word of Yahweh which was to . . . " It is placed over Hosea, Joel, Micah, and Zephaniah. In Hosea this is the third introductory element, but in the other three cases it is the first and only superscription.

A phrase, "in the days of _____ king of Israel and _____ king of Judah," is added to this superscription in Hosea, Micah, and Zephaniah (not Joel). It is also added to Amos, effectively tying Amos into the growing composition.

---

14 "The beginning of" is a construct form like בראשית in Gen 1:1. MT points דבר as a verb (like Gen 1:1), "in the beginning Yahweh spoke by Hosea." LXX reads the word as a noun: "in the beginning of the word of the Lord by Hosea."

Another superscription, מַשָּׂא, "a burden," is placed over Nahum, Habakkuk, Zech 9:1, 12:1, and Malachi. This effectively ties the last sections of the Twelve to the middle sections. Only in Habakkuk is מַשָּׂא the principal and sole superscription. In the other four, the word occurs in the level above other terms.

The clause אֲשֶׁר חָזָה, "which he envisioned," also functions at this top level. It is picked up from Amos and inserted in Micah and Habakkuk, creating another bond.

A string of prepositional phrases appears in the superscriptions. They may well have been inserted intentionally at this final stage to sharpen the focus of the Twelve. In Amos, Zech 12:1, and Malachi the phrases single out "Israel" as the subject of the prophecy. Micah points the word of the Lord against "Samaria and Jerusalem." Zechariah 9:1 points it against "the land of Hadrach." The same effect is provided in Nah 1:1, "burden of Nineveh." Habakkuk and Obadiah identify their subject in the text, as do other books.

Other prepositional phrases identify the prophet in Hosea, Jonah, Haggai, and Malachi.

Names of prophets also occur on this top level in Hos 1:1, Joel, Micah, Habakkuk, and Zephaniah. Also significant is that two superscriptions lack names: Zech 9:1 and 12:1. In the long book of Hosea, no superscriptions appear beyond 1:2. The skillful use of twelve names for prophets provides the number "twelve" for the book.

Conclusions

This study has shown the close relation between form and content among incipits in prophetic literature, including Jonah, Haggai, and Zechariah, and among superscriptions in Hosea, Joel, Micah, and Zephaniah.

It has shown evidence for superscriptions at three levels, two of which occurred when the Book of the Twelve was compiled.

It has shown the complexity and diversity of means used to unify the Book of the Twelve.[15] These include a series of overlapping devices that work toward the collection's unity; only Obadiah and the narrative books are not clearly "tied in."

---

[15] This unification is much more complex and diverse than in the books of Jeremiah or Ezekiel. It is more like Isaiah. But the Twelve uses superscriptions more extensively and consistently than Isaiah does.

The study of incipits suggests that the narrative books, Haggai, Zech 1–8, and Jonah, should be viewed as "literary precursors" to the Book of the Twelve. In addition, the Amos superscription suggests that Amos should be viewed in this light although redactional work was performed to tie Amos into the larger whole.

Incipits at the primary level are also found in Hos 1:1 and Zech 9:1–3. Prophetic formulas perform the introductory function in Obad 1 and Zech 1:1.

The study suggests that all the other superscriptions, at what I have called levels two and three, evidence the collaborative work that produced the Book of the Twelve. This work built on incipits and formulas in Hosea, Amos, Obadiah, Zech 9:1, and 12:1. It left the incipits in Jonah, Haggai, and Zech 1–8, without adding additional superscriptions. But the process of building the Book of the Twelve accounts for the development of superscriptions in Joel, Micah, Nahum, Habakkuk, Zephaniah, and Malachi.

The use of linguistic elements in the superscription to tie books together has been shown. But the importance of each element varies from book to book. In some books an element is primary, in the sense that it forms the basic superscription for that book. The same element may be secondary in another book.

משא, "burden," is primary for Habakkuk. But it is secondary to another linguistic element in Nahum and Malachi and tertiary in Zech 9:1 and 12:1. Together these elements helped group Nahum, Habakkuk, Zech 9–11, 12–14, and Malachi.

דבר יהוה, "word of Yahweh," is primary in Malachi, but secondary for Hosea, Zech 9:1, and 12:1. The use of this phrase links Hosea, Zech 9–11, 12–14, and Malachi.

חזון, "vision," is primary for Nahum, but secondary for Obadiah. Use of the verb in relative sentences links Amos, Obadiah, Micah, Nahum, and Habakkuk.

דבר יהוה אשר היה ל..., "the word of Yahweh which was to...," is primary for Joel, Micah, and Zephaniah, but tertiary for Hosea. In its incipit form it is primary for Jonah, Haggai, and Zech 1–8. The phrase groups Hosea, Joel, Jonah, Micah, Zephaniah, Haggai, and Zechariah.

"In the days of _____ king of Israel and _____ king of Judah" is primary in Micah and Zephaniah, but tertiary for Hosea and Amos. Use of the phrase added Amos to this cluster and gave a chronological reason for the order of books before Haggai and Zech 1–8.

אשר חזה, "which he envisioned," is primary for Amos, but secondary for Micah and Habakkuk.

That these language-linked groups exist but are not placed together in the Twelve shows that other factors were decisive for the shape of whole. But the way these common phrases are placed ties the books together in other ways. Hosea is a unit in the "word of Yahweh" group, but placing Hosea at the beginning of the Twelve and providing it with third layer of superscriptions helps relate it to Joel, Amos, Micah, and Zephaniah.

That "burden" appears in Nahum, Habakkuk, Zech 9–11, and Zech 12–14, a group separated by Zephaniah, Haggai, and Zech 1–8, means that the word ties the group of prophecies before Haggai–Zech 1–8 with those that follow.

Also instructive is that the use of these superscriptions to separate units does not produce twelve writings. It takes the use of prophets' names to do that.

The "independent" units, those that show no signs of having been included in these editing processes, Amos, Jonah, and Haggai-Zechariah, deserve special study as to how they function in the Twelve and how they influenced the writing and editing of the whole. Nogalski has already posited a "Jonah edition" with influence from Joel. The same could be suggested of the influence of Amos in the use of the "Day of Yahweh" in Joel and Zephaniah. Amos also influenced the use of superscriptions that mention eighth-century kings. Haggai–Zechariah 1–8 had direct influence on the "word of Yahweh" group. When one searches for what accounts for the power and meaning of the Twelve, it is possible to isolate a composition built around the three books that include stories about prophets, Amos 7, Jonah, and Zech 7–8.

If Amos and Haggai–Zech 1–8 are the poles around which the Twelve is built, and Jonah is seen as an interpolation that provided a distinct interpretation of events, we may be approaching an understanding of the Twelve. Amos then becomes the center for a prophetic interpretation, in terms of the "Day of Yahweh," of the eighth to the fifth centuries, which brought an end to the monarchies of Israel/Judah. Haggai-Zechariah introduces an interpretation of what God does in the following period. And Jonah opens the door to a universalizing understanding of God's interest in the nations, as well as in Israel.

More studies are needed. A first step must be to survey prophetic formulas, similar to this survey of superscriptions, in other prophetic books, and to study prophetic genres in the Book of the Twelve.

9

The Character of God in the Book of the Twelve

Paul R. House

Much of the work of the Seminar on the Book of the Twelve has been devoted to trying to understand the redactional layers behind the text, the literary unity of the Twelve, and the way segments of the Twelve are linked into a whole.[1] There has also been serious discussion about whether it is advisable to treat the twelve prophecies as one book, or whether it is more reasonable to examine each in its context. Time has been spent discussing the merits of the Septuagint over against the Masoretic Text, and vice versa.[2] Qumran texts have not been neglected altogether. Hermeneutical matters, such as the value of using words such as "unity" and "coherence," have at least been broached. One of the newer areas of exploration, however, is the theological coherence of the Twelve (or lack thereof). Rolf Rendtorff in 1997 offered the first treatment of the Twelve's theology,[3] and this essay seeks to follow in his large footsteps.

One seeking to analyze the Twelve's theology runs many of the same risks as those who attempt to examine the book's redaction, literary unity, or historical background. The fact remains that twelve separate prophecies must be treated as a single corpus. It is still true that two possible canonical traditions may be considered. The Twelve's thematic unity and diversity have not miraculously disappeared. These facts should not dissuade the theologian from pressing forward, but they should make that theologian humble in his or her assertions. Hopefully this essay will strike balance between the need to make assertions and the necessity of exercising caution while doing so.

---

[1] Several of the earlier papers have been adapted and published in *Forming Prophetic Literature: Essays on Isaiah and the Twelve in Honor of John D. W. Watts* (ed. James W. Watts and Paul R. House; JSOTSup 205; Sheffield: Sheffield Academic Press, 1996).

[2] On this subject see Barry Jones, *The Formation of the Book of the Twelve: A Study in Text and Canon* (SBLDS 149; Atlanta: Scholars Press, 1995).

[3] Included as chapter 6 in the present volume.

An analysis of the Twelve's theology, even a brief one such as this effort, ought to consist of three basic parts: an explanation of methodology, a treatment of relevant texts, and a unifying summary of common ideas or themes.[4] Each component is necessary for an informed discussion of the Twelve's theology, for each addresses a major concern of Old Testament studies in general and of Old Testament theology in particular. Old Testament theology, like its counterparts New Testament theology and systematic theology, is currently involved in methodological debates. Therefore, exegetical and theological reflection are often held in abeyance. Theoretical discussions are not inconsequential, but it is also appropriate for Old Testament theologians to state their chosen methodology, to offer their analyses, and to defend their work as the need arises.

At its heart, Old Testament theology is a study of what the biblical text says about God. In other words, God's character is the object of study. As is true in all compelling literature, the nature of a character in an Old Testament book is revealed through that character's actions, thoughts, statements, and so on. The person's character may also be revealed through what other individuals in the text think or say about the person in question. It is also true that a character's nature is developed by an author in tandem with the text's major themes and events. When these elements are taken into consideration, God's character in the Book of the Twelve unfolds alongside the book's main emphases. This fact means that characterization techniques used to convey warning dominate the depiction of God in Hosea through Micah, judgment terminology marks Nahum through Zephaniah, and renewal metaphors take precedence in Haggai through Zechariah.

Methodology

Though it is an overstatement to say that there have been nearly as many methodologies for Old Testament theology as there have been Old Testament theologians, this comment is not far from true. Scholars have employed categories of systematic theology, utilized a single theme as an organizing principle, sought ancient kerygmatic statements around which the whole of Old Testament theology can be gathered, and attempted to use the canon as an organizing principle for theological

---

[4] For my own approach to Old Testament theology and a more lengthy treatment of the Twelve's theology, see Paul R. House, *Old Testament Theology* (Downers Grove, Ill.: InterVarsity Press, 1998).

reflection. More recently, theological analyses have been written from a variety of reader-response perspectives and from pluralistic viewpoints. Clearly, there is no shortage of ways to approach the task.[5]

Because of the challenges in analyzing the Book of the Twelve, it is important to adopt a methodology that can account for unity within diversity. Historical matters should not be neglected altogether, but it must be remembered that the claims of the text itself matter most. Redactional issues are not unimportant, yet by definition they cannot be taken as the final point from which to make theological observations. Therefore it is appropriate to utilize a canonical approach to the Twelve's theology, since this methodology allows for reading the text as a coherent whole without losing a sense of each book's origins.

It is necessary to define what is meant by "canonical approach." This methodology has been rightly associated with the program set forth by Brevard Childs, though it has benefited from insights by Christopher Seitz, James Sanders, and John Sailhamer.[6] By "canonical" I mean analysis that is God-centered, intertextually oriented, authority-conscious, historically sensitive, and devoted to the wholeness of the Old Testament message. It means theological reflection that deals carefully with the Twelve in a manner that will make its influence on subsequent biblical texts more evident.

This type of canonical study also notes the individual prophecies' historical setting, structural details, and thematic emphases as together they build what becomes finally the Book of the Twelve. These elements aid understanding how each individual book supplements earlier and succeeding prophecies. There is no doubt that the first readers of the Book of the Twelve knew that the books, placed together, did not unfold in specific chronological order. Thus, familiar themes and descriptions of God, Israel, and the nations probably took precedence in their minds as they read. It makes sense, then, to examine how historical context and literary concepts help create the theology of this one book.

---

[5] For an summary of these viewpoints, see John H. Hayes and Frederick C. Prussner, *Old Testament Theology: Its History and Development* (Atlanta: John Knox, 1985); Gerhard F. Hasel, *Old Testament Theology: Basic Issues in the Current Debate* (4th ed.; Grand Rapids: Eerdmans, 1991); and Leo G. Perdue, *The Collapse of History: Reconstructing Old Testament Theology* (Minneapolis: Fortress, 1994).

[6] See Brevard S. Childs, *Old Testament Theology in a Canonical Context* (Philadelphia: Fortress, 1986); J. A. Sanders, *Torah and Canon* (Philadelphia: Fortress, 1972); John H. Sailhamer, *Introduction to Old Testament Theology: A Canonical Approach* (Grand Rapids: Zondervan, 1995); and Christopher R. Seitz, *Word without End: The Old Testament as Abiding Theological Witness* (Grand Rapids: Eerdmans, 1998).

Alongside this broad methodology must stand a more specific principle, which is that the Book of the Twelve describes only one God. A variety of perspectives on God's character is offered, but the authors all believe they are writing about the same deity. There is no sense that they are depicting rival gods. Rather, they all claim to speak for and with the God who has been uniquely revealed to Israel in the events and texts that mark their people's history. Therefore, it is appropriate to describe their theology as a whole, not as a group of unrelated parts, or as set of competing voices.

In practice, this canonical methodology gathers the primary statements about God in the Twelve. It collates these statements with previous and/or subsequent passages. It determines ways to state the text's common confessions about God as well as the unique contributions a prophecy or grouping of prophecies may make to Old Testament theology. In other words, this approach gathers exegetical data, draws together similar ideas from other contextually relevant texts, states propositions about what the texts claim about God, and attempts to present conclusions in a way that makes the data accessible. Such goals are beyond my ability to achieve even in a longer work, so the attempt to do so more briefly here is a worthy challenge.

Textual Analysis

Before noting some of the specific aspects of the Twelve's theology, it will perhaps be helpful to outline the book's general thematic emphases.[7] When one reads the Twelve as a canonical partner with Isaiah, Jeremiah, and Ezekiel, several common prophetic notions are readily apparent. These ideas help order an effective analysis of the book's theology. For instance, the fundamental sin of covenant-breaking receives significant treatment in all the prophetic books, and the Twelve is no exception. In the Twelve, however, this theme has particular significance in Hosea-Micah. This segment focuses on the specific and general ways that Israel suffered for its covenant infidelity. These prophecies define, describe, and denounce these infidelities. They threaten punishment for the transgressions, and they anticipate coming judgment for what has

---

[7] For a more detailed discussion of the Twelve's literary unity, see Paul R. House, *The Unity of the Twelve* (JSOTSup 97; Sheffield: Almond Press, 1990). If I were to write this book again, I would change the title to *Literary Unity in the Twelve* to reflect that literary unity is but one type of unity the Twelve exhibits. The book's conclusion makes this point (pp. 243–45), but the title does not.

been done. They do the same for Gentile nations as well. As a group, these six prophecies stress a God who warns of coming punishment for sin. The warning includes descriptions of devastating judgment and promises of ultimate renewal beyond the chastisement, but warning is the main notion nonetheless.

Nahum, Habakkuk, and Zephaniah move beyond the description of sin and threats of punishment to specific threats about the coming Day of the LORD. Here the LORD is depicted as a judge even more surely than in Hosea-Micah. All nations will be destroyed because of their sins, regardless of the people's size or current influence. Covenant and non-covenant countries alike are included in the destruction, for they are all accountable to the one God, who is their creator. All creation is swept away by the end of Zephaniah; all, that is, but a multinational remnant of faithful persons. The LORD remains the God who spares a remnant to serve the Creator and to inherit blessings.

Just as parts of Isaiah, Jeremiah, and Ezekiel look beyond judgment to a brighter future based on God's presence and the existence of a believing remnant, so Haggai, Zechariah, and Malachi point toward God's eventual transformation of judgment to glory. Temple, city, and people are all devastated by Israel's enemies. But God promises to restore all these aspects of Israelite life. The renewal will someday be as complete as the devastation, which has been hinted throughout the earlier portions of the Twelve. God's determination to forgive and restore reinforces the canon's insistence that punishment is meted out in order to effect cleansing and restoration. When Malachi closes, the Twelve has spanned three centuries and the full range of prophetic theology. Prophecy and reality are tightly woven.

The God Who Warns and Loves: Hosea

Perhaps no prophet pays a higher price for his or her calling than Hosea. Like other prophets, he preaches the covenant truths already stated in the canon. Like other prophets, he embodies his message. Unlike other prophets, however, he suffers profound personal agony through his wife's marital infidelity. By loving this woman despite her failure to remain faithful, Hosea demonstrates for Israel the persevering love of God for a constantly straying chosen people.

This love is portrayed in two basic ways in the two major sections of the prophecy. First, Hos 1–3 expresses the love God has for an idolatrous/adulterous nation. Second, Hos 4–14 describes the warnings a loving God extends to the corrupted people. All of the nation's sins in the first section are treated as a breach of faith akin to adultery, while the imagery in the second part expands to include judicial and parental metaphors.

Hosea's marriage to a compromised woman in chapters 1–3 fits other canonical depictions of God as a mistreated spouse. Ezekiel 20 considers Israel idolatrous even before the exodus, a view reflected in Josh 24:2 and in Amos 2:4, which says that Judah follows lies that its fathers pursued. Exodus 32–34 may also at least imply that the people had some prior knowledge of idolatry before leaving Egypt. Given these passages, it is plausible that Gomer engaged in premarital sexual deviancy and that, from the start, Hosea's marriage to her demonstrates the immeasurable, grace-oriented love God has for Israel.

Hosea's children's names indicate that the God who loves is also the God who warns. Each name, whether "Jezreel," "Not Pitied," or "Bastard," reveals God's anger at the Israelite monarchy and people. These names speak of terrible pain in Hosea's household and in God's heart. They also prefigure tremendous agony to come for a disobedient nation. The warnings have begun in earnest.

The spousal terminology is supplemented in Hos 4–14, yet the prophecy's tone changes little. Judicial language is used to describe the LORD in 4:1–3, in which God "contends" with Israel for ongoing transgression. The prophet declares a divinely initiated lawsuit against lawbreakers, a procedure that also occurs in 2:6–19 (Eng., 2:4–17), 4:4–6, and 5:3–15, as well as in Isa 1:18–20, Jer 2:5–29, Mic 6:1–5, and Mal 3:5.[8] The reason for the suit is the breach of the Sinai covenant (4:1–2), and the result is that the land mourns (4:3). Clearly, rejecting God for other gods leads to corrupt behavior. Israel's spouse is also Israel's judge, so the nation is forewarned of future punishment.

Parental imagery marks 11:1–11, a passage that surveys Israel's past and argues that the LORD has done more for Israel than the covenant demands. First, God chose Israel and delivered it from Egypt (11:1). Nowhere does any Old Testament text so much as imply that this election was anything other than the LORD's unmerited mercy toward Israel. Second, the LORD called Israel despite the people's constant descent into Baalism and other forms of idolatry (11:2). Third, God established the northern kingdom because of Solomon's idolatry (cf. 1 Kgs 11:1–40), yet the people turned from their healer, God (11:3). Fourth, God

---

8 Claus Westermann, *Basic Forms of Prophetic Speech* (trans. H. C. White; Philadelphia: Westminster, 1967), 199–200.

has sustained the nation. Fifth, the LORD will punish the people in the future (11:5–7). Sixth, after punishing the "son," God will again have compassion on the straying child (11:9–11).

Israel's history is presented as the story of a loving parent faced with raising a rebellious child. God called Israel, taught the Israelites how to walk, fed them, and guided them (11:1–5). This love has been spurned, yet the LORD cannot give them up completely. Judgment must give way — indeed must create — renewal (11:8–11). Ultimately, God will heal the people's infidelity, ingratitude, ignorance, and rebellion.

Hosea has been examined in more detail than subsequent prophecies because it sets the stage for the Twelve's characterization of the LORD. It portrays God as a loving yet betrayed spouse, dishonored parent, and mighty judge. It warns that unless faithfulness to God's kindness results, the nation can expect the reluctant, punishing judge to act.

Subsequent prophecies in the Twelve operate in a similar manner. A variety of techniques of characterization appear, all designed to discuss the nature and acts of the covenant God. Each technique reveals God's patience, yet at the same time stresses the limits of that patience. Threats, comfort, and promise coexist to demonstrate the magnitude of the LORD's person.

The God Who Warns and Promises: Joel

Joel has been and will continue to be an enigma in the Twelve. Historical and redaction critics have debated the prophecy's authorship, date, and original audience. Interesting theories about how Joel fits into the Twelve have been forwarded by Jim Nogalski.[9] This diversity of opinion has affected theological analysis as well, since Old Testament theology does not exist in a vacuum. What is apparent, however, is that Joel shares Hosea's concern to warn Israel to repent. It is also evident that Joel states that judgment will come, but that beyond the punishment lies great renewal. Thus, the prophecy's emphasis on the God who warns and promises is in keeping with Hosea's themes and with those in the rest of the Twelve.

Joel's chief means of warning is through description of the Day of the LORD. Having warned the people to fast and mourn in 1:1–14, the "day" is announced in 1:15. This proclamation closely parallels earlier canonical passages. The language echoes Isa 13:6 and Ezek 30:23, and

---

9 James D. Nogalski, *Literary Precursors to the Book of the Twelve* (BZAW 217; Berlin: de Gruyter, 1993), and *Redactional Processes in the Book of the Twelve* (BZAW 218; Berlin: de Gruyter, 1993).

brings to mind the terrible scenes depicted in Deut 27–28 and 32, in which God sends military defeat and plagues for persistent covenant-breaking.[10] In all there are at least sixteen passages that discuss judgment as the Day of the LORD.[11] Joel launches the Twelve's treatment of the subject. In each of the sixteen texts a quick, decisive return to the LORD is the only prudent response to the warnings.

Judgment is not God's final word, for the LORD promises to renew the people's fortunes in 2:18–4:21 (Eng., 3:21). God's love here mirrors Ezek 16 and Hos 11:1–9. God refuses to release the beloved nation. Why? As in Isa 45:5, 45:21, and 49:23, the answer is plain: to demonstrate that the LORD is God and there is no other (Joel 2:27). Devotion to this monotheistic principle will eliminate the transgressions that lead to judgment.

God's spirit will effect the promised renewal (3:1–5 [Eng., 2:28–32]). All God's people will receive the spirit of the LORD, an infusion Ezek 36:24–32 expects will turn the people's hearts from stone to flesh and create a restored land. Scott Hafemann concludes correctly that "it is the future bestowal of this life-giving (divine) Spirit which forms the core of the prophetic expectation for restoration."[12]

Significant for the issue of God's sovereignty is that the LORD will judge sinners both inside and outside Israel (4:1–15 [Eng., 3:1–15]). All nations should hear the LORD's warnings as if God were a roaring lion about to devour them (4:16 [Eng., 3:16]). The description of God as a roaring lion exercising universal jurisdiction appears in Amos 1:2, thereby serving as a linking image between prophecies.

Clearly, God's promises are two-edged in Joel. The LORD pledges good or ill depending on the peoples' level of repentance. Warning and hope coexist as time and the Twelve press forward. So far, God has warned and promised as a spouse, parent, judge, and healer — all to no avail.

---

[10] For a comparison of these texts, consult S. R. Driver, *The Books of Joel and Amos* (The Cambridge Bible for Schools and Colleges; Cambridge: Cambridge University Press, 1901), 19; Hans W. Wolff, *Joel and Amos* (trans. S. D. McBride, Jr., et al.; Hermeneia; Philadelphia: Fortress, 1977), 10; and Douglas S. Stuart, *Hosea-Jonah* (WBC 31; Waco, Tex.: Word, 1987), 228.

[11] See Gerhard von Rad, *Old Testament Theology* (trans. D. M. G. Stalker; New York: Harper & Row, 1965), 2.199–225.

[12] Scott J. Hafemann, *Paul, Moses, and the History of Israel* (WUNT 31; Tübingen: Mohr, 1995), 182. Hafemann's painstaking analysis of Paul's use of "the letter and the spirit" demonstrates that the New Testament interprets Joel 2:28–29 contextually and canonically.

The God Who Roars against Sin: Amos

Amos 1:2 picks up from Joel 4:16 (Eng., 3:16) the image of a leonine LORD roaring against the people. God's anger is directed at Israel and Judah, as well as at six other nations. The covenant people have broken faith with God in a manner similar to that described in Hosea and Joel. For their part, the nations have shown excessive cruelty in war, sold captives into slavery, cast off normal human compassion, and broken treaties made in good faith (1:3–2:16). God's roaring serves as a grave warning of imminent international punishment. It also prefigures a new way for the Twelve to describe the LORD's person and work.

God commands attention in this section by demanding that the people "listen" (3:1; 4:1; 5:1) to a stunning summary of their sins. By rejecting God they have rebelled against the Creator of all the earth (4:13; 5:8). As the Creator it is God's prerogative to turn the light to darkness or to send the waters from their boundaries into the land. Israel and the nations must bow before their maker. God deserves and demands exclusive worship. Having received neither, the Creator will become the Destroyer (5:18–27).

Amos 7:1–9:15 includes several images of God that coincide with emphases in Hosea and Joel. For example, God promises extraordinary punishment in 7:1–8:3, yet allows compassion to stay execution as in Hos 1–3 and 11:1–9. Likewise, the hopeful statements about the LORD's desire to renew the covenant people matches the bright future pledged in Joel 3:1–4:21 (Eng., 2:28–3:21). Further, the Day-of-the-LORD passages in Joel 4:1–21 (Eng., 3:1–21) and Amos 1:3–2:16 emphasize the universal scope of divine power. These examples are not cited to diminish Amos's theological achievement in its own historical context. Rather, this essay, like others employing similar methods, collects ongoing theological statements in the Twelve and does not try to pit one prophecy's achievement against the other.

In the context of the Twelve, Amos continues the book's emphasis on God's loving, kind, familial, and faithful character. At the same time, it stresses that the LORD is ruler and judge of all the earth. In mercy God sends prophets such as Amos to deliver the divine word, and in righteousness the LORD pledges to punish the earth's wicked and to bless those who obey the covenant.

The prophecy also works with new characterizations of the LORD. God is portrayed as a terrible lion about to devour the wicked. Amos stresses God's sovereignty over the whole earth, a theme that adds texture to the

Twelve's reasoning for God's power over the Gentiles. Amos's creation metaphors begin a trend that reoccurs later in the Twelve and links the prophecy to texts that span the Law, Prophets, and Writings.

The God Who Warns Against Pride: Obadiah

Pride has been denounced in both the Twelve and earlier prophecies (cf. Hos 9:1; 10:1; Joel 4:1–3 [Eng., 3:1–3]; Amos 6:1–7; Isa 14:12–16; Ezek 28:17; etc.). Thus it is no surprise that pride is singled out in Obadiah as the main reason for Edom's judgment. God's displeasure unfolds in three parts. First, Obad 1–9 announces Edom's impending doom for its pride and hateful attitude toward Israel. Second, Obad 10–14 denounces Edom's glee over Jerusalem's demise. Third, Obad 15–21 contrasts the fall of Edom with the blessing of the righteous remnant on the Day of the LORD. As in Amos, it is the Day of the LORD that will make sinners pay for what they have done, and that will vindicate the faithful by blessing them.

Without question, Obadiah furthers the Twelve's emphasis on the Gentiles' sin and on the LORD's right to judge the entire earth. Edom's activities demonstrate that only God's direct intervention can halt sin outside Israel's borders. Clearly, the Day of the LORD is as necessary beyond Israel as it is within it, since repentance is not forthcoming from either group. It is this direct action against the sin of pride and hatefulness that also provides the backdrop for Jonah.

The God Who Warns the Gentiles: Jonah

Jonah eases fears that God does not care for the Gentiles, fears that may have arisen due to statements in Joel, Amos, and Obadiah. Jonah shows that the LORD loves even the Assyrians, the most powerful and vicious of Israel's ancient foes. Of course, Isa 19:19–25 has already made this point canonically. God sends a prophet to alert the Assyrians so that they, too, can come to know the God who created the heavens and the earth. Jonah's reluctance to undertake this task continues the Twelve's emphasis on the hatred Israel and the nations have for one another, a situation that makes it unlikely that these enemies will be reconciled before the day of the LORD.

The contents of Jonah's clean narrative illustrate God's persistent warning and redemption of the Assyrians. First, Jonah 1:1–16 recounts God's call to Jonah and the prophet's desire to flee from the LORD. The God who calls is the God who cares for Nineveh. Second, Jonah 1:17–2:10 covers the prophet's time in the fish and his subsequent decision to undertake the preaching mission to Nineveh. Here the LORD is the Creator of the great fish, the God who coerces the prophet and who preserves the prophet's life. Third, Jonah 3:1–10 discloses Jonah's "ministry" to the Assyrians. Jonah's halfhearted effort highlights God's grace when Jonah's hearers repent. Fourth, Jonah 4:1–11 reveals the prophet's anger at the LORD's mercy. Again the point is that God loves all people. Their sins are God's concern. In contrast, Jonah complains about God's kindness, despite the fact that he himself has been a beneficiary of the LORD's mercy.

The opening segment underscores the LORD's direct action in the saving of human beings. Just as God intervened in the lives of Abraham, Isaac, and Jacob, so the LORD now moves on behalf of Gentiles. Sadly, the prophet does not accept the LORD's vision, nor does he resonate with texts such as Isa 19:19–25 or grasp the implications of his own confession that the LORD created the world. His view of God remains landlocked and culture-bound.

Jonah's time in and deliverance from the belly of the fish reemphasizes Amos's creation motifs. At the same time, the experience allows Jonah to comment that the LORD alone is a living, hearing, acting, saving God. The issue that remains unresolved is whether the prophet will translate this stated theology into active ministry.

Upon hearing Jonah's sermon, the people of Nineveh hope that the LORD is a merciful God, and they are not disappointed. God "relents," just like, for example, in the golden-calf incident, in which the LORD relents from destroying Israel and beginning anew with Moses (Exod 32:12). God's forgiveness in this instance is hardly a failure of prophecy. Rather, it fulfills the intent of prophecy in the whole canon. Hosea 6:1–3 counsels the people to repent and be forgiven, yet no change occurs. Joel 2:12–14 encourages repentance and hopes for renewal in language very close to that of Jonah 3:9. Amos 4:6–13 mourns the nation's refusal to repent and thereby to avoid judgment.

Prophecy is not offered simply to relieve God of the responsibility to warn before punishing. It intends to effect change in hearers and to make them part of God's faithful remnant. If Jonah believes he has failed because the city survives, then he does not grasp the purpose of prophecy any more than he understands the practical implications of creation theology.

The final scene captures the essence of the canon's description of God's nature. The same God creates, calls, reveals, judges, and forgives. There is no other deity able to do these things. In fact, there are no other gods who have ontological existence at all. Thus, God's character remains intact in Jonah. Sadly, it appears, however, that even an Israelite prophet intends to do little to alleviate the animosity between Israel and the nations. Sin continues to distort and impair international relationships even as the LORD continues to warn against such activities.

The God Who Testifies against Sin: Micah

Micah completes the first half of the Twelve's discussion of worldwide sin and its consequences by summarizing and expanding concepts already introduced in Hosea through Jonah. Set in the latter half of the eighth century B.C.E. (1:1), this prophecy rehearses the tragic fact that the punishment depicted in the next three prophecies of the Twelve need never have occurred. Repentance could have staved off judgment, as Jonah proves, but the covenant people fail to change, a trait they share here with the Gentiles. Therefore, as Obadiah has already shown, punishment will overtake them.

Micah portrays God as testifying against the earth for its inhabitants' refusal to heed divine warnings. Micah 1–3 highlights God testifying against the present sins of Israel and the Gentiles. This testimony constitutes a warning to change while change and forgiveness are yet possible. Micah 4–5 finds God testifying to the righteousness and future blessing of the remnant. Here the LORD guarantees a blessed future by sending an ideal Davidic ruler. Micah 6–7 describes the LORD as one who testifies to the eternal nature of the Abrahamic covenant. In this section God removes sin for Abraham's sake. In Micah, the LORD speaks against sin in the present and future by emphasizing past promises.

Micah 1–3 pronounces woe on the wicked by cataloging contemporary sins in ways reminiscent of earlier canonical texts. God's vehement anger over worldwide iniquity in 1:2–4 sounds very much like the powerful statements in Isa 1–6 and Amos 1–2, to name just two passages. Likewise, the cause of the divine anger, idolatry (1:5–7), recalls the complaints of Isaiah, Jeremiah, Ezekiel, Hosea, and Amos, and calling idolatry "harlotry" (1:7) reminds readers of Hosea. Though quite creative in its own right,[13] the list of towns to be destroyed in 1:10–16 is not unlike Amos 1:2–2:3 or even Isa 13–23 or Jer 46–51 in strategy or intent.

Though they are not objects of God's wrath, Mic 4–5 makes clear that

---

[13] For an excellent translation of this section, consult Hans W. Wolff, *Micah the Prophet* (trans. R. D. Gehrke; Philadelphia: Westminster, 1981), 14–16.

the remnant will suffer before being redeemed (4:1–7). They must endure exile, as well as political and personal travail (4:8–10). Their hope lies in God, whose plans cannot be thwarted (4:11–13). More specifically, Mic 5:1–15 concludes, much as Isa 7–12 has already stated, that renewal can only come through the emergence and ministry of a unique Davidic ruler. From Bethlehem will come one "whose origin is from old days, from everlasting days" (5:2). This king's realm will extend throughout the earth. His origins mark him as a supernatural figure, much like the description of the king in Isa 9:6 as a "mighty God" and "everlasting father." This king will provide rest, sustenance, and peace for the harried people of God (5:3–6). Idols will be removed from the earth (5:10–15), a sure sign of God's triumph.

Having staked out the future, Mic 6–7 returns to the present, and also reaches back into the distant past. It is significant that Micah concludes with a statement on the removal of sin as it relates to the Abrahamic covenant. By closing this way, Micah conceives of a history that spans from the patriarchal era to the final judgment at the end of time. By Micah's day, God's promises to the patriarchs had resulted in exodus, conquest, Davidic dynasty, national division, and impending destruction. Micah envisions an accompanying new exodus, new David, and new city of God. These promises mean that each successive generation has historically relevant pledges to sustain their present and to give hope to their future. Micah neither neglects the realities of the present nor the possibilities of the future.

As Micah closes, a host of warning images have been applied to God in keeping with the Twelve's thematic emphasis. God is spouse, parent, judge, healer, witness, lion, creator, deliverer, and only deity. God is merciful, loving, patient, and yet also holy, good, righteous, and firm. Each characterization undergirds the Twelve's belief to this point that judgment is not and never will be inevitable. The God who warns is the God who stands ready to heal and forgive.

The God Who Destroys Assyria: Nahum

Though the first six prophecies in the Twelve repeatedly stress the reality of judgment, their general place in history means that this punishment is either potential or lies mainly in the future. Obadiah is an exception to this rule, of course, but even there Edom's sins have yet to be addressed. In Nahum, Habakkuk, and Zephaniah, the Twelve turns to treating punishment as if it is a near certainty. Israel and the nations will indeed feel the sting of the LORD's justifiable wrath. Warnings have been spurned, so the consequences of rejecting mercy will now unfold.

Nahum begins this emphasis on the God who judges by stating that the end has come for Assyria, the very nation to whom Jonah had preached. From the outset the prophecy establishes the LORD's character as the basis for the announced punishment of Nineveh. In fact, 1:2–11 summarizes the divine qualities found in the Twelve and earlier canonical texts. God is jealous for good reason (1:2), as the explanation for the prohibitions against idolatry in Exod 20:4–5 has demonstrated. This jealousy amounts to zeal for righteousness. At the same time, the LORD is patient and just (1:3), points made in Exod 20:1–6, 34:6–7, and elsewhere. As Creator, God rules nature (1:3–5), as Amos has emphasized. God is good (1:7), and the wicked cannot endure the LORD's presence (1:6–8). Assyria's plotting against other nations amounts to scheming against God (1:9–11), so such activities will result in death. Pride and viciousness will bring down even the mightiest country.

Nahum 1:1–15 indicates that the repentance described in Jonah either did not spread or did not last. God sent Jonah to warn the Assyrians of punishment, so Nineveh cannot argue that God is patient with the Jews but not with them. The problem is that God's mercy has not been met with long-term commitment.

Nahum 2–3 reveals that God opposes and will humiliate Nineveh. These statements could appear vindictive had the previous prophecies and Nah 1:1–15 not set forth God's case against the nations. It will not surprise readers of Amos 1–2 to discover that judgment falls because Nineveh is filled with lies, violence, and oppression (3:1), or because Nineveh enslaves others (3:4) and is cruel (3:19). God may rightly expose their nakedness (3:5), make them an object of contempt (3:6), and render them powerless (3:8–9) because of their overwhelming cruelty.

There is no question that Nahum's depiction of God and Nineveh is plainspoken. God no longer roars. Now God devours. God is the universal LORD who saves and punishes. God's power and justice dictate the flow of history. God has been patient, yet has begun to move against evil in an evident and telling fashion. Lacking are the parental and spousal metaphors that have dotted the earlier texts. Characterization techniques to convey judgment now dominate the scene.

The God Who Inspires Faith in Crisis: Habakkuk

Through the use of a creative, dramatic structure, Habakkuk reworks a number of theological ideas already prominent among its predecessors. For example, the book announces national and international iniquity. It depicts God using a powerful nation, this time Babylon, to punish sinners in Israel, and highlights the prophet's relationship to the LORD. In Habakkuk, God acts as revealer, judge, comforter, instructor, deliverer, and sovereign LORD of history. These common notions are mixed with an uncommon depiction of a prophet to make a strong theological statement about how God inspires faith in the faithful even as crises unfold.

Habakkuk 1:2–11 reminds readers that God reveals the future to special messengers. When Habakkuk asks how long Israel's wicked will continue, the LORD responds by divulging that Babylon will destroy Israel's wicked. The prophet can be certain that sin will not remain unchecked forever. Just as Assyria receives its just rewards, so the covenant people will as well.

God's answer only partly satisfies Habakkuk. He is interested in the complete triumph of good over evil, so one wicked nation defeating another does not seem a proper solution to him (1:12–2:1). God's next reply helps clarify matters. Habakkuk may count on the fact that though final judgment seems to come slowly, it will indeed come and will devastate the wicked (2:2–3, 5). The correct posture of Habakkuk and of all who call on the LORD is that of faith. The just person lives by faith, just as the covenant person lives by every word that comes from God (Deut 8:3). Such faith, and such faith alone, can sustain the prophet and those like him. God will bring woe on Babylon (Hab 2:5–11). Habakkuk need not fear that God's character has somehow been diminished. Idolaters such as Babylon will be crushed (2:12–20).

Habakkuk concludes with a psalm of trust, which underscores God's ability to engender faith in the remnant. The psalm longs for God to redeem the faithful by removing the wicked. This act would mean mercy for the oppressed, and the prophet longs to see this work that only God can do. Habakkuk asks God to repeat the exodus deliverance, when God freed Israel from Egypt (3:3–15). Such would mean a renewal of divine, revelatory activity; it would constitute grace for the righteous who live by faith. For this sort of miracle the prophet is willing to wait (3:16). By faith he will wait, though everything around him seems bleak (3:17–19). He will live by faith despite the fact that Israel and Babylon must fall before his faith will be vindicated. God's word alone is enough to fuel this belief.

Nahum and Habakkuk leave readers with no question that the Day of the LORD is coming soon upon Assyria, Israel, and Babylon. Obadiah depicts Jerusalem's fall, and also pledges the destruction of Edom. The only comfort that appears in these books is for the faithful, and even they can expect tremendous difficulties that may cause searching, Habakkuk-like questions about God's nature.

The God Who Punishes
to Create a Remnant: Zephaniah

Zephaniah leaves no doubt whether God will limit judgment to the wicked in Israel, Assyria, and Babylon. All creation will suffer for their transgressions (1:2–3). Assyria and Babylon will be joined in judgment by other countries who have offended the LORD (2:4–12). Though God's just anger continues to be a main theme, that this wrath falls in order to forge a multinational remnant also receives major attention (3:6–20). The goal of God's judgment, then, is not simply punitive; it is ultimately redemptive.

Zephaniah 1:1–17a stresses that old sins such as idolatry will cause the LORD to sweep away everything created in Gen 1:1–26 (Zeph 1:2–3). While creation is the setting, the objects of God's anger are the wicked of the earth (1:3). God will reverse creation as in the days of the flood,[14] which will remove violence and fraud (1:8–9), apathy (1:12–13), and polytheism. This Day of the LORD will be as fearsome as Joel and Amos predicted.

Next, Zeph 1:17b–3:5 indicates that every wicked nation will be devastated on the Day of the LORD. But one group will survive the conflagration. The "humble of the land" who seek the LORD, the law, righteousness, and humility (2:3) will become the remnant that will possess the land (2:7, 9). Those mentioned in 2:3, 7, and 9 are clearly Israelites, but 2:11 offers the possibility of extending the identity of the remnant to people from other lands.

This potential is realized in Zeph 3:6–20. God states that divine indignation (3:8) will "change the speech of the peoples to pure speech" (3:9) and cause worshipers to come from "beyond the rivers of Ethiopia" (3:10). While 3:10 may refer specifically to exiled Israelites, the plural word "peoples" indicates that the remnant has a multinational identity. Given the presence of 2:11, the prophecy's overall context argues for this definition of "the remnant." And it is to this remnant that all the Creator's blessings are promised (3:11–20).

---

[14] Michael De Roche, "Zephaniah 1:2–3: The 'Sweeping of Creation,'" *VT* 30 (1980): 104–9.

Zephaniah concludes the emphasis on judgment begun in Nahum. At this point in the Twelve all polytheists stand under divine condemnation. The sins chronicled in Hosea through Micah will be eradicated. Still, renewal is the goal beyond devastation, so hope for the future is hardly gone. The Creator/Deliverer who reaches out to Nineveh remains concerned with all peoples. This hope rests unexplained, but the next three books address the matter of how the God who warns and judges is also the God who forgives and renews.

The God Who Renews the Temple: Haggai

Zephaniah concludes without stating exactly how renewal will occur in history. Haggai, Zechariah, and Malachi discuss this matter and offer a pattern for how complete restoration will unfold. Each written after the Jews' initial return from exile, the prophecies are honest about how preliminary and preparatory to total restoration their era is, but they are hopeful and confident in the foundations for the future.

Haggai contends that full national renewal cannot take place until the temple destroyed by Babylon is rebuilt. Ezra 3:8–4:24 indicates that earlier efforts to rebuild took place, but were stopped by political enemies. Haggai believes the time has come to try again, and offers four messages that motivate the people to build. First, 1:1–15 argues that God deserves honor, so the people should construct a temple that demonstrates their commitment to the LORD. Indeed, they will suffer hardship until they obey. Second, 2:1–9 presents God as the one who promises greater glory for the new temple. Though it is humble in size and origins, the people must not underestimate the importance of their fresh start. Their captivity is over. Their lives have begun anew. Greater days lie ahead. Third, 2:10–19 states that God purifies the people so that they can be a worthy remnant. Fourth, 2:20–23 claims that God renews the covenant with David. With the people back in the land, the temple in place, and the Davidic covenant reaffirmed, Haggai declares that full renewal is not only possible, but already under way.

Israel has persevered in exile because its God has remained constant. Unwilling to give up the people (Hos 11:1–9), the LORD has brought them home and given them a humble new beginning. There is no question in Haggai's mind that the same God operates in his day as in earlier eras. God continues to warn, explain, reveal, and heal. Now, however, the focus is on healing, and the people themselves seem more obedient to these divine overtures.

The God Who Renews Jerusalem: Zechariah

Zechariah is a magnificent and difficult prophecy. It has been divided in many ways by scholars through the years, and strong debates over issues such as authorship, date, and original audience have marked its history of interpretation. This essay cannot address these issues, nor can it do justice to Zechariah's multifaceted theological depth. Still, even a brief treatment must mention two specific ways the prophecy depicts God: as the one who is jealous for Zion, and as the shepherd of Israel.

Having begun with a defense of God's dealings with Israel in 1:1–6, the prophecy stresses that the people's recent repentance (1:6) signals a new era in Israelite history. God is once again jealous, or protective, of Jerusalem (1:14), which means the city's enemies will be scattered and impediments to its rebuilding removed rather than the Jews being scattered and destroyed. Eight visions follow, which together demonstrate that every important element of Israelite life damaged by defeat and exile will be mended (1:7–6:15).

A key to this renewal and a proof of God's interest in Israel is the emergence of a person God calls "my servant the branch" (3:8, 10). This individual will remove Israel's sin and allow its inhabitants to live in peace. He is a Davidic heir and will make the temple glorious again (6:12–13). There is little doubt that this individual is the same as the one promised in Isa 4:2, Isa 11:1, and Jer 23:1–8, passages which also utilize branch/root imagery for the coming ideal Davidic ruler.

Thus, Zech 3:8–10 and 6:12–13 combine royal and priestly metaphors to describe one who can rebuild the temple, destroy sin, and serve God and the people. As a result of the LORD's kindness, the branch's labors, and their repentance, the covenant people will be forgiven. God's jealousy for Jerusalem and Israel will make it so (cf. 7:1–8:23).

Zechariah 9–14 continues the picture of future glory begun in the previous chapters. Zechariah 9:1 begins a "burden," or oracle, that continues through 11:17. Another "burden" stretches from 12:1–14:21. This recurring term helps bond Zechariah and Malachi, which begins with a "burden" of its own. Zechariah's first "burden" explains that all Israel's oppressors and ancient foes will be defeated by the LORD (9:1–8, esp. 9:4). Coupled with 8:20–23, Zech 9:1–8 demonstrates God's sovereignty beyond Israel. All the earth belongs to the LORD (9:1), God watches the whole earth to make certain Israel is safe, and the LORD has determined to give the nations to the chosen people (9:7–8).

All these wonders will occur because of the coming king (9:9–10)

and because God shepherds Israel like a flock (9:16–17). The Jews suffer under poor shepherds (10:1–2), a common prophetic image for
wicked rulers (cf. Jer 25:34–38; Ezek 34:7–10). But now God will be their
shepherd, which means Israel will prevail over the shepherds/leaders of
other lands (10:3–11:3). No one is capable of frustrating the sovereign
shepherd's purposes, a fact Ezek 34:11–31 declares in an earlier passage
that connects the LORD's shepherding of Israel, the Davidic ruler, and
Israel's ultimate restoration. Worthless human shepherds will be driven
from the land as a prelude to that day (11:4–17).

Jerusalem's restoration will be complete only when God dwells in
Zion and all sin is eradicated. This action will drive wickedness from
the chosen city, priesthood, and throne. Then the nations will consider
Jerusalem, Zion, the dwelling place of God, their capital city. Then the
city will be entirely "holy to the LORD" (14:16–21). Before that time, the
God who created the heavens, the earth, and the human race (12:1) will
strengthen Jerusalem. All who oppose God's purposes will be destroyed
"on that day" (12:9), which is an obvious reference to the judgment-day
imagery in previous prophecies.

Clearly, Zechariah's characterization of God is much more like that
of Hosea than it is of, say, Zephaniah. God is once again a benevolent,
though not irresponsible, figure. The LORD is shepherd, healer, and the
one who sends the Davidic ruler to restore people and city. Restoration
themes require a change in the way the LORD is described, and these
changes take the text back to its warning mode.

The God Who Loves and Renews Israel: Malachi

Malachi expresses the cost of renewal and explains how barriers to
restoration may be removed. It does so in a creative style that utilizes
questions, answers, exhortations, oracles, and narrative-like description
while presenting its message. Questions form six distinct segments that
isolate the sins that God will overcome in achieving the people's renewal. To effect renewal, the LORD is presented as the God who loves
Israel (1:1–5), the God who instructs and corrects priests (1:6–2:9), the
God who denounces infidelity (2:10–16), the God who establishes justice (2:17–3:5), the God who never changes (3:6–12), and the God who
exposes arrogance (3:13–15). Following these foundational sections,
3:16–24 (Eng., 3:16–4:6) presents the LORD as creator of the remnant.
The emergence of the remnant at the end of the book highlights the
people's ultimate renewal. As in the earlier prophecies, however, only

the LORD's direct intervention in history through the Day of the LORD makes this renewal possible.

Malachi 1:1–5 emphasizes that God's love undergirds the coming renewal. In this way the last Book of the Twelve connects with the first. It was God's electing, patient love that made it possible for remnant persons like Hosea to exist, and possible for straying persons like Gomer to repent and come back to God. Here it is God's love that sustains the people. All hope is based on the belief that the God who has remained loving and faithful for three centuries will maintain that loyalty indefinitely. God's love cannot be in question. Any pain the nation encounters must of necessity originate elsewhere. Renewal, on the other hand, cannot originate anywhere but with the LORD.

Summary of the Characterization of God in the Twelve

Malachi brings both the Twelve and the Prophets to a close. As the last segment of the Twelve, the prophecy completes the book's charting of Israel's and the nations' sins, the just and inevitable punishment of that sin, and the renewal the judgment is sent to effect. Set near 450 B.C.E., Malachi finishes the Twelve's historical odyssey from before Assyria's defeat of Samaria, through Babylon's destruction of Jerusalem, to Persia's dominance over the chosen people and the promised land. Thus, the Twelve covers three centuries of decline, defeat, and initial recovery. Malachi also emphasizes the future envisioned by the rest of the Twelve, which focuses on God's intervention in history on behalf of the believing remnant.

To sustain these thematic threads, the Twelve has had to employ a fully developed portrait of the LORD. The warning texts require God to be both benevolent and menacing, depending on the messages' particular needs. The judgment passages dictate an emphasis on imagery that allows the LORD to act decisively in a punishing manner. Similarly, the renewal texts use characterizations that underscore the just and forgiving aspects of the LORD's nature. Thus, a full-orbed portrait of God includes images of God as spouse, parent, judge, healer, creator, sovereign ruler, shepherd, deliverer, and refiner of a sinful world.

Are these descriptions simply competing voices? No, for the writers depict what they deem to be the same God. Further, texts that summarize the LORD's person, such as Nah 1:2–8, include all these aspects of personality, or at least a majority of them. The writers of the Twelve do not consider it odd that a fully developed person may have several

characteristics. Finally, the depiction of God in the Twelve does not differ significantly from that of earlier books, nor from earlier summary
texts such as Exod 34:6–7. It seems reasonable, then, to conclude that
a single character can have many characteristics and remain consistent,
and that the canon as a whole accepts the notion that God is one, yet
not limited in personality. In this way the Twelve keeps faith with the rest
of the canon by linking God's character to specific texts and events, and
by using techniques of characterization relevant to the action it conveys.

10

"Israel" and "Jacob" in the Book of Micah:
Micah in the Context of the Twelve

Mark E. Biddle

Within the first several verses of the book of Micah, the reader encounters phenomena that raise questions to linger throughout the book. The clearly "Deuteronomistic" heading (1:1)[1] identifies the book as the words of a certain Micah, a Judean, roughly contemporary with Isaiah, who preached concerning Samaria and Jerusalem. The expectation that the book will address the fates of the capital cities of the northern and southern kingdoms, perhaps similar to the way 2 Kgs 17; Jer 3:6–11; and Ezek 23 employ the catastrophe in Samaria as an object lesson for Judah and Jerusalem,[2] is immediately met by a brief unit (1:2–4) describing YHWH's theophany in universal terms. Employing language related intertextually to the description of YHWH's judgment against the nations, especially Edom, found in Isa 34,[3] this theophany recalls similar announcements of YHWH's worldwide judgment throughout the *Dodekapropheton* (Amos 1:2; Nah 1:5; Zeph 1:2; cf. Zeph 3:8). Abruptly,

---

[1] For a recent discussion of these "Deuteronomistic" superscriptions, see Aaron Schart, *Die Entstehung des Zwölfprophetenbuchs: Neubearbeitungen von Amos im Rahmen schriftenübergreifender Redaktionsprozesse* (BZAW 260; New York: de Gruyter, 1998), 31–49.

[2] James D. Nogalski argues that Micah once constituted the third of four books (Hosea, Amos, Micah, and Zephaniah) in a corpus older than the Twelve (*Literary Precursors to the Book of the Twelve* [BZAW 217; New York: de Gruyter, 1993]). In this "Deuteronomistic" corpus, "Hosea and Amos record God's prophetic word to the Northern Kingdom while Micah and Zephaniah functioned as Southern counterparts.... Broadly stated, Hosea alternates between YHWH's pronouncements of judgment and salvation for Israel. Amos presumes Israel's recalcitrance in Hosea, and announces judgment on Israel. Micah assumes Samaria's destruction from Amos as a warning to Judah of a similar fate if it does not change.... Zephaniah centers its message on YHWH's judgment, like Amos, but that message is directed to Judah and Jerusalem" (James D. Nogalski, *Redactional Processes in the Book of the Twelve* [BZAW 218; New York: de Gruyter, 1993], 274).

[3] Mark E. Biddle, "Intertextuality, Micah, and the Book of the Twelve: A Question of Method" (paper presented to the Seminar on the Formation of the Book of the Twelve, SBL Annual Meeting, New Orleans, 1996).

146

a lengthy lament turns attention, as might have been anticipated from the heading, to the manner in which the sins of Samaria have reached and infected Judah (1:9). The introduction (1:5) to this lament, however, surprisingly refers to "Jacob," confusing the precise identity of the addressees. If Jacob's transgression is Samaria, are the "sins of the house of Israel" and the "high place of Judah" (= Jerusalem) parallel? This confusion of addressees continues throughout the subsequent lament. Why are the "sins of Israel" associated with Judean Lachish (1:13) and what benefit could the "kings of Israel" have hoped to derive from the southern village of Achzib (1:14)? Did Micah employ "Israel" as a synonym for "Judah" and reserve "Jacob" for the northern kingdom?[4]

In fact, the entire book of Micah manifests a curious tendency with respect to names of the people of God, a tendency characteristic of the *Dodekapropheton,* as well. The book refers to "Judah," Micah's presumptive addressee, only four times — only three times excluding the Deuteronomistic chronological information in the superscription (1:1, 5, 9; 5:1). Instead of this expected designation, references to "Israel" (12x) and "Jacob" (11x) predominate. Notably, this preference pertains both to sections of the book generally regarded "authentic" (i.e., 3:1, 8, 9) and to those widely held as redactional expansions (i.e., 2:12; 4:14; 5:6, 7). Were it not for the superscription, one might easily conclude that Micah was a northern prophet who addressed a northern audience. Instead, and governed no doubt by acceptance of the historical setting for Micah's ministry provided by this superscription, scholarship assumes, for the most part, that Micah employed the terms "Judah," "Israel," and "Jacob" interchangeably.[5]

---

[4] Interpreters adopt every possible position regarding the referents of these terms in Micah. For example, Theodor Lescow argues that Micah employs both "Jacob" and "Israel" to refer to Judah (*Worte und Wirkungen des Propheten Micha: Ein kompositions-geschichtlicher Kommentar* [AzTh 84; Stuttgart: Calwer, 1997], 39–47, 96). In support of this position he appeals, with respect to "Jacob," to parallels in Isaiah (48:1), and with respect to "Israel," to parallels in Jeremiah (2:4–6; 4:1–4; 5:15–17, 20–31; 18:1–6, 13–17). In contrast, W. D. Whitt ("The Jacob Traditions in Hosea and Their Relation to Genesis," *ZAW* 103 [1991]: 21) argues that "Israel" refers to both kingdoms in Mic 1:14–16 and that "Jacob" consistently denotes Judah, adducing other Jeremiah texts in support (10:25; 30:7, 10; 31:11; 46:27, 28). W. McKane employs historical criteria to draw the source-critical conclusion that "Micah was a Judean prophet and vv. 5a, 6–7 are not his work" ("Micah 1,2–7," *ZAW* 107 [1995]: 434). Ina Willi-Plein resolves the problem text-critically, arguing that Mic 1:5b is a gloss (*Vorformen der Schriftexegese innerhalb des Alten Testaments: Untersuchungen zum literarischen Werden der auf Amos, Hosea, und Micha zurückgehender Bücher im hebräischen Zwölfprophetenbuch* [BZAW 123; New York: de Gruyter, 1971], 70–71).

[5] Hans W. Wolff can argue, for example, that "Micah thinks in 3:8 with reference

Admittedly, these terms manifest a surprising fluidity in the Hebrew Bible. The general consensus holds that authors or speakers prior to the fall of Samaria usually reserved the name "Israel" for the northern kingdom,[6] whereas authors or speakers after the fall of Samaria, and especially after the exile, could appropriate the name for southerners as the surviving claimants to the patriarchal heritage.[7] Similarly, prior to the fall of Samaria, "Jacob" was often employed as a synonym for "Israel,"[8] while Judeans in the exilic and postexilic period seem to have favored "Jacob" as a designation permitting them to lay claim to the earliest tradition and to still avoid the negative political and historical connotations of "Israel."[9] Micah's usage, then, seems to conform to exilic and postexilic practice rather than to that of the eighth century. Does this circumstance reflect the preferences of Micah the prophet or the program of the tradents and redactors of the book?

If the explicit claim of the superscription and the evidence of the southern place-names in the lament (1:8–16) confirm not only the notion that Micah was a Judean, but, more significantly, that the editors and tradents of the book considered him so, this peculiarity deserves exploration and explanation. Two aspects of the phenomenon suggest that it represents a redactional program, not the redactional program that produced only the book of Micah, but also that produced the Book of the Twelve. First, "Jacob" and "Israel" dominate all sections of Micah, from the very confusing, and supposedly "authentic," opening chapter, to the equally ambiguous core chapter 3, and including the surely redactional expansions to chapter 2 (vv. 12–13) and the eschatological "Zion" oracles of chapters 4–5.

---

to 'Jacob' and 'Israel' exclusively of Judah and Jerusalem (cf. 3:1, 9)" and can conclude that the same is true of 1:5a. Micah 1:5b he then labels as an insertion designed to link the superscription with the existing material (*Dodekapropheton 4: Micha* [BKAT 14/4; Neukirchen-Vluyn: Neukirchener, 1982], 15–16).

    [6] For example, Hos 1:6; 4:1; and often; Amos 2:6; 3:14; and often; Isa 7:1; 9:8, 14.
    [7] For example, Isa 40:27; 41:8, 14; 43:1, 22, 28; 44:1; and often in Isaiah; Zech 12:1; Mal 1:1; Ezra 3:1; 7:7, 10; etc.; Neh 9:2; 12:47.
    [8] For example, Isa 8:17; 9:7; 10:20, 21; 17:4; Amos 3:13; 6:8; 7:2, 5; 8:7; 9:8; Hos 10:11; 12:3, 13.
    [9] For "Jacob" as a designation for southern exiles, see especially Isa 43:1; 44:1; 46:3; Jer 10:25; 30:7, 10; 31:11; 46:27, 28. For helpful summaries of the situation, see Hans-Jürgen Zobel, "יעקֹ(ו)ב," *ThWAT* 3.771–78; Whitt, "Jacob Traditions," 20–21; and Walter Maier, *The Book of Nahum: A Commentary* (St. Louis: Concordia, 1959), 228. Each occurrence of the terms must be evaluated very carefully. As Mic 1 demonstrates, the twin dangers of circular reasoning and easy assumptions may lead one to overlook the complexity of a given instance.

Second, a similar preference for the names "Jacob" and "Israel" characterizes the Book of the Twelve up to Nah 2:3. The distribution of these two names manifests an intriguing concentration at the front of the corpus. Of only twenty-eight instances of "Jacob," twenty-one appear in the four contiguous books of Amos (6x), Obadiah (3x), Micah (11x), and Nahum (1x). Hosea (3x) and Malachi (4x) account for the remaining seven usages. Interestingly, key references to "Jacob" in Hosea (12:3–4), the first book in the Twelve, and in Malachi (1:2–5), the last, focus on the patriarch's relationship with his brother, Esau/Edom. Nahum marks a similar dividing point in the distribution of "Israel" (Hosea through Nahum, 91x; Habakkuk through Malachi, 14x). By contrast, the sixty-three instances of the name "Judah" divide rather equally (Hosea through Nahum, 31x; Habakkuk through Malachi, 32x).

The substance and scope of this essay is thereby sharply circumscribed. What are the details of the pattern for usage of these names in Micah itself? Does this pattern participate in some scheme reaching into the books surrounding Micah in the Minor Prophets? For heuristic purposes, instances of the names "Jacob" and "Israel" in each of the three major literary divisions of Micah, Mic 1–3 (the "core" collection), Mic 4–5 (the eschatological "Zion" expansion), and Mic 6–7 (a divine lawsuit and prophetic liturgy composition), will be examined as distinct groups. Not coincidentally, characteristic formulae and phrases employing the names in these sections confirm the standard literary analysis and suggest parameters for an understanding of "Israel" and "Jacob" in the book of Micah and beyond.

"(House of) Jacob and (House of) Israel" in the Core Collection

On the face of it, the expression "house of Jacob and house of Israel" and its variants[10] would appear to be the common merism encompassing both kingdoms (Jacob would then be a reference to Judah). Several structural elements, however, establish a framework or *inclusio* around

---

[10] "House of Jacob … and house of Israel" appears in 3:9; "Jacob … and the house of Israel" in 1:5; 3:1; "Jacob … and Israel" in 3:8. "Israel" appears unaccompanied in 1:13, 14, 15 and "the house of Jacob" in 2:7. Since these uses appear in material that belongs, for the most part, to the same redactional layer as the binary expression, or, more appropriately, since their current position nestled among the binary expressions influences a homogenous reading, they can be provisionally understood as synonymous with their occurrences in the binary forms. "Jacob, all of you … and remnant of Israel" in 2:12 will be treated separately below.

Mic 1:5–3:12* and set the parameters for understanding the connotations of its use of "Jacob" and "Israel." The section opens with the announcement that "all this" is or will be "because of the rebellion (בְּפֶשַׁע) of Jacob" and "because of the sins (וּבְחַטֹּאות) of the house of Israel" (1:5), phrases echoed at the end in the prophet's description of his mission "to declare to Jacob his rebellion (פִּשְׁעוֹ) and to Israel his sin (חַטָּאתוֹ)" (3:8). The jarring reference to Jerusalem as the "high place of Judah (בָּמוֹת יְהוּדָה)" (1:5) not only relates back to the theophany of 1:2–4 (v. 3), but also prefigures the announcement that Zion will become a "ploughed field (שָׂדֶה תֵחָרֵשׁ)," Jerusalem a "ruin (עִיִּין),"[11] and the temple mount a "high place of the forest (לְבָמוֹת יָעַר)" (3:12). This framework, then, likens the fate of Jerusalem (3:10–12), the "high place of Judah," with that of Samaria (1:6–7) and, by virtue of the redactional linkage to the theophany opening the book, sets the fates of both in the context of the destruction of the "high places" and mountains of the world (1:2–4).

The unexpected reference to Jerusalem as a "high place" suggests the dependence of 1:5, where the term connotes the pejorative sense of the Canaanite cultic site, on 3:10–12, where the term emphasizes the aftermath of destruction. Provisionally, then, Mic 1:5, which sits very loosely in its context,[12] seems to have been composed specifically to link the Samaria (1:6–7) and Jerusalem (3:10–12) *inclusio* to the opening section of the book. These three distinct uses of the term "high place" (meaning "the world's heights," 1:3; a pejorative reference to Jerusalem as a cult site, 1:5; a description of Jerusalem as a barren hill, 3:12), while serving to bind this section as a compositional unit, also betray something of the redactional history of Micah.

In fact, this theme of the fate of the "high places" helps anchor Micah in the Book of the Twelve. Hosea 10:8; Amos 4:13; 7:9; and Hab 3:19 also discuss "high places" in ways that suggest literary relationship to the

---

[11] Cf. 1:6, "I will make Samaria a ruin of the field (לְעִי הַשָּׂדֶה)."

[12] It can hardly be read as the logical continuation of vv. 2–4, which speak of a worldwide cataclysm in association with YHWH's appearance. "All this" must refer to what follows. Concerning the problem of the discontinuity between vv. 2–4 and v. 5, see Wilhelm Rudolph, *Micha Nahum Habakuk Zephanja* (KAT 13/3; Gütersloh: Gerd Mohn, 1975), 39–41; Wolff, *Dodekapropheton 4*, 14–16; T. Lescow, "Redaktionsgeschichtliche Analyse von Micha 1–5," *ZAW* 84 (1972): 55–61; Nogalski, *Literary Precursors*, 129–37; Lescow, *Worte und Wirkungen*, 28–30; Burkard Zapff, *Redaktionsgeschichtliche Studien zum Michabuch im Kontext des Dodekapropheton* (BZAW 256; New York: de Gruyter, 1997), 262–68.

texts in Micah. Schart[13] has already called attention to the close parallels between Mic 3:12 and Hos 10:8, but the Hosea text and Mic 1:5 exhibit an even stronger resemblance. Hosea 10:8 identifies the "high place of Awen" appositionally as the "sin of Israel." The parallelism of Mic 1:5 similarly equates the "sins of the house of Israel" with "the high place of Judah." Amos 7:9 forms the third member in this chain of interprophetic allusions. Jeremias has already called attention to aspects of this brief pronouncement that seem foreign to the book of Amos, while at the same time demonstrating unmistakable affinities with the book of Hosea, and especially Hos 10:8.[14] It remains only to note the unusual relationship between Amos's condemnation of the "high places of Isaac," itself a peculiar reference to the northern kingdom,[15] and Micah's condemnation of the "high places of Judah."[16]

Thus, the Samaria/Jerusalem framework of Mic 1–3 employs "Jacob" and "Israel" as references to the North and the South, respectively. Do references within the framework conform to this pattern? "Israel" occurs, unaccompanied, three times in the lament of Mic 1:8–16. H. W. Wolff suggests that the phrase "glory of Israel" (1:15), usually a divine epithet,[17] should be understood here as a parallel to "king of Israel" (1:14). In his view, it recalls David's flight to Adullam at the "low point" of his life (1 Sam 23:13).[18] Since all the place-names that serve as the basis for the wordplays in the lament indicate locations in the Judean Shephelah, "Israel" must refer to Judah. Only Mic 1:13b falls outside this pattern. Although Mic 1–3 employs the familiar pair "rebellion"/"sin" (1:5; 3:8), the terms occur in reverse order, disrupting the terse rhythm of the

---

[13] *Entstehung*, 190.

[14] Jörg Jeremias, *Der Prophet Amos: Übersetzt und Erklärt* (ATD 24/2; Göttingen: Vandenhoeck & Ruprecht, 1995), 111–12.

[15] Jeremias remarks, "The use of the term 'Isaac,' that besides Amos 7:9, 16 never parallels Israel in the OT and is never used in reference to the northern kingdom, remains unexplained" (111, n. 13). He considers it likely that "Isaac" here is somehow related to the unusual double reference to Beersheba (Amos 5:5; 8:14).

[16] The picture in Amos 4:13 (one of three late doxological acknowledgments of the justice of YHWH's dealings with Israel/Judah) of YHWH, the Creator God who "bestrides the high places of the earth," on the other hand, more closely parallels Mic 1:3. The relationship between these two texts belongs, therefore, to a later phase in the growth of the Twelve. The enigmatic conclusion to Habakkuk's prayer celebrating YHWH's theophany (3:19) may also be related to this "theophany" layer of material. See the helpful discussion and summary of research on Amos 4:13; 5:8–9; and 9:5–6 in Dirk U. Rottzoll, *Studien zur Redaktion und Komposition des Amosbuchs* (BZAW 243; New York: de Gruyter, 1996), 242–50.

[17] Isa 17:3, 4; Ezek 10:19; 11:22.

[18] Wolff, *Dodekapropheton 4*, 33.

wordplays. Furthermore, the framework interprets Samaria's wound that has reached Judah (1:9) in relation to Israel's rebellion in Lachish, the sole instance in Mic 1–3 in which "Israel" refers unmistakably to the northern kingdom.[19]

The remaining three instances of the "Jacob"/"Israel" pair (3:1, 8, 9; disregarding 2:12 for the moment), along with the sole instance in Mic 1–3 of "house of Jacob" by itself (2:7), present another profile altogether. Schart rightly calls attention to a "summons to hear" series stretching across the books of Hosea (4:1; 5:1), Amos (3:1; 4:1; 5:1; 8:4), and Micah, and culminating in Mic 3:1, 3:9, and 6:2.[20] In his view, several intertextual connections suggest literary relationship among the three books: Mic 3:1 (הלוא לכם לדעת את־המשפט) picks up on the charge to the leadership in Hos 5:1 (כי לכם המשפט); Mic 6:2, the last in the series, cites Hos 4:1, the first in the series, almost verbatim (כי ריב ליהוה עם); like Amos 5:19 and 9:3, Mic 3:5 refers to the snake's bite; both Hos 4:2 and Mic 3:10 refer to "bloody deeds"; and the reference to threat posed by the fact that "YHWH is in the [people's] midst" (Mic 3:11) can only be understood against Amos 5:17 and 7:8, 10. Schart's observations can be expanded: (1) Citation of Micah's opponents who call for him to cease "preaching" (נטף) recalls Amos 7:16.[21] (2) Micah 3:2 (שנאי טוב ואהבי רעה) describes the wicked behaviors of Micah's audience in terms reversed in the call to repentance in Amos 5:15 (שנאו־רע ואהבו טוב). (3) In general terms, Micah and Amos adopt a similar stance on the theme of social and economic justice.[22]

The question of the nature of the relationship among these "summons to hear" (and their contexts) in Micah, on the one hand, and in Hosea and Amos, on the other, is inseparable from the question of the meaning of "Jacob ... and ... Israel" in Mic 3:1, 8,. and 9. Schart recognizes two possible interpretations of the significance of the "summons to hear" series and other intertextual links among Micah, Hosea, and Amos: either the hand responsible for Mic 3:1–12 knew a more or less

---

[19] So also Schart, *Entstehung,* 182–83.

[20] Ibid., 186–89.

[21] The second instance of the peculiar "house of Isaac" in Amos 7, clearly referring to the North. Is "house of Jacob" in Mic 2:7 meant as a counterpart? Is the reader of the Twelve to understand that, just as Amos's opponent called on him not to preach to the "house of Isaac" (= the North), Micah's opponent, the "house of Jacob" (= Judah), called on him stop proclaiming his message publicly?

[22] Note especially Mic 3:9 // Amos 5:10 [תעב]. Editors supplied Hosea with this theme, as well; see Hos 5:10.

final form of the Hosea-Amos "Book of the Two,"[23] or the editors responsible for combining Hosea and Amos on one scroll were themselves also responsible for the final form of Mic 3:1–12, that is, they included Micah along with Hosea and Amos from the outset (a "Book of the Three"). For Schart, who opts for the first explanation, the referent of "Israel" in Mic 3 provides the key. As he observes, "[I]f one has this [summons] series before one's eyes, then it becomes problematical to relate the expression 'house of Israel' in Mic 3:1, 9 to Judah."[24] Conversely, he concludes that since, in Micah, "Israel" refers to Judah, the tradents responsible for the summons texts in Hosea and Amos could not have authored the Micah texts. He reasons that, should "Israel" here refer to the North, one would be forced "to envision the scene as though the northern kingdom were an uninvolved spectator."[25]

In response to Schart, however, one might object that the book's superscription, the enigmatic redactional unit in 1:5, and the address to Samaria in 1:6–7 all presume that the northern kingdom is involved, *at least from the perspective of the fictive reality created by the book itself.* Grounds other than "historical" realities, namely the (literary) contexts of these address forms, must be adduced to resolve the question of the referents of Mic 3:1, 8, and 9. With respect to context, however, the two axes to which these "summons" texts relate, namely Mic 1, on the one hand, and the other "summons" texts in Hosea and Amos, on the other, are in conflict. In Micah, these summons call on the leadership of both North ("Jacob" = "Samaria," Mic 1:5) and South ("Israel" ="Judah," Mic 1:5, 14, 15); in the context of the Twelve, "Jacob" and "Israel" would be synonymous references to the North only. In neither case does a contextual reading justify understanding both terms as designations for Judah alone. The editor responsible for the superscription worked with a text that could be understood as referring to both North and South. If Mic 3:1–12 constituted part of that book, the editor, given the affinities with Hosea and Amos outlined above, will likely have understood Mic 3:1–12 as a blanket condemnation of both kingdoms, culminating in harsh words for Jerusalem (just as the body of the book begins with equally harsh words for Samaria).

---

[23] Jörg Jeremias, "Die Anfänge des Dodekapropheton: Hosea und Amos," in *Congress Volume: Paris, 1992* (ed. John Emerton; VTSup 61; Leiden: Brill, 1995), 87–106 = *Hosea und Amos: Studien zu den Anfängen des Dodekapropheton* (FAT 13; Tübingen: Mohr, 1996), 34–54.

[24] Schart, *Entstehung,* 186, n. 100.

[25] Ibid., 188, n. 111.

"Remnant of Israel" and "Remnant of Jacob" in the Eschatological/Zion Composition of Micah 4–5

As already anticipated in the oddly placed oracle in Mic 2:12–13, the book of Micah turns from theological interpretation of history (Mic 1:2–3:12*) to eschatological promises for Jerusalem (Mic 4:1–5:14). These Jerusalem promises attract particular interest for several reasons. First, if reconstructions of the growth of the *Dodekapropheton* such as those by J. Nogalski[26] prove accurate with regard to the "eschatologizing," or even "apocalypticizing," function of the book of Joel in the Twelve, Mic 4–5 will either represent the earliest concentration of such eschatological material in the "Deuteronomistic" corpus or will manifest evidence of having been incorporated into Micah at some point after Micah's inclusion in the protoscroll. Second, even a cursory reading of Mic 4–5 suggests that the preserved material originated in a variety of settings and reflects a variety of ideologies. The manifold connotations of the names "Jacob" and "Israel" may serve as a diagnostic criterion. Third, despite evidence of growth, Mic 4–5 displays a beautifully symmetrical structure, marred only at a few points (Mic 4:6–7; 5:4–8) which, significantly, include unique references to the "remnant of Jacob" (Mic 5:6, 7). This high degree of literary structure and the composition's location in the middle of the book must be considered in relation to whether it comprised part of the book when Micah joined the protocollection. Finally, individual units in Mic 4–5 resemble isolated redactional insertions in other books of the Minor Prophets. A taxonomy of these eschatological units in the *Dodekapropheton* will provide additional data for reconstructing Micah's role in the growth of the Twelve.

Before grouping and examining individual occurrences of the names "Israel" and "Jacob" in this eschatological composition, it will be helpful first to analyze its structure and second to suggest an initial taxonomy of eschatological texts in the Twelve. Against this background of the two primary contexts for "Israel" and "Jacob" in the book of Micah, the profiles of these figures should emerge with greater clarity.

The Macrostructure of Micah 4–5

Two features of Mic 4–5 lend it remarkable coherence. First, with few exceptions (5:3–8, 9–14; and, perhaps, 4:6–8), all of the units deal explicitly with the future of Jerusalem. Second, it exhibits a very sophis-

---

[26] Nogalski, *Redactional Processes,* 275–78.

ticated literary skeleton. Four types of introductory phrases mark the units of Micah's eschatological Jerusalem composition:

1. "Eschatological" formulae, such as "and it will be in the latter days (והיה באחרית הימים)" (4:1); "in that day (ביום ההוא)" (4:6); "and it will be in that day (והיה ביום־ההוא)" (5:9).

2. Vocative second-person masculine singular pronouns addressed directly to personifications of architectural features of cities or cities themselves, for example, "and you, O . . . stronghold of daughter of Zion/Bethlehem (ואתה...בת־ציון/בית־לחם)" (Mic 4:8; 5:1 [Eng., 5:2]).

3. A temporal adverb contrasting the current state with the future predicted in the "eschatological" units ("now [ועתה/עתה]," 4:9, 11, 14). The nearly homonymous pairing of the pronoun and the adverb is a masterfully poetic touch.

4. A series of "to be" verbs with the simple copula ("and . . . will be [והיה]," 5:4, 6, 7).

As the following chart demonstrates, chiasm accentuates the contrast between the present and the future, which dominates the structure overall, and, second, in its current state, the structure is imbalanced at precisely those points that do not deal explicitly with the fate of Jerusalem, the theme of the composition.

4:1	והיה באחרית הימים			
4:6				ביום ההוא
4:8		ואתה		
4:9			עתה	
4:11				ועתה
4:14			עתה	
5:1		ואתה		
5:4				והיה
5:6				והיה
5:7				והיה
5:9	והיה ביום־ההוא			

For the moment, the fact that four units (4:6–8; 5:4–5, 6, 7 [Eng., 5:5–6, 7, 8,]) disrupt this balanced chiasm will only be noted. The latter two units will become the focus of attention below.

A Taxonomy of "Eschatological" Texts in the Minor Prophets

Several themes that figure prominently in Mic 2:12–13 and 4:1–5:15 resurface elsewhere in the Minor Prophets.[27] Although these texts manifest considerable lexical similarity (e.g., in the vocabulary for "gathering [קבץ]" the Diaspora; Hos 2:2; Joel 4:2; Mic 2:12), specific treatments of these themes vary widely. The relationship among these texts may elucidate the relationship between the redaction history of Micah and the growth of the Twelve. Did Micah assume more or less its current form *before* joining the Minor Prophets scroll or *during* the formation of the corpus?

Micah 4:1–4, 11–13; 5:1, 14; Joel 4:2, 9–17; Zeph 3:8; Zech 12:2, 3–5, 6, 8, 9; 14:1–3, 12–15, 16–19 all deal with "the nations gathered in/against Jerusalem." In general, these texts can be divided into two major categories:[28] in one view, the nations will assemble against Jerusalem to lay siege, but, since they do not understand YHWH's plan for history, they will be surprised by the Day of YHWH (Mic 4:11–13; 5:1; Joel 4:9–17; Zeph 3:8; Zech 12:2, 3–5, 6, 9; 14:1–3, 12–15); in another view, the nations will make pilgrimage to Zion to worship YHWH or to submit to his lordship (Mic 4:1–4; Zech 14:16–19; cf. Zech 2:11; 8:22–23; 9:10). While none of the pertinent Micah texts employs the names "Jacob" or "Israel," and thus are not specifically germane to this study, several background observations regarding the interrelationships among texts that deal with this broad topic may illuminate the redaction history of Mic 4–5. First, the two viewpoints clearly conflict with one another, and may even represent competing ideologies. Second, a complicated system of interdependency links these texts across the Twelve.[29] Third, and per-

---

[27] These themes include the nations' pilgrimage to and siege against Jerusalem; the fate of the nations; YHWH's reign on Mount Zion; the restoration of the Davidic monarchy; and the gathering and return of the Diaspora. They resurface in Hos 2:1–2; Joel 4:1–3, 16–21 (Eng., 3:1–3, 16–21); Amos 9:11–15; Obad 8–10, 15–21; Zeph 2:7; 3:8–20; Zech 8:1–18, 9–15; 12:1–6; Mal 1:2–5.

[28] Joel 4:2 (Eng., 3:2) is eccentric. According to this text, YHWH will assemble the nations in the "Valley of Jehoshaphat" in order to plead with them to release the Jews of the Diaspora.

[29] For example, either Joel 4:10 (Eng., 3:10) or Mic 4:3 cites, and reverses, the other. The direction of the dependency is far from clear (for the priority of Joel, see Zapff, *Redaktionsgeschichtliche Studien*, 261, n. 84; in support of the contrary, see Erich Bosshard-Nepustil, "Beobachtungen zum Zwölfprophetenbuch," *BN* 40 [1987]: 42; Schart, *Entstehung*, 268–69). Similarly, Joel 4:12 and Mic 4:3 also allude to one another (YHWH judging the nations), and Joel 4:13 and Mic 4:13 seem to be related in some way. While no clear criterion for determining the direction of dependence between Joel 4:10 and Mic 4:3 seems to have been established, that Mic 4:1–5 and

haps most important, the conflict manifests itself within Micah (4:1–5 versus 4:12–13; 5:14).

Similar circumstances prevail with respect to the theme of kingship in Jerusalem: One group of texts rather simplistically expects the reestablishment of the Davidic monarchy (Hos 2:1–2; Amos 9:11–15; Mic 5:1–3; Zech 3:8; 6:12–13), while another focuses on the reign of YHWH (Joel 4:9–16 [implicitly]; Obad 21; Mic 4:1–5; Zeph 3:8–20; Zech 8:1–9; Zech 14:9, 16–17). Presumably, the focus on YHWH's reign reflects the community's embarrassment at the delayed restoration of the Davidic monarchy, an embarrassment that may explain the strange attitude toward the house of David expressed in Zech 12:7.[30] Once again, Mic 4–5 manifests ties with other sections of the Twelve;[31] once again, individual texts within Mic 4–5 adopt contradictory stances.

The theme of the return of the exiles or the Diaspora, in which use of the names "Israel" and "Jacob" plays a significant role, may provide criteria that will help clarify the intricacies of these intertextual relationships. The texts in question may be classified as follows:

Zech 14:16–19 stand out in the Twelve for their utopian vision deserves full consideration. It is tempting to hypothesize a development in postexilic thought from a bitter expectation of revenge on the nations to a more humanitarian hope for universal peace. The two ideas, however, could well have arisen and existed alongside one another. At any rate, Zech 14:16–19 makes a unique and valiant attempt to reconcile the two perspectives on the fates of the nations. It envisions a time after YHWH has exercised worldwide vengeance on Israel's enemies, when the survivors of that judgment will come annually to Zion to worship the Lord during Succoth. See Jeffrey Rubenstein, *The History of Sukkot in the Second Temple and Rabbinic Periods* (Brown Judaic Studies 302; Atlanta: Scholars Press, 1995), 45–50.

[30] Again, Zech 12–14 seems interested in balancing certain tensions in the Twelve. These observations concerning the commentary-like character of certain texts in Zech 9–14 is consistent with a growing body of scholarship that views Zech 9–14 as an anthology of extrapolations of earlier prophecy. See, for example, Magne Saebø, *Sacharja 9–14* (WMANT 34; Neukirchen-Vluyn: Neukirchener, 1969); Paul L. Redditt, "Israel's Shepherds: Hope and Pessimism in Zechariah 9–14," *CBQ* 51 (1989): 631–42; Odil H. Steck, *Der Abschluß der Prophetie im Alten Testament: Ein Versuch zur Frage der Vorgeschichte des Kanons* (Biblisch-Theologische Studien 17; Neukirchen-Vluyn: Neukirchener, 1991); Nicholas Tai, *Prophetie als Schriftauslegung in Sacharja 9–14: Traditions- und kompositions-geschichtliche Studien* (Calwer Theologische Monographien 17; Stuttgart: Calwer, 1996); Katrina Larkin, *The Eschatology of Second Zechariah: A Study of the Formation of a Mantological Wisdom Anthology* (CBET 6; Kampen: Kok Paros, 1994); Nogalski, *Redactional Processes*, 213–47; and Raymond F. Person, *Second Zechariah and the Deuteronomic School* (JSOTSup 167; Sheffield: Sheffield Academic Press, 1993).

[31] Micah 4:6–8 and Zeph 3:14–20 bear particularly strong resemblance to one another. Both focus on Zion/Daughter Jerusalem's wondrous restoration; both describe YHWH as king; and both refer to the gathering and return of the "lame (הצלעה)" and the "driven out (הנדחה)."

1. Hosea 2:1–2 (Eng., 1:10–11) focuses rather simplistically on the numerical growth of "Israel" (the North), the reestablishment of a single (Davidic) ruler over both houses of Israel ("the sons of Judah and the sons of Israel, together"), and the return from exile.[32] These emphases suggest that the text stems from before the Samaritan schism, when the hope for a reunited Israel would have required only the return of the exiles and the establishment of Davidic rule even over the North. The reestablishment of Davidic rule and the return of the "captivity (שְׁבוּת)" of Israel (the northern Diaspora?) also characterize the two units combined in Amos 9:11–15. Together these two texts may once have served as a linking framework around the early Hosea/Amos corpus.

2. Like Hos 2:1–2; Amos 9:11–15; and Joel 4:1–3, Obad 10, 15–21 (see especially v. 18) distinguishes between northerners ("the house of Joseph") and southerners ("the house of Jacob"), suggesting a historical setting prior to the Samaritan schism. Like Amos 9:11–15 and Joel 4:16–21, it expresses anger toward Edom. It differs from its kindred texts, however, in three key regards. First, it seems less interested in the restoration and reunification of the nation, which it seems to presume, than in vengeance against Israel's enemies. Second, although Obadiah targets Edom for its most severe disdain, its tone of universal revenge (v. 15) and climactic announcement of YHWH's sovereignty lends it an air of the apocalyptic. Third, avoidance of the straightforward terms "Israel" and "Judah" may betray a sensitivity that characterizes certain late exilic and early postexilic texts.[33]

Micah 2:12–13 employs the terms "Jacob" and "remnant of Israel" in a rather unique fashion. This passage, one of the more ambiguous in Micah,[34] contrasts "all" of Jacob with "the remnant of Israel" in a way that clearly suggests a distinction. Apparently, the author considered "all" of Jacob (= the Judean exiles) worthy of return, while only a few of the survivors of the northern kingdom would have been involved in the

---

[32] See Jörg Jeremias, *Der Prophet Hosea: Übersetzt und Erklärt* (ATD 24/1; Göttingen: Vandenhoeck & Ruprecht), 34–36.

[33] Note especially the care taken to establish the "proper" referents of these terms in Isa 48:1, for example.

[34] Partly because it appears in the midst of Mic 2–3 — the "accusation" section of Micah — and partly because of the linguistic difficulty presented by vv. 12b–13, interpreters disagree as to whether this saying offers hope (return from exile) or judgment (going into exile). Zapff surveys the positions taken in the literature (*Redaktionsgeschichtliche Studien*, 16–17). The distinction between "all" of Jacob and "the remnant" of Israel provides a clue to interpretation of the passage, as does the parallelism between "their king before them" and "YHWH at their head."

restoration. Zapff has recently called attention to a possible solution to the text-critical problems of vv. 12b and 13a and to the passage's rich intertextualities. He argues that the passage bears a strong relationship to a number of texts (including Amos 9:11–15; Joel 4:16–21; Mal 1:2–5; see especially Isa 34–35; 63:1–6) that, as O. H. Steck has argued,[35] demonize Edom. Zapff argues, quite convincingly, for accepting the MT reading "Bozrah" and repointing "from man/men" to "from Edom." Two allusions recall patriarchal promises — תהימנה alludes to the promise of offspring made to Abraham, Gen 17:4–5; פרץ likewise recalls the promise to Jacob in Gen 28:14.[36] In the eschatological schema outlined by these texts, Edom will be the staging area for the final return of the exiles. Edom's destruction will usher in universal judgment on the nations, and the returning exiles will then pass through Edom's territory unhindered. Micah 1:2–4, which, as mentioned above, fits awkwardly in its current context and gives every indication of having been a late insertion, shares with Mic 2:12–13 an interesting syntactical feature. Micah 1:2 begins with a summons, addressed to the nations, that includes an awkward third-person pronominal suffix: "Hear, O nations, all of them (כֻּלָּם), draw near, O earth and all its fullness." Similarly, Mic 2:12, in which YHWH promises to "assemble Jacob," includes the incongruous second-person pronominal suffix, "all of you (כֻּלָּךְ)." Unless emended, for which there is little manuscript support, the two suffixes can best be understood *as asides to the reader* and testify to the work of a common hand in the two texts.

If Zapff is correct that Mic 2:12–13 resonates with Steck's anti-Edom schema, it comes as no surprise that Mic 1:2–4 also demonstrates a number of textual links with Isa 34, a key text.[37] A late redactional

---

[35] *Bereitete Heimkehr: Jesaja 35 als redaktionelle Brücke zwischen dem Ersten und dem Zweiten Jesaja* (SBS 121; Stuttgart: Katholisches Bibelwerk, 1985), 42–44, 49–50.

[36] Zapff, *Redaktionsgeschichtliche Studien*, 23–30.

[37] Only these two texts summon (קרב and שמע) the nations along with "the earth and its fullness (ארץ ומלאה)" to hear a pronouncement of YHWH's judgment on all the nations of the earth. Both introduce descriptions, with affinities to theophany traditions, of YHWH's intervention. In both, the sins of a single people have prompted the universal Day of YHWH. Both contexts refer to the "jackal" and the "ostrich." In addition, certain themes and phrases in Isa 34 parallel other passages in Micah and further suggest some intentional relationship. The nations stand under YHWH's חֵרֶם (Isa 34:2; Mic 4:13); YHWH has a day of vengeance (נָקָם) on Edom/the nations (Isa 34:8; Mic 5:14 [Eng., 5:15]). Cities under YHWH's judgment become overgrown wastelands (Isa 34:13; Mic 3:12; 5:11). The unusual legitimizing expression, "for the mouth [of YHWH] has commanded/spoken (כי פי יְהֹוָה] צוּה/דבר)" is very intriguing. Isaiah 34:17 speaks of YHWH "casting the lot (גורל hiph. נפל)" and "apportioning by

layer of the book of Micah, then, sought to relate the book to the Amos/Joel/Obadiah/Malachi discussion of Edom's role in universal history. The text's apparent partiality to "all" of Jacob is an additional indicator of this redactional layer's relationship to the book of Isaiah, especially.[38]

3. Joel 4:1–3 (Eng., 3:1–3), on the other hand, distinguishes between the "captivity of Judah and Jerusalem" and the "Israelites who are dispersed among the nations." It envisions a period when YHWH will have restored (שׁוּב) the "captivity," but the "dispersion" remains among the nations, and may well reflect the circumstances of the Persian period, after the rebuilding of the temple.

4. Joel 4:16–21 (Eng., 3:16–21) employs the terms "Judah" and "Israel" in yet a third sense, identifying "sons of Israel" (v. 16) — the Zion reference in the context of a theophany establishes the Jerusalem orientation of this text — with "Judah" (v. 20; Zion is YHWH's dwelling place). The book of Zechariah also consistently treats "Israel" and "Judah" as synonyms (see 12:1–6). These texts reflect a period remote enough from the eighth-century crisis, on the one hand, and also from the Samaritan schism, on the other,[39] so that the name "Israel" has no negative connotations.

This synonymous usage also characterizes Mic 4:14 (Eng., 5:1), 5:1–2. Micah 4:14 belongs to the oldest core of Mic 4–5,[40] and may even

---

the line (חלק בקו)" when assigning Edomite territory to the wild animals and desert demons. Micah 2:5 speaks of YHWH disinheriting the greedy in Israel, leaving them with no one "to cast the line (חבל hiph. שׁלךּ) by lot (בגורל)."

[38] On the relationship between the redactional history of the book of Isaiah and the formation history of the Twelve, see Bosshard-Nepustil, "Beobachtungen zum Zwölfprophetenbuch," 30–62; Bosshard-Nepustil and Reinhard G. Kratz, "Maleachi im Zwölfprophetenbuch," *BN* 52 (1990): 27–46; Steck, *Abschluß.*

[39] It reflects not a tension between Jew and Samaritan, but conflict between Jerusalem and Judah. Cf. Larkin, *Eschatology of Second Zechariah,* 40–41, 140–45, 147–58.

[40] Wolff, *Dodekapropheton 4,* 108; T. Lescow, "Redaktionsgeschichtliche Analyse von Micha 1–5," *ZAW* 84 (1972): 65–74; Lescow, *Worte und Wirkungen,* 140–48. Rudolph (*Micha Nahum Habakuk Zephanja,* 93–94) associates Mic 4:14 with the Assyrian siege of Jerusalem described in 2 Kgs 18:17ff., 19:8. Zapff (*Redaktionsgeschichtliche Studien,* 125) comments that "none of the texts in Mic 4–5 is to be attributed to the prophet Micah himself. Instead, the oldest components of these chapters are to be dated, in any case, to the late pre-exilic period, more precisely in the period of the neo-Babylonian threat to Judah. That is, an original collection of the words of Micah, which is probably to be sought primarily in Mic 1–3, was actualized in the late pre-exilic period through references to the eighth-century threat (for example, by Mic 4:9, 10a, b, cα, 14)."

preserve a historical memory of the treatment of some Judean (Zion references) king at the hands of a foreign invader (the Babylonians?). Even the oldest portion of Mic 4–5, then, would date no earlier than the exilic period (cf. esp. Lam 3:30). Micah 5:1, on the other hand, while still employing "Israel" and "Judah" synonymously, reflects a period when expectations for the restoration of the Davidic monarchy ran high. Several allusions to other passages in the Twelve, especially Amos 9:11 and several "messianic" texts in Zechariah, establish the late exilic period as the intellectual milieu of Mic 5:1. The expression "as in the olden days" (Mic 5:1 [Eng., 5:2]) does not refer to the eternity of the Davidic line, but, synonymous with the usage in Amos 9:11, looks forward to the reestablishment of the throne. Avoidance of the term "king" characterizes late exilic/early–Persian period texts, written as they were in a period of heightened sensitivity to rebellion on the part of the imperial powers (for מושל see, for example, Zech 6:13). On the other hand, Mic 5:2, which refers to the exilic inhabitants of Eretz Israel as the "sons of Israel," seems to be motivated by a different source of embarrassment altogether, namely the delay in the restoration of the Davidic house. Micah's insistence on the insignificance of the Davidic house (which is never named) recalls Zech 12:6–14, which is also concerned with establishing that, despite the importance of the Davidites, the tribe of Judah (אלפי יהודה) is even more significant (Zech 12:4–6). It evidences, then, the common intellectual milieu of Mic 5:1–2 and portions of the book of Zechariah.

This use of "Israel" as a synonym for "Judeans" coincides substantially with usage in Mic 1, but not Mic 2–3. Given the composite nature of Mic 1, this resemblance suggests that the redaction responsible for the core of Mic 4–5 may also have given Mic 1:6–16 its current shape.

5. The precise connotation of "remnant of Jacob" in Mic 5:6, 7 depends entirely on (a) the significance of the metaphors of dew and rain in 5:6; (b) relatedly, whether v. 6 and v. 7 are to be understood synonymously; (c) whether v. 8 summarizes both vv. 6 and 7, v. 7 only, or is a later comment; and (d) what the phrase, repeated in both units, "in the midst of many nations," signifies. Metaphorically, "dew" can represent several notions in the Hebrew Bible. Because of its mysterious appearance, it can be likened to an ambush (1 Sam 17:12). In the arid Levant, it can symbolize fecundity (Gen 27:27–29; Deut 32:2; 33:13; Hos 14:6; Ps 133:3). Scholarly opinions range from Wolff's conclusion that "the first saying asks, then, not about what the 'remnant of Jacob' means for the nations, but about the wondrous origin of its future existence in

the midst of the nations,"[41] to Zapff's suggestion that "the promise of blessing given Jacob will be transferred, as it were, via the personified 'remnant of Jacob' to all the nations who...adopt a positive attitude toward the remnant of Jacob."[42]

Both vv. 6 and 7 supply the metaphors with an interpretive clause calling attention to the likeness. The remnant of Jacob will be like a lion in that it will "tread down and tear in pieces so that none can deliver." The similarity between the remnant and the dew and rain, on the other hand, hinges around the indifference of the dew and the rain to those whom it benefits. People hope for dew and rainfall; dew and rainfall "do not look for man, nor await the sons of man." They simply fall where they fall. The implication, then, seems to be that the remnant among the nations is indifferent to its impact upon them — certainly an unusual sentiment in the Hebrew Bible!

How does this sentiment relate to that expressed in v. 7? It may be significant that the explanatory clause in v. 7c is conditional: "if he [the lion] should pass through..." Verses 6–7 can be understood then as something of a warning not to disturb the remnant that wishes simply to be left alone. Should the nations disturb Jacob, the lion may well "tear, with none to deliver."

This sayings couplet concludes with a summary statement addressed to an unspecified masculine figure, presumably Jacob. Grammatically, if the conclusion means to continue vv. 6–7, it should address "the remnant," a feminine noun. Metaphors give way to idiomatic expression. Therefore, although v. 8 understands vv. 6–7 unambiguously, it can best be taken as the earliest commentary on these two units.

Finally, the phrase "in the midst of many nations (עמים רבים)" may be understood diametrically to mean either "in the midst of [each of] many nations" — that is, as the Diaspora (the image of the remnant spread abroad as the dew supports this interpretation) — or as a group gathered in one place, presumably Eretz Israel, whose place is "in the midst of the many nations." The seemingly redundant "among the peoples (בגוים)," likely a variant reading preserved in the MT, points to the former understanding.

---

[41] Wolff, *Dodekapropheton 4*, 129.

[42] Zapff, *Redaktionsgeschichtliche Studien*, 100–102. He considers it especially significant that the imagery of "dew" and of the "lion" both appear in the context of patriarchal promise ("dew," Gen 27:27–29) and blessing ("lion," Gen 49:9–10).

Israel and Jacob in the Prophetic Liturgy: Micah 6–7

Only one occurrence each of "Israel" and "Jacob" appears in the final section of the book. In both instances, the appeal to traditions common to the twelve tribes (exodus, Balaam, Abraham) obscures any political connotations for these terms. In fact, the universally Israelite tone of this material, probably the intentional result of the canonical redaction, points to the danger of overreliance on the presumed historical setting of the prophet's career as an interpretive key. These books have been consciously edited for use by later generations of any who call themselves "Israel."

Conclusions

In the book of Micah, as elsewhere in the Hebrew Bible, the terms "Jacob" and "Israel" may be seen as variables. The reader of Micah who seeks to establish their value confronts a bewildering situation. Read synchronously, the book sets the values of these terms in Mic 1:5 such that "Jacob = the northern kingdom" and "Israel = Judah." This equation, however, cannot be sustained throughout the book, and, since Mic 1:5 is clearly redactional, the critical reader may appeal to another basis for establishing the values of the key terms. Usually, interpreters privilege the prophet's assumed historical setting (established by the superscription to the book) and stipulated kerygmatic purpose (usually identified with the message of Mic 2–3). Read in this fashion, the book sets the values of the terms in Mic 3:1 such that "Jacob = Israel = Judah." This equation, however, seems ridiculous on its face and can be applied nowhere else in the book. Obviously, therefore, the ambiguity and variability of the terms "Jacob" and "Israel" in Micah point to its redactional history and give evidence of the relationship between Micah and the Minor Prophets.

The preliminary observations offered above yield at least five (also preliminary) conclusions. First, the Deuteronomistic heading assumes a book concerned with the fates of the capital cities of Israel and Judah. In fact, a significant portion of the book addresses these cities directly, often personifying them (Mic 1:6–16; 3:10–12; 4:1–14; 7:8–13). Notably, these passages do not employ the term "Jacob"[43] and use "Israel" in its broadest sense to include Judah. Consequently, the Deuteronomistic heading provides little data for understanding the terms as employed

---

[43] Disregarding the cultic phrase "God of Jacob" in 4:2.

in Micah, except to establish that the Deuteronomistic editor(s) worked with a book which could be considered to have joint addressees.

Second, Mic 1:5, which equates "Jacob" with the North and "Israel" with the South, gives every appearance of having been a late addition, itself concerned with clarifying the confusion in addressees in a preexisting book of Micah. It is particularly striking in its negative attitude toward Jerusalem, an attitude not otherwise attested in the Minor Prophets (cf. Isa 57).

Third, setting aside the question of "authentic" Mican usage — since the earliest form of the book possible to reconstruct will have been the form incorporated into a corpus, probably by the "Deuteronomistic" editors responsible for the heading — the vexing "summons to hear" formulae in Mic 3:1, 8, 9 must be interpreted in the *literary* context of the book of Micah and the Twelve. In other words, that the prophet may have been a southerner who would surely have addressed his message to his compatriots is of no consequence. In the context of the book, and certainly in the context of the Twelve, nothing prevents, and a great deal encourages, understanding Mic 3 as an accusation leveled at the leadership of both houses of Israel, whether "Jacob" and "Israel" are understood as a merism or as synonyms for all Israel.

Fourth, much of Mic 4–5 — excluding perhaps those portions of Mic 4:9–14 which may have figured in the accusation against Jerusalem in the earliest form of the book — displays significant affinity, lexically and theologically, with Zech 12–14. This material focuses on the remnant, whether designated "Jacob" or "Israel." Typical of late eschatological/ early apocalyptic works, these texts describe the nebulous situation in which the remnant found itself: amidst the nations, at enmity with them, hopeful of restoration, but unsure of the traditional foundations for that hope.

Fifth, Mic 2:12–13 (and Mic 1:2–4) also participate in a much broader program within the Twelve and within the prophetic corpus as a whole. Like Isa 34–35 and 63, and commenting on texts in Amos, Joel, Obadiah, and Malachi, these interrelated passages portray Edom as the first to suffer in the coming universal judgment against YHWH's enemies.

Finally, this analysis of the names "Israel" and "Jacob" in Micah suggests that the book of Micah contains materials related to its broader context in the Book of the Twelve on at least three levels, representing perhaps three distinct redactional phases: (*a*) Micah 1:16–3:12* and 4:9–14*, together with the "Deuteronomistic" superscription, seem to function, as Nogalski and others have argued, as a continuation and broadening of the accusations of Hosea and Amos (especially) to include Judah. (*b*) Micah 1:2–4 and 2:12–13 link the book to the Edom polemic, which stretches across the Twelve, adding to Micah an interest in universal judgment. (*c*) The final form of Mic 4–5 seems to be an "anthology"[44] of late postexilic reflections on the fate of the remnant, somehow related to Zech 12–14.

---

[44] On "anthologizing" as a late technique for extrapolating/exegeting existing prophecies, see Larkin, *Eschatology of Second Zechariah*, 32, 35–37.

11

The Zion-Daughter Oracles:
Evidence on the Identity and Ideology of
the Late Redactors of the Book of the Twelve

Byron G. Curtis

Words differently arranged have a different meaning,
and meanings differently arranged have a different effect.
— BLAISE PASCAL (1623–1662), *Les Pensées* #23.

Introduction

The final form of the Book of the Twelve presents the books of
Haggai, Zechariah, and Malachi as the closing portions of a large and
substantial work comprised of a dozen brief prophetic books. How
did this placement come about, and by whom was it accomplished?
In a 1993 SBL paper, "Social Location and Redaction History in the
Haggai-Zechariah-Malachi Corpus," I presented a theory of a multistage
redaction history of the Twelve, building in part on R. E. Wolfe's 1935
article on the editing of the Twelve, D. A. Schneider's 1979 dissertation
on the unity of the Twelve, and D. N. Freedman's 1987 article, "Headings in the Books of the Eighth-Century Prophets."[1] There I defended
a new proposal which in part claimed:

> By the end of the exile, then, a set of at least six, but likely seven, books already
> existed, promulgated in two groups of three, a Hezekian-era set [= Hosea-Amos-
> Micah] and a Josianic-era set [= Nahum-Habakkuk-Zephaniah], along with the
> insertion of Obadiah, composed just after Jerusalem's destruction and linked
> programmatically and intertextually with Amos, which it immediately follows.

---

[1] Roland E. Wolfe, "The Editing of the Book of the Twelve," *ZAW* 53 (1935):
90–129; Dale A. Schneider, "The Unity of the Book of the Twelve" (Ph.D. diss.,
Yale University, 1979); David N. Freedman's article now conveniently appears in *History and Religion* (ed. John R. Huddleston; vol. 1 of *Divine Commitment and Human
Obligation: Selected Writings of David Noel Freedman;* Grand Rapids: Eerdmans, 1997),
367–82.

Whether Joel or Jonah yet appeared within this collection is doubtful: post-exilic origins for these two books seem reasonably assured.[2]

My 1993 paper also identified a social location for the final stages of this redaction, namely, within a prophetic traditio-circle which was heir to the restorationist prophetic movement begun by the historical Haggai and Zechariah.

My proposal ran counter to the statement by P. D. Hanson, among others, that an early form of the Book of the Twelve once ended with Zech 8.[3] Rather, I proposed that the books of Haggai-Zechariah-Malachi comprised a single prophetic corpus at an early stage in their history and were added *as a group* to the preexisting collection that became the Twelve, a collection that ended with Zephaniah. Like J. Nogalski, whose Zurich dissertation also appeared in 1993,[4] but which I had not even heard of yet, I argued for several discrete literary precursors to the Twelve. Nogalski identified these as a Deuteronomistic group containing Hosea, Amos, Micah, and Zephaniah; and as a Haggai-Zechariah corpus ending with Zechariah 8. Also, as Nogalski did, I discerned a major redactional seam connecting Zeph 3 with the Haggai-Zechariah corpus. Like Nogalski, I was convinced (following Meyers and Meyers) that Haggai–Zech 1–8 once circulated independently.[5] Unlike Nogalski, I believed that this latter corpus was likely not attached to the body of the Twelve until it came to include Zech 9–14 and Malachi as well.

This essay seeks to augment my earlier proposal by examining the concluding portion of Zephaniah, the Zion-Daughter oracle of Zeph 3:14–20, and to relate this oracle to two later redactional seams in the Book of the Twelve, the new unit that begins in Zech 9, and the concluding "hem" in Mal 3:22–24. I argue that the Zion-Daughter oracle of Zeph 3:14–20 bears clear marks of redactional linking to the Haggai-Zechariah-Malachi corpus, and that this redactional work shows us something about the ideology and social location of these late redactors.

My essay proceeds first by interacting with some of the scholarship on the late redactions of the Twelve, especially by taking a fresh look at

---

[2] Byron G. Curtis, "Social Location and Redaction History in the Haggai-Zechariah-Malachi Corpus" (seminar paper, SBL, 1993), 4.

[3] Paul D. Hanson, *The Dawn of Apocalyptic* (rev. ed.; Philadelphia: Fortress, 1979), 386, n. 68.

[4] James D. Nogalski, *Literary Precursors to the Book of the Twelve* (BZAW 217; Berlin: de Gruyter, 1993). Part Two is separately entitled, *Redactional Processes in the Book of the Twelve* (BZAW 218; Berlin: de Gruyter, 1993).

[5] Eric M. Meyers and Carol L. Meyers, *Haggai–Zechariah 1–8* (AB 25B; Garden City, N.Y.: Doubleday, 1987).

Roland E. Wolfe's foundational 1935 paper on the subject;[6] second, with a detailed examination of the Zion-Daughter oracle in Zeph 3:14–20; third, with a tentative proposal that this redactional work is closely and intentionally related to the similar Zion-Daughter oracles in the Twelve, especially Zech 9:9–10; fourth, by arguing that the Zion ideology of this material comports well with the ideology and socio-literary ethos of the appendices to Malachi in 3:22–24 (Eng., 4:5–6); and fifth, by concluding that we perhaps may best look to the Zion-Daughter oracles and to the appendices of Malachi, taken together, as our clearest light on the latter redactors of the Twelve.

Review of the Scholarship

Modern discussion of the redaction history of the Twelve hearkens back to the important but unacceptably speculative work of Roland E. Wolfe. Prior to the publication of Wolfe's 1935 article, most discussion proceeded along the lines of an individual accumulation of scrolls.[7]

Wolfe proposed two distinct processes at work in the formation of the Twelve as a single composite scroll. First he proposed a source-critical analysis that divided the books into strands, with a separate redaction to incorporate each strand. The dozen strands he identified included an "anti-idol polemicist," a "doxologist," a group of "eschatologists," a "messianist," a "nationalist school," a "Judaistic editor of Hosea," and a "late exilic editor," among others, each assigned to a particular time and setting.

Second, he discerned stages to the collection of books. Thus the books of Hosea and Amos formed an original nucleus, a book of two. This was later expanded to form a "Book of the Six" comprised of Hosea, Amos, Micah, Nahum, Habakkuk, and Zephaniah. Later still, according to Wolfe, a single editor inserted Joel, Jonah, and Obadiah "at inopportune places," thus forming a "Book of the Nine." The final stage of adding whole books came with an alleged third-century scribal school that appended Haggai, Zechariah, and Malachi to form the Twelve. Supplementation and revision, he says, continued at least until the time of Ben Sira.[8]

---

6 Wolfe, "Editing of the Book of the Twelve." Wolfe's article is a condensation of his 1935 Harvard dissertation.

7 So Karl Budde, "Eine folgenschwere Redaktion des Zwölfprophetenbuchs," *ZAW* 39 (1921): 218–29.

8 Wolfe, "Editing of the Book of the Twelve," 93, 95, 107 and 118–22.

Wolfe succeeded in giving a new direction to scholarly research on the Twelve, but his documentary approach, modeled closely on the Graf-Wellhausen hypothesis, proved to be "too sweeping to be convincing."[9] Wolfe had merely identified common themes, phrasings, and genres within the prophetic collection and attributed each to a common source, in a mirror image of the Graf-Wellhausen hypothesis.

R. E. Wolfe also undermined the traditions of attribution within the Twelve, in which the origins of the individual books are carefully preserved by the attribution of authors' names. The final form of the scroll presents Hosea, Amos, Micah, Haggai, Zechariah, and so on as real individuals and as authors of portions of the whole. This point says nothing decisive against the common view that Malachi is an anonym, although it does stand in tension with E. Ben Zvi's view that the prophet Zephaniah is at best a shadowy figure loosely attached to the pre-compositional stage of the book that now bears his name.[10] But after all the historical, literary, and redactional analyses of the last hundred years are sifted, this tradition of named attributions remains our most powerful set of evidences about the origins of the Twelve. We should be loath to give it up. At the same time, the widespread realization that the Twelve has its own composite unity must surely alter the way we view the production of the individual books as we now possess them.

Wolfe himself may have been less than persuaded by his own proposal: although he claims to discern the redactional layering of the Twelve "almost as accurately as the various geological strata on a hillside slope," the concluding paragraph of his article calls it "merely a hypothetical reconstruction of an obscure chapter in the history of prophecy," a point ironically noted in W. Rudolph's response.[11]

Few have followed R. E. Wolfe in discerning so many redactional stratifications common to the books of the Twelve. But despite serious weaknesses, Wolfe asked many of the right questions and shed light on the path. For my purposes it is sufficient to point out a few of his proposals regarding redactions of Zephaniah, and their relationship to Zechariah.

---

[9] Elmer Dyck, "Jonah among the Prophets: A Study in Canonical Context," *JETS* 33 (1990): 63–73.

[10] Ehud Ben Zvi, *A Historical-Critical Study of the Book of Zephaniah* (BZAW 198; Berlin: de Gruyter, 1991).

[11] Wolfe, "Editing of the Book of the Twelve," 125, 129; Wilhelm Rudolph, *Haggai—Sacharja 1–8—Sacharja 9–14—Maleachi* (KAT 13/4; Gütersloh: Gütersloher, 1976), 299.

Wolfe believed, perhaps in spite of himself, that Zephaniah was an authentic seventh-century Judean prophet whose collected oracles — though much altered by many redactors — once concluded "the Book of the Six," and later "the Book of the Nine," to which Haggai-Zechariah-Malachi was then added. I think there is merit to this supposition.

He also believed, as have many both before and after, that Zeph 3 had undergone considerable redactional change over the generations. Zephaniah 3:5's paean to the righteous Yahweh who "does no wrong" and whose justice goes forth "morning by morning," accordingly, is ascribed to the psalm-loving eleventh editor, working between 275 and 250 B.C.E.[12] Yahweh's announcement of doom to the nations in Zeph 3:8, when he stands to testify against them on the day of his "burning anger," is attributed to the inspired redactor of protest, editor seven, the "Day of Yahweh" redactor who also penned the parallel "Day of Yahweh" passages in Amos, Obadiah, Joel, and Zeph 1–2, around 325 B.C.E. The remaining interpolations in Zeph 3, Wolfe says, are all attributable to an editorial school of "eschatologists," eighth in historical order, who worked around 300 B.C.E. These writers were also responsible for Zech 9:16–17's announcement that "on that day" Yahweh will "save his people like a flock." They also wrote virtually all of Zech 12–14, as well as many other passages from Hos 1 onward. It is to these prophets of eschatological salvation that Wolfe also attributes two portions of our Zion-Daughter oracle: Zeph 3:15b, and 3:18–20.

Several others members of the SBL's Seminar on the Formation of the Book of the Twelve have turned their attention to the difficult problems in the history of the Twelve, and with some similar results. J. Nogalski, for example, agrees that the book of Zephaniah once concluded what he has identified as one of two major "multi-volume corpora," which he usefully labels as "precursors" to the Twelve.[13] In 1996, Aaron Schart carried the case of the superscriptions a little further than D. N. Freedman had, by arguing that the unifying system of superscriptions in Hos 1:1, Amos 1:1, Mic 1:1, and Zeph 1:1 is matched by other unifying features such as the summons, "Hear...!" found in three of them, and by the "futility curses" found in all four, and thus the four books should be viewed as having been copied on one scroll.[14] Schart's

[12] Wolfe, "Editing of the Book of the Twelve," 114.

[13] Nogalski, *Literary Precursors.*

[14] Aaron Schart, "The Combination of Hosea, Amos, Micah, and Zephaniah on a Single Scroll: Unifying Devices and Redactional Intentions" (seminar paper, SBL, 1996).

view would seemingly support Freedman's generally early dating of the prophetic books. E. Ben Zvi, on the other hand, pushes the "compositional stage" of the book of Zephaniah into the postmonarchical era, and, with it, probably most of the Twelve.[15] Ben Zvi's distinctive approach is received with appreciation, though not full endorsement, by A. Berlin in her 1994 Zephaniah commentary, which leaves the dating issue unresolved.[16]

In my own view, I think it is significant that two of the presumably seventh-century books do not share the dated superscription form of the books surrounding them. Instead, "oracle" (מַשָּׂא [maśśā']) headings introduce the books of Nahum and Habakkuk. This incipit form does not persist in Zephaniah, which, in the order of reading, returns to the formulae of the books dated to the eighth-century kings, though, of course, updated to the late-seventh-century reign of King Josiah (1:1). No other book among the Twelve except for Zephaniah returns to employ the eighth-century superscription form.

In this regard, then, if we posit with Hans Walter Wolff an exilic-era Deuteronomistic redaction for the body of the Twelve ending with Zephaniah,[17] we then have no adequate way to account for the *Rezeptionsgeschichte* of Nahum and Habakkuk. Instead, I posit with F. I. Andersen and D. N. Freedman a Hezekian-era collection of three, and with Schneider a Josianic-era collection of three, which were then combined. In this way we may account for a greater number of the books within the Twelve.

Accordingly, I propose that an early version the Twelve, containing two preexilic collections of three books each (minus Isaiah), once circulated independently, a collection whose order was Hosea, Amos, and Micah followed by Nahum, Habakkuk, and Zephaniah. If this hypothesis is true, then Zephaniah's heading once would have formed an *inclusio* with the earliest headings in the collection. Nogalski calls this grouping of four headings a "framing device," and surely this is correct.[18] Such a literary linkage may provide further occasion for the relative clause's lengthy genealogy in Zeph 1:1. This clause, which links the prophet to an ancestral Hezekiah, also links this incipit to the eighth-century collection, whose incipits also contain the name Hezekiah (Hos 1:1; Mic

---

15 Ben Zvi, *Zephaniah*, 347–52.

16 Adele Berlin, *Zephaniah* (AB 25A; Garden City, N.Y.: Doubleday, 1994), 33–42.

17 Hans Walter Wolff, *Joel and Amos* (Hermeneia; Philadelphia: Fortress, 1977).

18 James D. Nogalski, "Intertextuality and the Twelve," in *Forming Prophetic Literature: Essays on Isaiah and the Twelve in Honor of John D. W. Watts* (ed. James W. Watts and Paul R. House; JSOTSup 235; Sheffield: Sheffield Academic Press, 1996), 118–19.

1:1). Presumably, since Hezekiah is an unusual name, the prophet is of the royal house, although, of course, this cannot be proved.[19]

Zephaniah's oracles of stern judgment and reform provide a fitting conclusion to the body of the Twelve in its late preexilic form. Since no allusion to Jerusalem's fall appears in these three books, and since their concern is, in Gottwald's words, with "the international power shift" from Neo-Assyria to Neo-Babylonia,[20] I think their first promulgation probably took place before 587. For these prophets and their early promulgators, Jerusalem may have been threatened, but it was not yet destroyed.

Zephaniah 3:14–20

Scholars have proposed many further expansions, supplementations, and redactions in the individual books of the Twelve. Most of these proposals proceed without particular regard for the scope of the whole collection, but only in light of the individual book or unit.[21] However, several passages evidence such substantial redactional shaping as to provide significant clues to the character of the redactional groups that lie behind them, and therefore have significant bearing on the social location and social-historical questions.

I propose then to discuss Zeph 3:14–20, with some reference to Zech 9 and Mal 3:22–24 (Eng., 4:4–6). The first and third of these stand as codas to the books that contain them; the second appears as the opening unit of Zech 9–14, which is (at least) a major compositional unit in its own right. All three units, therefore, stand at significant points in the overall compositional structure of the Twelve.

It has long been thought that the ending of the Zion-Daughter oracle in Zeph 3 contains exilic or postexilic supplementation. I think the coda of Zeph 3 provides evidence of supplementation that may supply a substantial clue to the identity of the final or near-final promulgators. In 1987, R. J. Coggins proposed a linkage between the close of Zeph 3 and the prophet Haggai:

---

[19] Joseph Blenkinsopp, *A History of Prophecy in Israel* (rev. ed.; Louisville: Westminster/John Knox, 1996), 113; Otto Eissfeldt, *The Old Testament: An Introduction* (trans. Peter R. Ackroyd; New York: Harper & Row, 1965), 425.

[20] Norman K. Gottwald, *The Hebrew Bible: A Socio-Literary Introduction* (Philadelphia: Fortress, 1985), 390.

[21] For recent discussion see Blenkinsopp, *History of Prophecy in Israel*.

In our present study we have seen links between Haggai and Zechariah and be-tween Zechariah and Malachi, and it is surely also legitimate to see Haggai's concern for the proper ordering of the temple as owing something to the hymnic passage in Zephaniah which immediately precedes it, promising a great festival in the temple on Zion when God himself would be in the midst of his people (Zeph 3:17f.). In just the same way Haggai's community could look forward to God's presence with them when all his commands had been carried out (Hag 2:5).[22]

I would like to suggest the specific manner in which such a linkage took place. As we shall explore below, Zeph 3:14–20 may serve as a linchpin in the latter phases of the growth of the Twelve. The text, with poetic delineation and prose-particle analysis, is reproduced below. Prose-particle analysis will be briefly explained thereafter.

Zeph 3:14–20: Text

Poetic-Accent Count	Prose-Particle Count	Poetic Delineation	
2+2		הָרִיעוּ יִשְׂרָאֵל	¹⁴רָנִּי בַּת־צִיּוֹן
3+1		בַּת יְרוּשָׁלָ͏ִם׃	שִׂמְחִי וְעָלְזִי בְּכָל־לֵב
3+2		פִּנָּה אֹיְבֵךְ	¹⁵הֵסִיר יְהוָה מִשְׁפָּטַיִךְ
3+3		לֹא־תִירְאִי רָע עוֹד׃	מֶלֶךְ יִשְׂרָאֵל יְהוָה בְּקִרְבֵּךְ
2+2	ה=1	יֵאָמֵר לִירוּשָׁלַ͏ִם	¹⁶בַּיּוֹם הַהוּא
2+2		אַל־יִרְפּוּ יָדָיִךְ׃	אַל־תִּירָאִי צִיּוֹן
3+2		גִּבּוֹר יוֹשִׁיעַ	¹⁷יְהוָה אֱלֹהַיִךְ בְּקִרְבֵּךְ
		יַחֲרִישׁ בְּאַהֲבָתוֹ	יָשִׂישׂ עָלַיִךְ בְּשִׂמְחָה
3+2+3			יָגִיל עָלַיִךְ בְּרִנָּה׃
transition to oracular prose?		מִמֵּךְ הָיוּ	¹⁸נוּגֵי מִמּוֹעֵד אָסַפְתִּי
2+2+3			מַשְׂאֵת עָלֶיהָ חֶרְפָּה׃

Prose-Accent Count	Prose-Particle Count	Delineation as Oracular Prose
5	את־ה=2	¹⁹הִנְנִי עֹשֶׂה אֶת־כָּל־מְעַנַּיִךְ בָּעֵת הַהִיא
4	את+ה+ה=3	וְהוֹשַׁעְתִּי אֶת־הַצֹּלֵעָה וְהַנִּדָּחָה אֲקַבֵּץ
5	ה=1	וְשַׂמְתִּים לִתְהִלָּה וּלְשֵׁם בְּכָל־הָאָרֶץ בָּשְׁתָּם׃
7	ה+את+את=3	²⁰בָּעֵת הַהִיא אָבִיא אֶתְכֶם וּבָעֵת קַבְּצִי אֶתְכֶם
5	את+ה=2	כִּי־אֶתֵּן אֶתְכֶם לְשֵׁם וְלִתְהִלָּה בְּכֹל עַמֵּי הָאָרֶץ
5	את=1	בְּשׁוּבִי אֶת־שְׁבוּתֵיכֶם לְעֵינֵיכֶם אָמַר יְהוָה׃

---

[22] Richard J. Coggins, *Haggai, Zechariah, Malachi* (OTG; Sheffield: JSOT Press, 1987), 85.

Zephaniah 3:14–20: Translation

poetry

14Shout for joy, O Zion-Daughter!
    Raise the triumph-call, O Israel!
Be glad and exult with all your heart,
    O Jerusalem-Daughter!
15Yahweh has cleared away your punishment,
    Swept away your enemies!
The King of Israel, Yahweh, lives among you;
    You shall fear disaster no more!

16On that Day
    It will be proclaimed to Jerusalem:
"Fear not!"—and to Zion:
    "Be not discouraged!"
17"Yahweh your God lives among you,
    A Hero who rescues!"
He delights over you with gladness;
    He is quiet in his love;
    He rejoices over you with singing.

18Those who were afflicted   [?]
transition   because of the appointed feasts
to oracular   —I have gathered [them].
prose??   They came from you;   [?]
        [But such] reproach [was] a burden on her. [?]

oracular prose

19"I will surely deal with all your oppressors at that Time!
I shall rescue the lame; and the scattered I shall gather!
I shall turn their shame into Praise and Fame in all the earth!

20At that Time I will bring you [home];
at [that] Time I will gather you.
For I shall make you Fame and Praise
among all the peoples of the earth,
when I restore your fortunes before your very eyes!"
    —says Yahweh.

The method of prose-particle analysis, though still in some respects experimental, produces significant results in distinguishing Hebrew poetry from Hebrew prose. This method was developed around 1980 by F. I. Andersen and D. N. Freedman, and based on massive computerized analyses of the Hebrew text.[23] The prose particles are the relative particle אשר, the definite direct-object marker את, and the definite article ה. It has long been noted that these particles are common in prose, but

23 F. I. Andersen and D. N. Freedman, "'Prose Particle' Counts of the Hebrew Bible," in *The Word of the Lord Shall Go Forth* (ed. Carol L. Meyers and M. O'Connor; Winona Lake, Ind.: Eisenbrauns, 1983), 165–83.

rare in poetry. The method measures the frequency of these three prose particles within any given text, and yields a percentage figure which represents the prose-particle density (PPD) of that text.

Freedman concludes, after a close comparison of the statistics with passages generally accepted as poetry and those generally accepted as prose, that "practically everything with a reading of 5% or less will be poetry," and "practically everything with a reading above 15% will be prose."[24] My own testing of the data sufficiently confirms this thesis to sustain the proposal as a good working hypothesis in adjudicating disputed texts and in discerning more precisely the boundaries between poetry and prose. Andrew E. Hill, who made his name as a scholar in the historical linguistic analysis of the book of Malachi, makes rich use of this method in his recent commentary. He uses the method to help determine Malachi's literary genre.[25]

Most oracular material happens to fall between Freedman's two limits, into a category many now call "oracular prose," a form of exalted prose speech that owes much to the line structure and ornamentation techniques employed in poetry.[26] On the other hand, M. O'Connor considers the book of Zephaniah to exemplify what he calls "prophetic verse," a style that A. Berlin calls "not formally metrical," but containing many poetic rhythms and tropes, enough for the book to qualify. Thus for O'Connor and Berlin, Zephaniah *is* verse, but of the prophetic variety.[27]

I shall not attempt to resolve the apparent incongruity between the two positions and their preferred terms, "oracular prose" and "prophetic verse." It is sufficient for this essay simply to note that regardless of the term, prophetic speech is dissimilar in some important respects from both the Hebrew of prose narrative, and from the Hebrew of the books universally recognized as poetry, such as the Psalms, Job, and Lamentations.

---

[24] David N. Freedman, "Another Look at Biblical Hebrew Poetry," in *Poetry and Orthography* (ed. John R. Huddleston; vol. 2 of *Divine Commitment and Human Obligation: Selected Writings of David Noel Freedman;* Grand Rapids: Eerdmans, 1997), 215. Freedman's article originally appeared in 1987.

[25] Andrew E. Hill, *Malachi* (AB 25D; Garden City, N.Y.: Doubleday, 1998). See the book's bibliography for Hill's published articles on the historical linguistics of Malachi and Zech 9–14.

[26] So Meyers and Meyers, *Haggai, Zechariah 1–8*, lxiv; and most recently, Hill, *Malachi*, 26.

[27] Michael O'Connor, *Hebrew Verse Structure* (Winona Lake, Ind.: Eisenbrauns, 1980), 240–62; Berlin, *Zephaniah*, 11.

Freedman also suggests that prose-particle counts (PPCs) may help us distinguish earlier poetry from later poetry. He writes: "There is some evidence to show that the so-called prose particles are almost entirely absent from the earliest poetry, while they increase in number in late poetry."[28] This tool has limits, however: while no early poetry features high PPCs, some late poems have low PPCs.

The Masoretic Text of Zephaniah contains 767 words, of which 94 are prose particles. Thus the PPD for Zeph 1–3 is 12.3 percent, which lies within Freedman's designated range for oracular prose. Detailed examination of the individual units of Zephaniah yields a more complex picture. If we follow the delineation of units presented in *BHS*, with only a few revisions, the following picture appears:

Zephaniah 1–3, Prose-Particle Density

Unit	Descriptor	PPC	Words	PPD (%)
Zeph 1:1	superscription	1	20	5.0
1:2–3	against all earth	9	27	33.3
1:4–6	against Judah	19	43	44.2
1:7	"Hush!..."	0	14	0.0
1:8–9	against Judah's princes	7	28	25.0
1:10–11	against merchants	5	27	18.5
1:12–13	against the complacent	6	35	17.1
1:14–16	"Yahweh's great Day..."	7	39	17.9
1:17–18	"I will bring distress..."	3	36	8.3
Subtotal for Chapter 1		57	269	21.2
Zeph 2:1–3	"Gather the nations..."	4	43	9.3
2:4–7	against Philistia	2	39	5.1
2:8–11	against Moab & Ammon	5	80	6.3
2:12	against Cush	0	6	0.0
2:13–15	against Assyria	6	54	11.1
Subtotal for Chapter 2		17	222	7.7
Zeph 3:1–5	"Woe to the city..."	2	54	3.7
3:6–8	"I have cut off nations..."	3	58	5.2
3:9–13	"I will purify..."	2	70	2.9
3:14–18	"Shout, Zion-Daughter..."	1	55	1.8
3:19–20	"At that Time..."	12	39	30.8
Subtotal for Chapter 3		20	276	7.2
Zephaniah Total		94	767	12.3

---

[28] Freedman, *Poetry and Orthography*, 214.

According to the charted analysis, the book of Zephaniah's highest PPD occurs in the cluster of units from 1:2 to 1:16. There the PPD ranges as high as 44.2 percent. One single line, the "Hush..." of 1:7, contains no prose particles, but the remainder is rich with them. The highest densities are found in the oracles of judgment against all the earth (1:2–3 = 33.3), against Judah (1:4–6 = 44.2), and against Judah's princes (1:8–9 = 25.0). This pattern breaks off in 1:17–18, where the PPD is only 8.3 percent, in a passage which otherwise looks like a continuation of the "Day of Yahweh" oracle of 1:14–16. The high PPD is peculiar for a prophetic book, and more closely matches the PPD of prose-narrative books.

The 8.3 percent PPD of this last unit of Zeph 1, 1:17–18, comports well with Zeph 2, which averages a PPD of 7.7 percent, with a plus-or-minus deviation of only 3.4. On these grounds, perhaps Zeph 1:17–18 should be associated more closely with Zeph 2 than with Zeph 1 in future analyses of the book's rhetorical structure.

Every rhetorical unit of Zeph 2, with the exception of the single-line oracle against Cush in 2:12, falls within Freedman's 5 percent to 15 percent range for oracular prose, and in this respect its PPD of 7.7 percent is unremarkable.

Zephaniah 3, however, bears a remarkable feature. The whole chapter averages a PPD of 7.2 percent, very close to the previous chapter's 7.7 percent. But this percentage masks an important difference. The whole chapter, except for 3:19–20, has a very low PPD. Factoring out the last unit, Zeph 3:1–18 has a PPD of 3.4 percent, with a deviation of a mere plus-or-minus 1.8. Zephaniah 3:19–20, on the other hand, has no less than 12 prose particles in 39 words, yielding a PPD of 30.8 percent, a very high figure.

As Berlin's discussion of the divisions of the text of Zephaniah indicates, the majority of interpreters take Zeph 3:14 to be the beginning of a new rhetorical unit; many consider the unit to extend to the end of the chapter, to 3:20.[29] But the prose-particle analysis suggests that 3:19–20 is a prose elaboration of a poetic oracle. To my mind it looks like a commentary on a previously existing poetical text. Note the PPD figures for Zeph 3:14–20:

Unit	Descriptor	PPC	Words	PPD (%)
3:14–18	"Shout, Zion-Daughter..."	1	55	1.8
3:19–20	"At that Time..."	12	39	30.8

[29] Berlin, *Zephaniah*, 18–19.

Ivan J. Ball observes that most of Zephaniah is written with a low density of parallelism and meter, but that twice the book reaches "a high density of parallelism and meter, at the two most significant and climactic points in Zephaniah, breaking into 'pure' poetry." The first occasion appears in what he calls the "great hymn on the 'Day of Wrath'" in 1:15–16; the second appears in the "Zion hymn of YHWH's kingship" in 3:14–17.[30] Ball uses these observations as a rhetorical argument for the strong authorial unity of the book. Such unity is also advocated by O. Palmer Robertson.[31]

I am reluctant to separate out supposedly "secondary" material embedded within otherwise original prophetic oracles. I think that it is better to err (if it is to err) on the side of caution with the claim that the collections of prophetic oracular and visionary material we now call books were preserved with comparatively little redactional supplementation to the oracles and prophetic speeches themselves. Editorial activity, of course, is abundant in the collection, least obtrusively in the shaping and framing of the material. But the newer approach to the Twelve, reading the book as an editorially constructed composite, as exemplified by the members of this SBL Seminar, permits us to see a broader range of redactional activity at work.

Supplementation, when it does occur, is more likely at the links between groups and collections of oracles, and at the opening and closing of particular books. Thus we ought to look for supplementation in the penning of editorial superscriptions and in introductory marks at the heads of books, in closing appendices, summaries, parting exhortations, or colophons at the ends, and at the seams between the collected portions of whole books, as Mark Biddle argued in this seminar in 1996, and as J. Nogalski's work, *Literary Precursors to the Book of the Twelve* and *Redactional Processes in the Book of the Twelve,* amply displays.[32] This is difficult work, and finding supplementation elsewhere is even more difficult work, as any perusal of J. Nogalski's work will show.

In making this claim, I do not wish to rule out the kind of editorial

[30] Ivan J. Ball, *A Rhetorical Study of Zephaniah* (Berkeley, Calif.: Bibal Press, 1988), 12–13.

[31] O. Palmer Robertson, *The Books of Nahum, Habakkuk, and Zephaniah* (NICOT; Grand Rapids: Eerdmans, 1990). P. R. House argues for a thematic unity to the book. See his *Zephaniah: A Prophetic Drama* (Sheffield: Almond Press, 1989).

[32] Mark E. Biddle, "Intertextuality, Micah, and the Book of the Twelve: A Question of Method" (seminar paper, SBL, 1996). For a published discussion along similar lines, see David N. Freedman, "Headings in the Books of the Eighth-Century Prophets," *AUSS* 25 (1987): 9–26. See n. 4 above for Nogalski's works.

activity described by R. E. Clements in his insightful essay, "The Prophet and His Editors." While emphasizing the role of the redactors as *re-* appropriaters of the prophetic word for new generations, Clements can still write: "Fundamentally, we encounter prophetic literature as a written record based on messages that prophets originally spoke to their contemporaries."[33] I think that — even after Nogalski — this claim is still sustainable.

Arguments for authorial unity such as Ivan Ball's bear more weight if Zephaniah, Ball's example, is seen as an isolated literary unit. But the Book of the Twelve bears an editorially constructed aspect as a collected and composite work. If, as I have argued, the body of the Twelve probably once concluded with Zephaniah, in a book of six or probably seven prophets, then the closing oracle of Zephaniah is a very likely place to look for a bridgelike editorial link between the preexilic/exilic collection and the postexilic concluding trilogy.

Many scholars have seen supplementation in the conclusion of Zephaniah, usually arguing on historical and ideological grounds. A recent proposal along these lines comes from Mária Széles, who posits a long development of the book, from original preexilic sayings to a final postexilic arrangement and editing. Regarding Zeph 3:14–20, she writes:

> Finally, in several stages, prophecies on salvation [appear] in 3:14–20.... The latest sections are to be attributed to a period after the return from exile...the closing declaration being 3:16–20. Here there appear the typical eschatological motifs of the later period — the overcoming of the power of the enemy, the restoration, the gathering together of the diaspora, the promise of a safe and peaceful life, and the enhancement of the chosen people before the eyes of the pagans.[34]

And:

> It is probable that verse 17 is a gloss originating from the captivity or from a period after it. On the basis of the influence of the previous verses, the editor has here written down his own witness to the promised future.[35]

Széles attributes 3:18–20 to a late postexilic editor of the whole book. That such views are commonly held is attested by their presence in the 1973 *New Oxford Annotated Bible*'s notes on Zeph 3, which remain unre-

---

[33] Ronald E. Clements, "The Prophet and his Editors," in *The Bible in Three Dimensions* (ed. D. J. A. Clines et al.; JSOTSup 87; Sheffield: JSOT Press), 205.

[34] Maria Széles, *Wrath and Mercy: A Commentary on the Books of Habakkuk and Zephaniah* (trans. G. A. F. Knight; International Theological Commentary; Grand Rapids: Eerdmans, 1987), 64–65.

[35] Ibid., 113.

vised in the 1991 edition. Both editions report that the whole of 3:14–20 is held to be a later addition.

At the extreme we may take Louise P. Smith and Ernest R. Lacheman. Their professed aim is to consider the book "as a whole" with its "chief emphases," yet in the process they find a complex series of layerings, from a single old and original Zephaniah oracle to heavily redacted late apocalyptic material, dating to the crisis of Jerusalem's Hellenists of 200 B.C.E. "Luckily the survival of a name (1:1, Zephaniah) in connection with the old oracle (1:4ff.) gave it its place in the Book of the Twelve."[36] Smith and Lacheman do not appear to be troubled by Ben Sira's reference to the Twelve ca. 180 B.C.E., comfortably surmising that he refers to a recent production, newly enrolled in the collection of sacred books.

The only prose particle within 3:14–18 is in the formulaic ביום ההוא of 3:16. If the thirty-nine words of 3:19–20 are analyzed separately from the fifty-five words of 3:14–18, the percentage yield for prose particles for 3:14–18 then equals a mere 1.8 percent, while it equals 30.8 percent for 3:19–20. It is possible that Ball is right in seeing artful rhetorical work here, an original prose elaboration of an original poetic oracle. However, another solution also seems possible. The low percentage for 3:14–18 is generally consistent with early oracular and poetic material; the high percentage for 3:19–20 is generally consistent with later oracular prose.

Seen in this light, it is possible to read Zeph 3:14–20 as an early poetic oracle with its own late prose commentary, suffused with restorationist ideology. Zephaniah 3:14–18 contains the generic language of the victory hymn in which no fixed events can be identified. The unit's themes of expulsion of the enemy and Yahweh's victorious habitation of Zion are common eschatological motifs with a long history in Israel's prophetic literature, as G. von Rad and many others have shown. Only in 3:19–20 do the historically specific themes of return from exile and Zion's restoration appear.

In making this observation I do not claim, as many have, that prophetic sayings of return to the homeland must be late in origin. The punitive policies of the Neo-Assyrians included population deportation, and render credible both the threats of deportation and the promises of return found in even the earliest prophetic books.[37] The Akkadian

---

[36] Louise P. Smith and Ernest R. Lacheman, "The Authorship of the Book of Zephaniah," *JNES* 9 (1950): 137–42, at 137.

[37] Francis I. Andersen and David N. Freedman, *Amos* (AB 24A; Garden City, N.Y.: Doubleday, 1989), 893.

"Poem of Erra," dated to no later than about 750 B.C.E., features the themes of national remnant and national restoration, including, like statements in the Hebrew prophetic books, promises of renewed fertility, rebuilt temples, and hegemony over enemy peoples.

Accordingly, as in Zeph 3 and in the endings of several of the individual books, the Erra poem concludes with the god Erra decreeing the restoration of the ravaged country and promising to the decimated Babylonians a great victory over their enemies. Erra promises the scattered Babylonian remnant that they shall again be great, and receive the tribute of all the surrounding countries.[38]

Also, as Hans Walter Wolff pointed out, the expression שׁוּב שְׁבוּת, "restore the fortunes" (only in Hos 6:11; Joel 4:1 [Eng., 3:1]; Amos 9:14; and Zeph 2:7 and 3:20 among the Twelve), so often attributed only to late sources, has an eighth-century parallel in the Sefire treaty stele (line 3.24), in which the cognate phrase הֵשִׁיב שְׁבִית, "to cause the restoration of," is attested.[39] The concluding *topoi* of return and restoration in Zeph 3:19–20, however, provide an ideal bridge to the restorationist oracles of Haggai, and, indeed, to the remaining corpus of the Twelve: Haggai, Zechariah, and Malachi. Zephaniah 3:14–20 thus serves not merely as an appendix to Zephaniah, but as an introduction to the prophets of Zion's restoration.

Zephaniah 3:14–20 and the Book of the Twelve

R. J. Coggins's suggestion has led us to propose a specific manner in which Zeph 3 relates to the subsequent body of restorationist prophecy of the Twelve. Zephaniah 3:14–18 stand as an early oracle pointing to the restorationist hope. This was the unit that concluded the body of the Twelve in its exilic and early postexilic form. I wish to hypothesize, then, that Zeph 3:19–20 is the late, editorial addition *created specifically by the promulgators of the restorationist prophecy now located in the concluding trilogy*

---

[38] G. W. Lambert, "The Poem of Erra," *Iraq* 24 (1962): 119–25.

[39] Wolff, *Joel and Amos*, 76 n. 19. An impressive collection and discussion of deportation themes in ancient Near Eastern literature, drawn from Egyptian, Hittite, Sumerian, Mari, Nuzi, Babylonian, Assyrian, Neo-Assyrian, and Israelite sources, can be found in J. B. Diggs, "Implications from Ancient Near Eastern Deportation Practices for an Understanding of the Authorship of עַד־בָּבֶל in Micah 4:10" (Ph.D. diss., Southwestern Baptist Theological Seminary, 1988). Some of this material is also surveyed in Gerhard Hasel, *The Remnant: The History and Theology of the Remnant Idea from Genesis to Isaiah* (Berrien Springs, Mich: Andrews University Press, 1974).

of the Twelve. Our holistic and redactional reading makes this conclusion plausible, perhaps probable, though far from certain.

This reading of the Twelve may be pressed still further. The Zion-Daughter oracle of Zeph 3 has a literary connection to the Zion-Daughter oracle of Zech 9. I suggest that these two units were editorially and thematically significant for the redactors responsible for appending Haggai-Zechariah-Malachi to the trunk of the preceding books. The two Zion-Daughter oracles thus appear in strategic redactional points within the Book of the Twelve.[40] The first, Zeph 3:14–20, bridges the gap from the preexilic prophets to the restorationist prophets; the second, Zech 9:9–10, bridges the gap from the early restorationists, Haggai and Zechariah, to the later restorationist prophets represented in Zech 9–14 and Malachi.

The prose-particle count for this unit, Zech 9, is 3 out of 196 words, yielding a PPD of 1.5 percent. This count is exceedingly low for postexilic Hebrew literature. How may one account for this phenomenon?

The Zion-Daughter oracle tradition, a kind of microcosm within the whole Zion tradition, plays a key role.[41] Both oracles represent a relatively early linguistic stratum; both appear in contexts that include much later material. The late prose commentary on the early poetic oracle of Zeph 3 matches the postexilic context of the reuse of Zech 9. I wish to hypothesize, then, that the oracle in Zeph 3:14–18 is early, roughly matching the original date for the oracle now contained in Zech 9, and that the prosaic material of Zeph 3:19–20 is a late editorial addition to that book, roughly matching the date at which the original and irrecoverable form of Zech 9 found a significant reuse in the early Persian period, as suggested by C. L. Meyers and E. M. Meyers.[42]

There is, I think, little merit in the oft-repeated conclusion that Zech 9:13's oracle against Greece points to a fourth-century origin or later for that portion of the book. The oracle declares that Yahweh "will arouse

---

[40] The expression בת־ציון ("Zion-Daughter") appears elsewhere within the Book of the Twelve only at Mic 1:3; 4:8, 10, 13; and Zech 2:7, 10. Micah 4 is a loose collection of Zion oracles; 4:9–11 may be seen as the converse side of the בת־ציון tradition. There the woman-figure, bereft of king and counselor, cries out in agony. In Zech 9:9–10, she cries out for joy when the king appears. In both oracles the verb used is the hiphil of רוע, "cry out, shout," but with opposite rhetorical effect.

[41] Elsewhere in Zechariah, the appeal to the exiles in 2:10f. (Eng., 2:6f.) depends on the בת־בבל / בת־ציון ("Babel-Daughter"/"Zion-Daughter") wordplay of 2:11 and 14.

[42] C. L. Meyers and E. M. Meyers, *Zechariah 9–14* (AB 25C; New York: Doubleday, 1993).

your sons, O Zion, against your sons, O Greece, and wield you like a warrior's sword." This declaration comports well with what we now know about the early Persian period.

The Greeks posed a significant threat to Persian interests from at least the time of the revolt of the Ionian cities (500–494 B.C.E.). Athens and Eretria aided the Ionians against Persia, starting in 499 B.C.E. Herodotus viewed the later campaigns of Darius I and Xerxes as punishment against Athens' intervention.[43] Athens also aided the Libyan chieftain, Inaros, in his Egyptian-based revolt against the Persians in 464 B.C.E., at great expense to both sides.[44] Persian loyalists such as Zerubbabel, Ezra, and Nehemiah, most likely would have sided with their Persian masters against any perceived Greek threat. It is in this historical setting that we likely ought to understand the reference against Greece in Zech 9:13. The sole historical marker in Zech 9 — the reference against Greece in 9:13 — and the prose-particle analysis of the unit both permit an early–Persian period setting for the unit.

Conclusion

The Zion-Daughter oracles of Zeph 3 and Zech 9 may then mark the seams of the closure of the Twelve, standing as they do between the seventh- and the sixth-century prophets on the one hand, and between the sixth- and the fifth-century prophets on the other. They therefore provide a clue to the redactional intent in the collection and juxtaposition of these prophetic books: a single group may well have been responsible for this late stage of the work. That group had a devoted theological and political interest in the restorationist program announced in the Zion-Daughter oracles; the group believed that the prophets Haggai and Zechariah had pioneered in the fulfillment of the restorationist ideal; and the group believed that the restorationist ideal had been betrayed by the later generations.

This profile of the group's ideology and identity corresponds well with the majority-view profile of the leadership group represented in the postexilic historical sources by the social-reformer figures of Ezra and Nehemiah, and in the prophetic sources by their contemporary,

---

[43] See the discussion in R. Sealey, *A History of the Greek City States, 700–338 B.C.* (Berkeley: University of California Press, 1976), 169–94.

[44] Kenneth G. Hoglund, *Achaemenid Imperial Administration in Syria-Palestine and the Missions of Ezra and Nehemiah* (SBLDS 125; Atlanta: Scholars Press, 1992), 137–64.

the figure of Malachi, Yahweh's anonymous "Messenger."[45] It is, I think, to this generation that we may look for the first promulgators of the collection in its now achievable twelve-part form. Hence the terrible threat found in the collection's editorial conclusion calls Judeans back to the enduring prophetic word, which has now found a new canonical shape as the Book of the Twelve:

> *Behold, I will send you Elijah the prophet*
> *before the great and terrible Day of Yahweh comes*
> *And he will turn the hearts of the fathers to their children*
> *and the hearts of the children to their fathers,*
> *lest I come and smite the land with a curse.*
> — Mal 3:23–24 (Eng., 4:5–6)

---

[45] Ibid.; H. G. M. Williamson, *Ezra and Nehemiah* (OTG; Sheffield: JSOT Press, 1987); Coggins, *Haggai, Zechariah, Malachi,* 72–74.

12

Remnant, Redactor, and Biblical Theologian:
A Comparative Study of Coherence
in Micah and the Twelve

Kenneth H. Cuffey

Introduction

Modern critical scholarship has both dissected and reassembled the books of the prophets. As a result of seeing discontinuities in the text, studies have portrayed fragmented books, each composed of pieces from various periods and hands. More recently, redaction-critical analysis has sought to understand not only the disparate origins of the pieces, but also the ways in which they were brought together to form the collections we now have.

Of late, there has been a new trend in biblical studies in general. This trend begins with the text in its final form and tries to explain what the text means, as it now stands. The interest is not only in how it got to be this way, but also in what the significance of the present shape might be for understanding the message and theology of whoever put it into that form. Correspondingly the focus shifts from the recovery of the *ipsissima verba* of the prophet to the interpretation of the final form, or, beyond that, of the "canonical" form.

Consider Micah as an example. The book of Micah has been mined for many discontinuities in critical research and is viewed as having a complicated redactional history. Possibly as a result, it has also been the focus of a number of studies which look at the book as a whole and attempt to discover if it can be understood as a complete interpretive unit. This research asks questions about issues of coherence such as whether or not the final form evidences a central, unified theme/message, what

With an initial note of gratitude to Dr. John Watts both for his influence in the Seminar on the Formation of the Book of the Twelve and his personal encouragement to me to pursue the following project.

185

connections between the parts hold them together, or what progression of thought can be traced through the final form of book.

Paralleling these researches into the literary coherence and canonical shaping of individual books has been a desire to trace the canonical process in larger portions of the Hebrew Bible. One specific field of inquiry has been the exploration of interconnections (i.e., coherence) within the Book of the Twelve. In focus here is how one reads the Twelve as a unity, and whether or not anyone ever intended for the Twelve to be regarded as a whole and complete literary work itself.

This essay seeks to compare and contrast the types of coherence found by scholars in studying a particular Book of the Twelve, Micah, with the coherence being claimed for the Book of the Twelve as a whole. Are these coherences similar or of a different kind altogether? In what ways? What do the likenesses or dissimilarities imply about the editing of the Twelve or the quest to find an overarching coherence among the books of the Twelve?

As a framework for discussion, the first task will be to define coherence and to offer a framework for understanding its varieties. Due to its limited scope, this essay will only present one case for seeing a thoroughgoing coherence in Micah and then compare this with a few significant studies that do the same for the Twelve as a whole. It is hoped that the comparisons and contrasts drawn will serve as a basis for further discussion about the nature of what is found and the directions this finding suggests for the future.

The Nature of Coherence

For the purposes of this study, "coherence" refers to the connectedness of a work. Any features which connect individual parts with each other, or all the parts into a whole, contribute to coherence in a work of literature. For discussion, I propose and use the following classification of the different types of coherence that may be found in works of prophetic literature.[1]

First, there is *internal coherence*. Recurrent features of style or the specification of transitions or connections can clarify the relations of section

---

[1] This system for classifying coherence is explained, documented, and illustrated in more detail in my dissertation, "The Coherence of Micah: A Review of the Proposals and a New Interpretation" (Drew University, 1987), 124–64. This work also contains a detailed exposition of the proposal I make in this essay for understanding the coherence of Micah in its final form.

to section or to the whole. Examples of indicators that would contribute to such coherence would be a consistent style of writing, the use of coordinate conjunctions and words that specify transitions (e.g., "moreover," "however," "or," "then," "next," "first," "thus"), repetition, catchwords, parallelism, or synonyms.

Second, literary works may have a *structural coherence*. In this case, the arrangement, or ordering, of the parts makes the work a connected whole. The arrangement, by placing the sections in a larger framework, indicates the way each part is to be construed. The larger context of the whole book can determine the meaning of a part, possibly in a way that differs from the reading we would have given that part in isolation. The parts are subordinated, then, to the purposes of the whole by means of the order. For example, the parts of a work can be arranged according to an order that is chronological, spatial, logical, rhetorical, natural, associational, or climactic.

Third, there is *coherence of perspective*. The perspective which underlies a work is another potential source of coherence. Common assumptions held throughout a piece of literature, a common situation as background, or the consistent outlook/viewpoint of an author or redactor may serve to connect the parts together into a whole.

Fourth, the parts of a work can be connected by *coherence of theme*. A key theme, or themes, may serve as a center around which all the parts are united and integrated. All the parts talk about the same thing. The common meaning found in the recurrence of a significant concept, of a dominant motif, or of a developed plot or argument all may serve as indicators of coherence of theme. One may look for a principle that creates oneness for a literary text, and then evaluate how the different components of the piece are integrated around that principle.

Coherence in the Book of Micah

Before examining the coherence found in the Book of the Twelve as a whole unit, it will be beneficial to look at the coherence of the final form of the book of Micah. Numerous attempts have been made to discover coherence in Micah.[2] Coherence of each type, or on every

---

[2] The most thorough works devoted to this topic have been those by John Willis and David Hagstrom. See especially John Willis, "The Structure of the Book of Micah," *SEÅ* 34 (1969): 5–42; and David Hagstrom, "The Coherence of the Book of Micah: A Literary Analysis" (Ph.D. diss., Union Theological Seminary in Virginia, 1982). The dissertation has since been published under the same title as SBLDS 89

level, has been proposed. This particular proposal for understanding the connectedness of the text will begin by making a case for a clear structuring of the materials in the book. Internal coherence will serve as confirming evidence for the existence of this structural coherence. The structure itself will suggest a primary theme or message that runs from start to finish through Micah as we now have it. Naturally this unified message, enforced by a particular ordering of the materials, will give rise to speculation about a coherent perspective which informs the whole of the book in its final form.

Structural Coherence

Several understandings of the overall structure of Micah have usually been advanced in commentaries and introductions. These structures have often been based on critical concerns about the development of the collection before the book attained its present form. Though this is an important issue, framing the question in this manner does not address the literary arrangement of the final form. The book of Micah, it has been argued, was arranged according to the following patterns:

(*a*) Micah 1–3/4–7. This outline has been based on the old critical judgment about the growth of the book, that the genuine material is in Mic 1–3 and the secondary, later materials are to be found in 4–7.[3] Note, however, that this is not an evaluation of the literary ordering of the final form. Rather it reflects the conclusions of certain scholars concerning the origins of the oracles.

(*b*) 1–3/4–5/6–7. Usually this arrangement has been based on grouping the contents into a section of threat (dismissing 2:12–13 as a later addition), followed by promises (4–5), followed by both threat and promise (6–7).[4] At least two issues must be raised regarding this

---

(Atlanta: Scholars Press, 1988). In addition, a recent commentary by Bruce Waltke does an outstanding job of cataloging and analyzing the textual data that lends a sense of connectedness to the book of Micah ("Micah," in *The Minor Prophets: An Exegetical and Expository Commentary* [ed. T. McComiskey; Grand Rapids: Baker, 1993], 2.591–764).

[3] Examples of scholars who advance this understanding would be Paul Haupt, "Critical Notes on Micah," *AJSL* 26 (1910): 201; idem, "The Book of Micah," *AJSL* 27 (1911): 15–16; Karl Budde, "Verfasser und Stelle von Mi. 4,1–4 (Jes 2,2–4)," *ZDMG* 81 (1927): 156–57.

[4] So Theodore Robinson, *Die Zwölf Kleinen Propheten: Hosea bis Micha* (trans. Otto Eissfeldt; 3d ed.; HAT 14; Tübingen: Mohr, 1964), 127–28. Also Ina Willi-Plein, *Vorformen der Schriftexegese innerhalb des Alten Testaments* (BZAW 123; New York: de Gruyter, 1971), 110; A. van Hoonacker, *Les douze petits prophetes* (Études bibliques; Paris: J. Gabalda, 1908), 340, 347, 353.

structure. If the question is the coherence of the final form, any proposal must treat Mic 2:12–13 where it stands. In addition, Mic 4–5 does not read as a uniform section of promise. Significant segments of these two chapters sound like threat and doom (e.g., Mic 4:9–11; 5:1, 3).

(c) 1–3/4–5/6:1–7:6(7)/7:7(8)–20. Actually a variation of (b), this ordering brings out the double alternation of threat and promise by subdividing Mic 6–7 on the same criterion used in the first two sections.[5]

(d) 1–5/6–7. This arrangement attempts to deal with the difficulty of dividing between Mic 1–3 and 4–5. These chapters are too closely tied by an *inclusio* (the nations in 1:2; 5:14), discussion of leadership issues in chapter 3 and again in 4:1–8, and the consistent message. This reading also brings out the contrasts between chapters 1–5 and 6–7.[6] Yet it overlooks the shifts in tone from negative to positive between Mic 2:11 and 12, as well as between 3:12 and 4:1. In addition, this proposal masks the transition from positive to negative at Mic 2:13–3:1 and the intermixing of hope and doom in 4:9–5:14.

(e) 1–2/3–5/6–7. This arrangement accounts for the apparent hope in Mic 2:12–13, divides the material so that each section starts with "Hear!" and maintains consistent alternation between condemnation and salvation. The shift takes place three times.[7] On the other hand, this proposal must explain occurrences of the summons to hear which do not begin major sections (Mic 3:9; 6:2, 9) and the differences in content, including both judgment and promises of salvation, in chapters 3–5.

Retrospect on Structure

Structural coherence interrelates with the other types of coherence. The order of the parts, for example, may suggest that a particular theme is being emphasized. Or the internal links in the text may build a case for the overall structuring.

---

[5] Artur Weiser, *Die Propheten Hosea, Joel, Amos, Obadja, Jona, Micha* (vol. 1 of *Das Buch der zwölf Kleinen Propheten;* 5th ed.; ATD 24; Göttingen: Vandenhoeck & Ruprecht, 1967), 231; Hans Walter Wolff, *Micah: A Commentary* (trans. G. Stansell; Continental Commentaries; Minneapolis: Augsburg, 1990), 17–26; Georg Fohrer, *Introduction to the Old Testament* (initiated by Ernst Sellin; trans. D. Green; Nashville: Abingdon, 1968), 444.

[6] James Mays, *Micah: A Commentary* (OTL; Philadelphia: Westminster, 1976), 2–12; also Hagstrom, "Coherence," 39–48, 193–201, 203–4.

[7] See Willis, "Structure"; also Wilhelm Rudolph, *Micha-Nahum-Habakuk-Zephanja* (KAT 13/3; Gütersloh: Gütersloher, 1975), 24, 65, 108; Leslie Allen, *The Books of Joel, Obadiah, Jonah, and Micah* (NICOT; Grand Rapids: Eerdmans, 1976), 257–60; Brevard Childs, *Introduction to the Old Testament as Scripture* (Philadelphia: Fortress, 1979), 431.

Since the text of Micah is difficult, uncovering an intended arrangement is not simple. A proposal for structural coherence in the final form
must account for all the textual data.

It must:

1. account for each passage where it stands in the final form,
   including Mic 2:12–13;

2. allow the contrasts (i.e., the shifts from doom to hope) between
   2:11 and 12, 3:12 and 4:1, and 7:6 and 7 to have full effect, and
   account for the shifts from hope to doom between 2:13 and 3:1,
   4:8 and 4:9, and 5:14 and 6:1;

3. understand the intermixed presence of doom and hope throughout chapters 4–5;

4. account for the differences between sections; and

5. explain all instances of the summons to hear.

The Integrating Principle: The Promises to the Remnant as Indicators of Structural Coherence

Most of the above-mentioned proposals for the structure of Micah
understand the book to be arranged in either two (*b, c, d*) or three (*e*)
sequences of doom alternating with hope. It is true that the interweaving
of judgment and hope can be found throughout Micah. However, in
any of these schemes there are several difficulties in explaining the final
form. Some overlook the placement and function of Mic 2:12–13. To
simply assign it a later date does not do justice to the final form. My
concern is with potential coherence in the text as we now have it. In
addition, Mic 4–5 is not a section of unmixed promise. Micah 4:1–8
presents the bright prospect of God's future rule from Zion. But are
Mic 4:9–10, 11; 5:1, 3 all positive? In this section, something different
seems to be happening, for the negative and the positive are interwoven.

Each of these commonly argued proposals for understanding the text
overlooks one crucial piece of evidence. In the final form, there are
four sequences of doom followed by hope. The primary indicator of
this ordering is the appearance of four promises to the remnant. These
four promises allow us to sense the flow and development of thought
throughout the book. Grasping their significance will delimit the sections and clarify the connections between them, as well as make plain
the way in which each part has been integrated around a central theme.

Except for the first, each of these promises, in Mic 2:12–13; 4:6–7; 5:6–7; and 7:18, occurs in a larger positive section. The larger units are 4:1–8; 5:1–14; and 7:7–20; these constitute the Mican words of hope. Such limits mark off the sections of doom — Mic 1:2–2:11; 3:1–12; 4:9–14; and 6:1–7:6.

Each negative portion deals with a topic unique to that part, but it always portrays the results of human sin — whether in the people's dislocation (1:2–2:11), in their corrupt leadership (3:1–12), in their inability to triumph in battle (4:9–14), or in the spiritual realm (6:1–7:6). The truly remarkable aspect of the organization is that each positive portion offers direct divine resolution to the problem raised in the preceding oracles of doom.

In the first section (1:2–2:13), God leaves heaven to descend to earth. God touches the mountains, changes geographical features, bewails the fate of the towns, and underlines the sins of the people which have brought this to pass. Each sin relates to location and geography, whether the oppressors are taking fields or homes (2:2, 9). The sentence on the people is exile, the loss of their land and familiar surroundings (2:3–5, 10). But then, the word of hope assures the reader that God will regather the exiled people (the remnant) to their proper surroundings, which their sin had once defiled (2:12–13).

The spiritual and political leaders are unqualified, since their primary interest is in serving themselves (ch. 3). Yet the next passage containing promise assures the reader that the Lord will replace the wicked leadership and rule as king (4:1–8). The Lord will rule over the remnant in Mount Zion and restore the former dominion to the daughter Jerusalem (4:6–8).

The situation does not look promising in the following subsection (4:9–14). God's people cry aloud in battle (4:9–10) and are led into exile (4:10; cf. 5:1). Although the people are unable to meet this crisis, the following subsection of promise assures that God will lead the people to victory (5:1–14). God will use a "shepherd-king" from Bethlehem (5:2, 4–5a) and multiple leaders (5:5b–6) to ward off the enemy and bring peace. So the remnant is pictured as inexorable in its progress to victory (5:6–7).

Thereupon the text returns to the proclamation of doom (6:1–7:6). In succession, Micah gives the reader a glimpse of the Lord's case against the people (6:1–8) and exposes the pervasive nature of their sins, as well as the devastating consequences this sin has caused (6:9–7:6). To resolve the problems created by the people's inability to please God, the final subsection looks beyond the judgment to God's shepherding care, vindication, and gracious forgiveness (7:7–20). The promise to the remnant is the climax of this final section of hope, as well as of the entire book. In language that evokes the covenant promise to Abraham (Gen 12:1–3) and the revelation of the meaning of the name of the LORD at Sinai (Exod 34:6–7), the prophecy assures that God will forgive the sins of the remnant of his inheritance (7:18–20).

This arrangement is confirmed by several other features that become apparent in light of this reading. The size of the sections of hope increases as one moves from the beginning to the end. There is a movement from external concerns to internal and spiritual ones, resulting in a climactic order. The highlight of the whole is the final passage, which anticipates God's faithfulness to the promises to the patriarchs and complete forgiveness of the people.

Such an understanding accounts for the data noted above. It allows Mic 2:12–13 to occur in sequence; these two verses are the hopeful response to Mic 1:2–2:11 and thus are surrounded by negative subsections. This reading allows the contrasts between Mic 3:12 and 4:1, as well as between 7:6 and 7, to have their natural function as shifts from doom to hope. The transition from hope to doom (between 2:13 and 3:1; 4:8 and 9; 5:14 and 6:1) then signals a new section. The three summonses to "Hear!" mark new sections at Mic 1:2; 3:1; and 6:1. Seeing the significance of the promises also opens new possibilities for understanding chapters 4–5 that are sensitive to the arrangement. In addition, this reading accounts for the different topics that appear through the book.

Coherence of Theme

Evidenced by the structuring around the four promises, whoever arranged the book of Micah into its present form had a theological intent. Each section has been arranged and edited to develop one thematic center.

This person desired to communicate something about the Lord as the God who (punishes yet) restores. Human rebellion unravels our surroundings and lives, and God punishes those transgressions. Eventually, however, in each area of life God will resolve and restore. The remnant is the focus of the Lord's restoring work.

The connectedness that comes from each section that examines the same theme is reinforced by the presence of several recurring themes of secondary importance. These themes contribute to the focus on God as the restorer. First, there is a consistent theology, as seen, for example, in the repeated ways in which human rebellion against God has consequences — for example, in the exile and defeat of Mic 1:2–2:11 and 4:9–14 or in the deterioration of lives in 7:1–6. Second, significant concepts recur — leadership, human or divine, is emphasized in each section (2:1–2, 9, 12–13; 3:1–12; 4:1–8, 9; 5:1–4a, 6–8; 6:16; 7:14); the nations are present as enemies, obedient pilgrims, or God's audience (1:2; 2:4; 4:1–5, 10–14; 5:4b–5, 6–8, 14; 7:10, 13, 16–17); and "a day," whether of punishment or deliverance, is anticipated (2:4; 3:4; 4:6–7, 10, 11, 14; 5:2, 4, 6; 7:4, 11, 12, 20). Third, the whole book seems oriented to an audience whose ties are with the southern kingdom and its capital, Jerusalem. Note references to Jerusalem (1:5; 3:12), the Temple Mount (4:1–5) or locations in the South (1:10–16), as well as the way in which northern places or customs seem to be viewed from a southern perspective as corrupting influences (1:6–7, 9, 13; 5:4b–5; 7:14).

Internal Coherence

Given that the book of Micah has such a clear-cut structure and theme, it would not be surprising if the redaction(s), which gave the book its outline and then its final form, also touched the words, concepts, and arrangements on a scope narrower than that of the whole book. Indeed, a number of recurrent literary features and links tie the different sections and their subunits together. These features would be less convincing if they existed in isolation, apart from any discernible structure or theme. Yet since these features have this larger context, they indicate the thoroughgoing nature of the redaction.

To thoroughly study these indicators of internal coherence would entail a massive amount of data, since one must analyze connections between smaller units of text. Obviously, this is beyond the scope of this essay.[8] Space will only allow for evidence that can make the case for internal coherence in the final form, especially as seen in the connections between the major sections.

Coherence within the Sections

One must examine what makes each of the sections coherent in and of itself. What holds each section together and makes that particular section, as differentiated from the others, a unit? For example, the

---

[8] Besides which, the works of Willis and Hagstrom (see n. 2 above) have both thoroughly detailed these links on the lowest levels. There is no need, let alone space, to repeat all their work.

first section, Mic 1:2–2:13, is a coherent piece because of the following features.

First, an overwhelming predominance of terms refer to the surroundings — land, locations, or spatial concepts. In no other section of Micah do these so clearly predominate. Geographical features and locations help describe the Lord's descent (1:2–7); the lament is dominated by place-names (1:8–16); accusations and judgments talk of crimes affecting houses and fields (2:1–11). Punishment is portrayed as the loss of land and the loss of heirs to whom to pass the land (2:3–5, 10). Then restoration is described as leaving an enclosed space, with the Lord as king in the lead (2:12–13).

Second, in the background is the assumption of a single situation — sins with the land (not specified until 2:1–2, 9–10) bring God to judge and the resultant destruction of and separation from the land.

Third, thought progresses from pericope to pericope. Our gaze steadily lowers throughout the subsection of doom. God comes down from heaven to the mountains, then to the capitals (1:2–7). The lament tells of the terrible nature of that coming judgment (1:8–16). Finally, the text exposes the sins which are the reasons for that judgment (2:1–11).

Fourth, there is a repeated connection between and juxtaposition of sin and consequent punishment (2:1–2 and 3–5; cf. 1:5, 7b with 1:6–7a; 1:13 with 1:9, 11, 12, 14, 15, 16; 2:6–9, 11 with 2:10). This connection is not pointed out as frequently or carried out as consistently in other parts of the book (e.g., 4:9–14 or 6:1–7:6).

Fifth, the section is unified by the recurrence of the word כל (*kol*) at the beginning of the negative (doom) and positive (hope) segments. We find כלם (*kullam*) (1:2) at the start of the section and כלך (*kullak*) in the oracle of promise at the end (2:12). These two occurrences may even be an *inclusio* that binds the material in between.

Sixth, this section is unique in that it has the most disproportionate contrast between the lengths of the hope and doom subdivisions. The section of judgment (1:2–2:11) is quite long in comparison to that of promise (2:12–13). In addition, the segment of judgment is unique within Micah, in that it is the longest of the four subsections of doom.

The same case can be, and has been, made for the other three sections of the book — Mic 3:1–4:8; 4:9–5:14; and 6:1–7:20.[9] Each section is unique compared with the other sections, and each section is bound internally by the links between its parts.

---

[9] Cuffey, "Coherence of Micah," 342–61.

Coherence between the Sections

On a wider scope, what are the links between the sections? What binds each major section together with the other three? Coherence on this level can be examined between contiguous sections (1:2–2:13 and 3:1–4:8; 3:1–4:8 and 4:9–5:14; 4:9–5:14 and 6:1–7:20), as well as between sections that are not (1:2–2:13 and 4:9–5:14; 1:2–2:13 and 6:1–7:20; 3:1–4:8 and 6:1–7:20). To fully detail the large number of connections between sections is far beyond the scope of this essay.[10] Examples will need to suffice.

There is good evidence for the interconnectedness of the first and second sections of Micah. First, Mic 1:2–2:13 anticipates the theme of leadership that is the central feature of 3:1–4:8. References to leaders set the tone for Mic 3:1–4:8, whether references to the kings of Israel (1:14) or to the Lord as the king who leads a reconstituted people (2:13). Second, the offenses of chapters 2 and 3 have a harmful effect. In Mic 2, judgment comes because the powerful have appropriated lands, houses, and garments (2:2, 8, 9). The accusations of chapter 3 are directed more specifically against the leaders, but the people still suffer, for the leaders mercilessly take advantage of and hurt the people for personal gain (3:2, 3, 5, 9–11). Third, the vocabulary of "stripping off," so prominent in Mic 3:2, 3 (גזל [gzl] and פשט [pšṭ]), has already been used in chapter 2 (2:2, 8 — the same verbs!). Fourth, "house" (בית [bayit]), is prominent in both sections, although used in different senses. In Mic 1–2, we see the "houses of Achzib" (1:14) and eviction from homes (2:2–9). The leaders of Mic 3 rule the "house of Israel/Jacob" (3:1, 9). Judgment approaches the "mountain of the house" (3:12), which will eventually be exalted (4:1) and become the goal of the nations' pilgrimages (4:2). Thus, although centered on different themes, the first two sections do share vocabulary and concepts.

The transition between the two sections (2:12–3:1) fulfills two functions. It separates the two sections and also bridges the gap, so that there is continuity and development. The two are distinguished by the change from surroundings to leadership, by the shift from promise to doom, and by the presence in Mic 3:1 of the summons to hear and אמר (ʾmr). The continuity is emphasized by the catchword ראש (rōʾš). In Mic 2:13, the Lord in regathering the people is "at their head" (בראשם; bᵉrōʾšām), while 3:1 addresses the corrupt "heads of Jacob" (ראשי יעקב). Notice, too, the way in which this catchword ties the themes of the re-

---

10 Ibid., 361–73.

spective sections, contrasting God's leadership of the reclaimed people
to their restored surroundings (2:13) with the leaders indicted in the
next section (3:1–12).

Coherence of Perspective

The coherence of structures, theme, and within and between sections
allows speculation about a coherence of perspective. Seeing connections
throughout the book indicates that at some stage the material was arranged to speak to a particular situation. When did this happen? Is the
arrangement secondary? Has it been imposed on the material? What
community would have found the text meaningful?

Since the central kerygmatic point is the function of God as the one
who restores, the book probably received its final form when restoration
was a significant concern. Military defeat (4:9–14) and exile (2:4–5, 10;
4:10) weigh heavily on the people's minds. The audience must have
been aware of its need for restoration, which would readily explain why
it would treasure a text about a God who restores. Through theological
interpretation of earthly events, the people sought to provide a fuller
meaning for their experiences — for example, by seeing disaster as a
punishment for sin in Mic 2:1–2 and 3–5, or in 3:9–11 and 12. The leadership is inadequate, compromised by corruption (3:1–12) or absence
(4:9). The nations are pressing in hard (4:9–5:14; 7:10, 16–17). The
hoped-for restoration as not taken place; the "day" is still future (7:11–
12). The book has a predominantly Judean background throughout, as
seen in the places (1:10–16) and concerns (e.g., 3:12; 4:1–5).

What points in history would adequately explain these themes and the
book of Micah's apparent assumptions? The text's final form would fit
well with redactional activity in the exilic era, whether of those dispersed
or of those still in the land. Alternatively, it could have arisen prior
to the exile, from a person or group in Judah under the influence of
Micah's prophetic ministry, whether a contemporary or a later disciple.
The picture of the crisis is so vivid possibly because it reflects experience
of the Assyrian invasions (733–732 B.C.E.? 725–722 B.C.E.? 701 B.C.E.?).
The bright promises of hope, then, would not be for survivors of the fall
of Jerusalem, but for the faithful "remnant," looking beyond impending
disaster to future restoration.

Full analysis of these possibilities is beyond the limits of this essay.
Although it is difficult to speak with certainty about redactional history,
these proposals show how such reconstruction can offer a coherent sit-

uation, outlooks, or views that a single author, redactor, or school might have held.

Reflection

The book of Micah is coherent, and the text evidences several types of connectedness. Once aware of the relationship between hope-filled subsections and preceding oracles of doom, it becomes clear that the book manifests structural coherence in four parts. Then it becomes possible to grasp the final form's coherent theme. The presence of a number of features which contribute to internal coherence helps confirm what has already been observed. All coherences in the text relate to a coherence of perspective.

Coherence in the Book of the Twelve

Several significant recent studies have argued for coherence in the Minor Prophets, indicating that these were, at some point, intended to be read as one literary unit. These studies seek coherence, not within one canonical book, but coherence that can be traced throughout the twelve-book unit. The work of two scholars, Paul House and James Nogalski, will serve as examples of this type of study. Is the coherence the same as found in a single book, as in Micah? Or is this coherence of a different nature, and in what ways might it differ? What would these variations imply?

Paul House suggests that "the minor prophets are arranged as a unified literary work."[11] All twelve books can be characterized as "written prophecy," or "minor prophetic written literature," which is characterized by three traits. First, throughout the corpus, poetry and prose are used interchangeably. Second, the narrative voice is either third person or first person. Third, common elements recur throughout, consisting of the sin of God's people, their approaching punishment, and the restoration.[12]

The Minor Prophets, as arranged in the canon, display a clear structure that derives from shared elements of a common message. The books in sequence focus, first, on the various types of sin in Hosea through Micah, second, on the logical consequences of sin in Nahum through

---

[11] P. House, *The Unity of the Twelve* (JSOTSup 97; Sheffield: Almond Press, 1990), 243.

[12] Ibid., 37–62.

Zephaniah, and, third, on restoration in Haggai through Malachi.[13] The reader can trace a comic plot by following each of the appropriate stages — introduction, complication, crisis, falling action, resolution.[14] Study of the characters reveals a consistent pattern. Yahweh serves as the hero, Israel and the Gentiles as comic foils; the prophets fulfill several roles.[15] The implied author behind the whole, of course, is God, and so the point of view attempts to match God's point of view. Each prophet serves as narrator, while the remnant is the implied audience.[16]

In a rather different pair of works, James Nogalski has detailed the evidence that, at a particular stage of development, the individual books of the Twelve were intended to be read together as one. In his first volume, Nogalski presents evidence that two corpora of minor prophetic material existed prior to the linking of the twelve books. First there was a Deuteronomistic corpus consisting of Hosea, Amos, Micah, and Zephaniah. These books (or, more specifically, the sections which proclaim judgment) were brought together during the exile to explain the fall of Jerusalem in the light of God's prior judgment on the northern kingdom (Israel). The redaction unified the texts with literary devices such as superscriptions, catchwords at the end or beginning, common Deuteronomic patterns, and editorial expansions. During the early postexilic period, this corpus was augmented by eschatological expansions that anticipate the day of restoration. A second corpus (Haggai and Zech 1–8) responded to the needs of the people as they rebuilt the temple.[17]

In his second volume, Nogalski seeks textual support for the idea that these two preexisting corpora were combined with Joel, Obadiah, Nahum, Habakkuk, and Malachi at a still-later stage. Joel serves as the literary anchor of this new corpus — the prophetic material throughout these books was adapted by incorporating intertextual references to Joel (and Isaiah). Finally, at some point after Alexander's invasion, Jonah and Zech 9–14 were added. These inclusions, along with the accompanying editing, brought the Book of the Twelve to its final form.[18]

Nogalski finds an impressive amount of evidence for these processes by observing an extensive catchword phenomenon, in which virtually

---

[13] Ibid., 63–109.

[14] Ibid., 111–62; note the chart on 124.

[15] Ibid., 163–219.

[16] Ibid., 221–41.

[17] James D. Nogalski, *Literary Precursors to the Book of the Twelve* (BZAW 217; New York: de Gruyter, 1993).

[18] James D. Nogalski, *Redactional Processes in the Book of the Twelve* (BZAW 218; New York: de Gruyter, 1993).

every book's ending is linked to the beginning of the subsequent book in the canon by the recurrence of catchwords, which can either continue a theme or contrast/juxtapose one theme with its opposite. In addition, he uncovers a number of other intertextual references, which might show that the books were edited with reference to each other as part of a comprehensive intention that the Twelve should be read as one literary piece.[19]

The Nature of Coherence
in the Twelve Minor Prophets as a Unit

Both House's reading of the Twelve and Nogalski's proposed redactional development have pointed to many connecting features among the Minor Prophets. These linkages provide evidence for all four types of coherence discussed earlier. House examines the whole corpus to determine whether certain literary features are found consistently. He proposes, first and foremost, an internal coherence, seen in the recurrent features of the "written prophecy" genre and in the appearance of a standard cast of characters. That one can trace a comic plot from segment to segment suggests a coherence of structure and of theme. The consistent viewpoint from which the story is told provides a coherence of perspective. The perspective all the parts share is that of the implied author, which no doubt would reflect the view of the individual or group that gave these books their present arrangement.

Nogalski's work, as it unfolds in his books, begins with internal coherence and reasons to a coherence of perspective.[20] The evidence for internal links consists of numerous catchwords, which link almost every book with the books preceding and following. Such coherence is also evidenced by references to other books of the Twelve or to other parts of the Hebrew Bible.

The reconstruction of a redactional history in which the editors of a certain stage intended that the Minor Prophets be read together as

---

[19] For the catchword phenomenon, see especially Nogalski, *Precursors*, 20–57. Later, Nogalski classifies the major ways in which intertextuality is expressed ("Intertextuality and the Twelve," in *Forming Prophetic Literature* [ed. J. W. Watts and P. House; JSOTSup 235; Sheffield: Sheffield Academic Press, 1996], 102–24). Besides catchwords, he points to quotes, allusions, motifs, and framing devices.

[20] "These writings implore investigation of productive editorial shaping through cross-references and catchwords as a means to discover the literary and theological intentions of this corpus" (Nogalski, *Literary Precursors*, 281).

a book offers a possible coherence of perspective. Actually, this perspective exists in several layers. At first, a coherence of perspective is in evidence for the preexisting corpora. The Deuteronomists read their four-book corpus as an explanation for the fall of Jerusalem. The early postexilic redaction of these works added eschatological materials to reassure a beleaguered and uncertain community. The Haggai-Zechariah corpus was formed in relation to the rebuilding of the temple. In later stages, a common perspective underlies the entire Book of the Twelve. Redactors of the Joel-related layer added significant internal links to the books of the other Minor Prophets (catchwords and intertextual references). The interests brought together in the book of Joel integrate a common set of views and concerns in evidence through the Book of the Twelve. Nogalski seems less concerned to propose a comprehensive structural or thematic coherence. There is no overall structure, other than the sequence of the books, that intends to communicate a single message.

Coherence in Micah and the Twelve: Comparison and Implications

All four types of coherence have been found in the book of Micah and in the Minor Prophets. The types of coherence proposed for a single prophetic book also seem to describe what is found in the whole corpus. Each type of coherence confirms that the Minor Prophets are to be read as one work.

Are there differences in the types of coherence in Micah and the Twelve? At first, these two sources seem to generate the same indicators. But at least two differences, with potentially significant implications, become apparent on further reflection.

First, there is a difference of scope. The coherence in Micah appears within a unit marked by a superscription, unique stylistic features, unique emphases, and a centuries-old tradition of being treated as a literary work, as a book. The coherence claimed for the Twelve is found outside of one clearly marked book. Rather, indicators of coherence are distributed throughout another "book," yet at a different level and on a grander scale. Reasons for positing the existence of this "book" are these same indicators of coherence, and not clear textual markers that unambiguously direct the reader to perceive these twelve minor prophetic books as one unified entity. There is the tradition that the Twelve was found on one scroll, but the implications are not clear. Was one scroll merely a matter of convenience and efficiency? Need it imply that the books were intended to be read as a unit?

Second, there is a resultant difference in certainty about an author's or redactor's intentionality. A modern interpreter is much less certain that the connections which apparently link the Minor Prophets were put there for that purpose. Most would agree that someone (a redactor? a school?) gave a particular book, such as Micah, its final form. Many would affirm that a person or persons arranged and adapted the materials with a particular motivation — a desire to communicate a theological message in relation to the circumstances of that time, through combining materials. As a result, the redactor(s) would have given the canonical book the very linkages and connections that we looked for in our summary of Micah. That someone probably put the links there motivates and validates our search for them. That they are confined to one book, which gives directions to read it as a book, assures that these links will not only be easier to find (in that they are drawn from a much smaller compass), but also more likely to correspond with someone's intentionality, in at least one stage of development.

With the Twelve, on the other hand, there are no clear markers (such as a superscription) which direct us to read it as a unified piece of literature, nor is there a clear scholarly consensus that would hold that it was ever intended to be read as such. So although similar evidence of coherence can be found, confidence that it was intentional is a step removed from the certainty of coherence in an individual book.

How clearly does the canonical connection imply the books are to be linked? How are we to interpret the connections we find in the text? Do the links reflect an author's or editor's intention? Or might we impose our own expectations and presuppositions on the text? Might the linkages merely be the result of chance associations noticed by the modern interpreter, but that were never anyone's intentional design? Any two books may simply have a shared fund of terms. And if these are intentional, what was the intention?[21]

For example, near the end of Joel is a reference to the LORD roaring from Zion, including cataclysmic natural effects (Joel 4:16 [Eng., 3:16]). The following book, Amos, begins with virtually an identical statement about the LORD roaring and thundering from Jerusalem, but with a slightly different set of natural events (Amos 1:2). The question is why

---

[21] Note the discussion in E. Ben Zvi, "Twelve Prophetic Books or the 'Twelve'?" in Watts and House, *Forming Prophetic Literature*, 139–40.

these two statements are juxtaposed at the end of one book and the start of the next.

Unfortunately, the evidence is inconclusive. It is possible that one of the two passages was composed to link two adjacent books and to provide a verbal (and possibly thematic) transition. Or were the two books placed next to each other because the two sections were already there? Further, the editor(s) might have been suggesting something by making the juxtaposition — perhaps a theological point — or the editor(s) might have had no message; rather, it seemed logical to order the two because of similar wording. It is also possible, though unlikely, that the two passages are grouped due to chance. But when the modern scholar comes searching for linkages, these expectations suggest a conscious link. In this case, we are imposing our own conclusions on a text that may offer little help in determining whether the juxtaposition was intentional.

There is tremendous uncertainty in almost all instances. A similarity or a quote can be explained in many different ways. Did *A* quote *B*? Did *B* quote *A*? Or did both *A* and *B* draw on a common tradition? Could the same group have edited both passages? Might *A*'s tradents have known the tradition of *B*, or vice versa?[22]

The case becomes even harder to prove when there is only an allusion or similar vocabulary appears in isolation.[23] Obadiah 15–21 and Mic 1:2–7 have "mountain," "fire," "Jacob," and "field" in common.[24] This might suggest intentional linkage. Yet, in each case, these are four common words spread over several verses. Do these passages allude to each other? Or is this an unintended coincidence? These connections hardly have the same weight that the shared quote has in Joel 4:16 and Amos 1:2, or in Mic 4:1–4 and Isa 2:2–4. In these latter cases there is clearly an intertextual reference. The difficulty is in determining source and intention.[25]

---

[22] For example, notice the relations posited between Mic 4:1–4 and Isa 2:2–4.

[23] Nogalski, "Intertextuality and the Twelve," 108–10, has a well-thought-out discussion on determining the validity of apparent allusions.

[24] See the discussions in Nogalski, *Literary Precursors,* 31–33, and *Redactional Processes,* 78–79.

[25] House, *Unity of the Twelve,* 245, readily acknowledges the difficulty: "There is absolutely no way to verify that the pattern I have proposed was *exactly* what the original shapers of the Book of the Twelve had in mind. Because of the literary evidence, however, I do not believe this pattern is a contrived scheme forced on the text."

A Random Case Study

The inherent dangers are aptly demonstrated by a case study. I chose two chapters at random — Hos 6 and Mic 3. Few (if any) would suggest that these two chapters were edited to refer to each other or to provide any basis for juxtaposing them in an earlier version of the Twelve. Yet on cursory examination, I was able to isolate four "significant" examples of the catchword phenomenon.

First, both passages use violent and graphic language to describe what is done to God's people. In Hos 6, God has "torn" them "to pieces" (טָרַף, ṭārap) and "struck" (יַךְ, yak) them (6:1). God has "hewn" (חָצַבְתִּי, ḥāṣabtî) them through the prophets (6:5). In Mic 3, the heartless leaders of Judah oppress the poor. They are pictured as tearing off their skin, eating their flesh, breaking bones, and chopping them up for the pot (3:2–3). The contrast is that, in Hosea, God acts to bring the people to repentance, while in Micah the greedy leaders oppress the common people.

Second, the role of true prophets is emphasized. In Hos 6:5, they are instruments to bring God's word and to announce the consequences of sin. In Mic 3:8, Micah describes himself as a prophet empowered by the Spirit of the LORD to call for justice and expose sins. The importance of this theme is reinforced in Micah in that the description of true prophecy is set in sharp contrast to the prophets of the day, who prophesied (and led the people astray) as long as they were paid (Mic 3:5, 11).

Third, both chapters address the defection of spiritual leadership. In Hosea, bands of priests ambush and murder (Hos 6:9). Micah, along with the exposé about prophets, tells of priests who teach for a price (Mic 3:11).

Fourth, both passages use imagery of light and dark. Hosea 6:3 refers to the certainty of the sun rising as a picture of God's dependability, which is echoed in Mic 3:6. The doom pronounced on the prophets is that the sun will set and the day go dark. They will be enveloped in night.

One could argue that these connections link the two chapters. Yet these chapters are far separated in canonical location. Or are the similarities cross-references? Or do they result from use of common prophetic themes and terminology? The exegete could doubtless find apparently meaningful parallels between almost any two passages in the Minor Prophets. Some of these links were intended, others were not. How can we tell the difference? In the interest of furthering the discussion

of the criteria necessary to validate such connections, I close with the
following suggestions and reflections.

Suggestions and Reflections

First, it is important to ask about the validity of connections from
the perspective of what the author/editor intended and what would
guide the audience in reading it. Ben Zvi is certainly correct to note
that we overemphasize the first angle.[26] If our concern is the authorial/
editorial end, it is far too easy to find coherence and to assume that
these connections exist because of someone's intention. We lose sight
that in writing literature, usually the desire is to communicate. To do this
with success there must be clarity, which is communicating "efficiently."
Hence, it is also vital to view a text from the reader's perspective. What
would have helped the reader understand? What allusions would the
reader have recognized?

Second, it would be beneficial to discuss and consistently use criteria for evaluating intentionality in coherence. This approach would
give some sense whether these phenomena are a proper foundation for
theories about how to read the text and about its development. The
judgment as to what is "hard" evidence will never be easy, but there
ought to be standards. What criteria exist for evaluating coherence for
literary or redaction-critical purposes?

The evidence must be *textual.* It must derive from the text and reflect
an accurate understanding of the language of the original.

The evidence must be *historically accurate.* The usages and connections proposed should fit the circumstances and concerns of their time.
In addition, the modern interpreter should expect that the author/
editor operates according to ancient conventions and sensibilities as to
what is good literature and effective communication. Allow them freedom from our conventions. What appear to be quirks in a composition
may have been perfectly acceptable in that culture — for example, the
frequent changes in person characteristic of the prophets may be one
such instance.

Valid evidence needs to be the *product of logically sound reasoning* and
not of circular thought. A hypothesis can become the lens through
which we read the text, which then yields numerous confirmations of
the hypothesis. It is startling how easily an interpreter can find what

---

26 Ben Zvi, "Twelve Prophetic Books," 149.

he/she sets out to find. The data from the text must determine the conclusions. Otherwise, the hypothesis will determine the data and will itself become the conclusion.

Beginning with a hypothesis and its accompanying presuppositions is unavoidable. It is important, however, that we acknowledge our presuppositions and test whether the hypothesis is valid, without allowing it to explain all the data.

Another logical limit is the uncertainty of all reconstructions of a text's development. We do have the final form, but not samples of each of the postulated stages. Until there is an earlier text to study, redactional schemes are hypothetical by nature. As such, although redactional proposals may be useful for thinking about the text and its historical background, their limits also introduce significant uncertainty.[27]

Solid textual evidence can receive *statistical confirmation*. A high density of shared terms indicates higher likelihood of intended intertextual reference than isolated occurrences. Similarity of style might confirm an intertextual relationship.

The evidence is likely to be *confirmed structurally* within a particular book. Where do these reputed links occur? Are they at significant junctures, and hence likely to have been placed as guides for the reader? For example, the catchwords Nogalski has pointed out at the beginning and end of books heightens the likelihood that these connections played a role in the shaping process. In addition, it is conceivable that the proximity of two texts with apparent links indicates an author's or editor's intentions. This may be proximity in the canon, in historical period, or in theological teaching. If located close to each other in the canon, the connections may be obvious. If the two texts are more distant, there needs to be reason to think that a reader would have "cross-referenced" the ideas (as in the striking parallels between Isa 2:2–4(5) and Mic 4:1–4[5]).[28]

To be valid, evidence from the text must be *consonant with its context*. In the hierarchy of importance, of first priority is the immediate context. If the interpreter finds the same or similar words in two different books, each should be explained first in its immediate context, rather than

---

[27] For example, Ben Zvi notes that discontinuities in the final form may reflect redactional activity or may arise from the use of prior sources (ibid., 146, n. 48).

[28] One might also posit a conceptual proximity — that the goal is to find more overt formal correspondences, whether these derive from contrast or similarity. See Ernst Wendland, "Text Analysis and the Genre of Jonah (Part I)," *JETS* 39 (1996): 191–206, esp. 202.

looking outside that work. If the word and its usage are understandable in the immediate context, need we posit the textual link to grasp what is being said? Would the word have been comprehensible without "cross-referencing?"

Second priority is the context of the book in which the passage(s) is (are) located. Indicators such as the title/superscriptions, or connection throughout with a particular personage (the prophet), show that this work was intended as a book in its own right.[29] Reading in this context is more urgent than including other books, since when the book attained its final form it was intended unambiguously as an independent unit. We do not yet have that certainty for the Book of the Twelve as a whole.

Awareness of concentric layers of context also allows the exegete to acknowledge the uniqueness of each text. Part of an oracle's message may be discovered by seeing, not how it is paralleled, but how it is unique.[30]

The question of a proposed link's consonance with its context will also arise when words/phrases/concepts are used in two passages in different ways. For example, Amos 9:11 uses the phrase "in that day" (ביום ההוא; *bayyôm hahu'*). So does Obad 8. Is this an example of a catchword?[31] The phrase is the same, but each appears in a completely different context. In Amos, the reference is to the time of restoration, while in Obadiah it depicts Edom's destruction. It is important to recognize the interpretive dilemma. Is the contrast in usage evidence that these two references were intentionally juxtaposed to carry forward the argument of the Twelve? Or is the fact that the usages make perfectly good sense on their own solid evidence that they are not parallel and were not meant to be construed as keywords?

It also seems appropriate to point out the dissonance between levels of context. Take, for example, the message of Micah. House reads Micah as part of a section in the Twelve that focuses on various types of sin. Although he acknowledges the promises of restoration, why judgment occurs "constitutes Micah's major theme."[32] Yet, as argued above, Micah in its final form is not primarily proclaiming doom for God's people. The fourfold structure around promises to the remnant reinforces that God will restore the people after discipline has been endured. The context of the book makes the message one of hope, while the context of the Twelve results in a negative perception. The dissonance in two different

---

[29] Ben Zvi, "Twelve Prophetic Books," 152.
[30] See Ben Zvi's argument about the uniqueness of Obad 21 (ibid., 141–42).
[31] Nogalski, *Literary Precursors*, 27–30, and *Redactional Processes*, 67–68.
[32] House, *Unity of the Twelve*, 139.

levels — in the book itself and the Twelve — should make us question
the connections in the broader context.

Finally, valid evidence should *"make sense to the reader."* For example,
Nogalski amasses evidence that the book of Joel is the literary anchor of
the Twelve. In this scheme, much rests on the reconstructed historical
role and literary/theological place of the book of Joel.[33] However, when
one reads the Twelve in sequence, Joel does not appear to have an
anchoring role. Might the textual links with Joel through the Minor
Prophets be the result of prophetic language and ideas from a prophet,
editor, or circle? Might the book have been shaped with reference to the
larger world of prophetic language and thought, rather than as literary
center for a developing corpus?

The third suggestion is that scholars need to learn from comparative study. For example, comparisons — examination of other explicit
links — outside the prophetic literature but within the Hebrew canon
may be helpful. Can insight be drawn from the colophon which links
Chronicles with Ezra (2 Chr 26:22–23 and Ezra 1:1–3)? These are two
works connected outside what was apparently regarded as one book. Instead of catchwords sprinkled through a larger swath, the link is a direct
quote of significant length. Might this case have implications for prophetic literature? Can fruitful insights be gleaned from parallel ancient
literary conventions within the canon or in other ancient literature?

Another fruitful comparison would be with past interpretations. How
did another commentator explain the data that I am anxious to see as
support for my ideas? Usually there are interpretations that diverge from
my own cherished readings. It is vitally important to ensure that I have
not overlooked something important. For example, the expanded literary horizon of the Twelve might explain some phenomena; however,
apparent coherence might be due to chance or a common circle of
tradents.[34] Conversely, our chronological/cultural remove from the ancient world may result in missing the real connections obvious to people
in that setting.

A more extensive study, juxtaposing more passages than just Hos 6
and Mic 3, would be fascinating. Are there intertextual references? If
so, what might they imply? Are the connections intentional references
outside the immediate context? Or do these links originate elsewhere?

---

[33] Nogalski, *Redactional Processes*, 1–57.
[34] Ben Zvi, "Twelve Prophetic Books," 136, 154–55.

Do they arise from a common vocabulary, possibly a common prophetic vocabulary?

Comparisons with the history of interpretation also serve as a check. If convinced of having found a marker for a desired reading, why has no one else, in all these centuries, seen it?

A fourth suggestion would be to explore connections between the methods of redaction criticism and the methodologies in biblical theology. Each discipline seeks coherence, and it should not be overlooked that this quest among redaction critics of the Twelve parallels the task of the biblical theologian, who tries to synthesize teaching on a broader basis than the individual passage or book. Both disciplines seek intertextual links that transcend immediate boundaries.[35] That the Seminar on the Development of the Book of the Twelve has significant implications for a biblical theology of the prophets needs to be explored in much more depth.

---

[35] In a similar vein, Dr. Barry Jones observed (in a conversation subsequent to the delivery of this paper) that theological commonalities may predispose many in the Seminar to confirm the Twelve as a literary unity.

13

A Frame for the Book of the Twelve:
Hosea 1–3 and Malachi

John D. W. Watts

Some major Old Testament books have been composed in frames, employing significant literary forms at the beginning and end. The Book of Job, for instance, begins with the story of Job, which presents the setting for the entire book (chs. 1–2). The narrative returns in 42:7–16 to complete the frame and to end the book.

Isaiah also has a frame, which begins with the issue of rebellious children (1:2–3). The frame closes with return to the same issue in 63:1–65:16.[1]

This essay investigates whether Hos 1–3 and Malachi compose a similar frame for the Book of the Twelve. I begin by recalling a passage which, I think, was influential in creating the idea of the Twelve: Zech 7–8. Zechariah answers the question, brought by the delegation from Bethel, about when to fast by questioning their motive for fasting. Then he says:

> " 'Are these not the words the LORD proclaimed through the earlier prophets when Jerusalem and its surrounding town were at rest and prosperous, and the Negev and the western foothills were settled?' " And the word of the LORD came to Zechariah: "This is what the LORD Almighty says: 'Administer true justice; show mercy and compassion to one another. Do not oppress the widow or the fatherless, the alien or the poor. In your hearts do not think evil of each other.' But they refused to pay attention, stubbornly they turned their backs and stopped up their ears. They made their hearts as hard as flint and would not listen to the law or to the words that the LORD Almighty had sent by his Spirit through the earlier prophets. So the LORD Almighty was very angry. 'When I called, they did not listen; so when they called, I would not listen,' says the LORD Almighty. 'I scattered them with a whirlwind among all the nations, where they were strangers. The land was left so desolate behind them that no one could come or go. This is how they made the pleasant land desolate.' " Again the word of the LORD Almighty came to me. This is what the LORD Almighty says: "I am very jealous for Zion; I am burning with jealousy for her." This is what the LORD says: "I will return to Zion and dwell

---

[1] Katheryn Pfisterer Darr, *Isaiah's Vision and the Family of God* (Louisville: Westminster, 1994).

in Jerusalem. Then Jerusalem shall be called The City of Truth, and the mountain of the LORD Almighty will the called the Holy Mountain." (7:7–8:3 NIV)

This passage contains in compressed form the essential message of each of the Latter Prophets. It brackets the word and ministry of the preexilic prophets with the words and ministry of Zechariah and his colleagues in the postexilic community of Jerusalem. The book of Haggai–Zech 1–8 was certainly a "precursor" of the Book of the Twelve.[2] The expansion of the sense of Zech 7–8 led to linking the book (Haggai-Zech 8) to another preexisting literary "precursor," the book of Amos. They became the poles around which groups of new literature developed.

The Relation of Hosea 1–3 to Malachi

Two years ago I read a paper before the Formation of the Book of the Twelve Consultation, "Superscriptions and Incipits in the Book of the Twelve."[3] I noted that superscriptions in Hosea and in Malachi are multilayered. In each the formula in the second layer is the same: "The word of YHWH."[4] This may well suggest that in one stage of the development of the material that became the Book of the Twelve they were part of a small corpus of prophetic writings gathered under the title "the word of YHWH." This suggests a relationship between them that their present positions at opposite ends of this large book does nothing to reveal. The "word of YHWH" corpus developed the idea inherent in Zech 7–8, bringing the message of preexilic prophets and postexilic prophets together and focusing the latter on Jerusalem.

Both Hos 1–3 and Malachi speak strongly to the theme of the love of God for Israel, a theme that is, in so many words, not a part of any other book in the Twelve. Both use the figure of domestic relations to speak about this theme.

Hosea speaks to the issue under the figure of Israel as God's wife. Hosea's second child by Gomer is named לא רחמה ("not compassioned").[5] The name is the basis for the message that God's relation to Israel is to be fundamentally altered. The following name spells this out: "Not My People." The basic confession of faith for Israel had been

---

[2] James D. Nogalski, *Literary Precursors to the Book of the Twelve* (BZAW 217; Berlin: de Gruyter, 1993).

[3] That paper is printed in this volume. See ch. 8.

[4] A form that appears again in Zech 9:1 and 12:1, both in the second layer.

[5] NIV translates "not loved." Note, however, the distinction in Hebrew, with the word "love" in the next chapter and in Malachi. It is proper to view these terms as synonyms, but they should be kept distinct from each other.

"I, YHWH, am your God and you, Israel, are my people." Now that is to
be negated, nullified. Yet the text hastens to look to a time when Israel
will again be called "children of the Living God" (Hos 1:10).

The "love" theme continues in chapter 2, picturing Israel as the adulterous wife and YHWH threatening to withhold compassion from the
children of this adulterous marriage (2:6 [Eng., 2:4]).[6] In 2:7 (Eng.,
2:5), Israel is quoted referring to her paramours as "my lovers" using
the direct word for "love" (מאהבי). The word repeats in 2:9, 12, 14, 15
(2:7, 10, 12, 13) with the same reference. In 2:16–25 (2:14–23), YHWH
tells what he proposes to do about this. In 2:16–17 (14–15), he determines to play the lover, courting Israel anew. In 2:18–25 (16–23), YHWH
addresses Israel. The paramours, no longer called "lovers" are identified
as the Baals. The key statement appears in 2:21–22 (19–20) (NIV):

> I will betroth you to me forever.
>   I will betroth you in [or with] righteousness and in justice
>   in faithfulness (חסד) and in compassions (רחמים).
> And I will betroth you to me in truth (אמונה) and the knowledge of YHWH.

The chapter moves to complete the frame, which ties it into the message
of chapter 1:

> I will have compassion (רחמתי) on the one not receiving compassion,
>   and I will say to Not My People "you are my people,"
>   and they will say "My God." (2:25 [2:23]).

The mask of literary allusion is stripped away and the real subject of the
relation of God and people is revealed.

Chapter 3 tells the story from the prophet's viewpoint, in the first
person. It uses the word "love" for both the love of husband as well as
of lovers:

> Then YHWH said to me: "Go again and love (אהב) a woman, one loved (אהבת)
> by another and an adulteress like Yahweh's love (כאהבת) for the Israelites while
> they are turning to other gods and are lovers of (אהבי) sacred raisin cakes." (3:1)[7]

---

[6] The verse numbering in the English translations varies from that of the Hebrew
in both Hosea and Malachi. Hebrew Masoretic numbering is given first, English in
parentheses or brackets.

[7] In the original group of four "word of YHWH" books, Hosea and Malachi were
also the frame. The inside material is composed of Zech 9–11 and 12–14. These units
deal with God's involvement with the entire process of the wars, but they concentrate
on the role of Jerusalem and of the Davidic house. Hosea 1–3 deals with Israel, the
people of God, not the kingdoms. Hosea 4–14 provides two inner frames comparable
to Zech 9–11 and 12–14, which deal with the mystery of YHWH's early relation to
Israel. They speak in high poetic hyperbole of the exodus and the wilderness journey,
and of the beginnings of Israel as the people of God.

Malachi begins almost as a continuation of Hos 3:

> "I have loved (אהבתי) you," says YHWH.
> But you say: "How [In what] have you loved us (אהבתנו)?" (1:2)

The dialogue continues with a definition of "love" in contrast to "hate."

> Was not Esau brother of Jacob? Oracle of YHWH.
> And then I loved (ואהב) Jacob but Esau I hated (שנאתי).

The word "love" (אהב) in all its forms occurs twenty-eight times in the Book of the Twelve. Most of them speak of loving to do something. Love connotes God's love for the people only in Hos 3:1; 9:15; 11:1, 4; 14:3, 4;[8] and Mal 1:2 (3x).[9]

Malachi returns to speaking of the relation of YHWH and Israel in terms of domestic relations.[10] Having spoken of God's love for the people in 1:2–3, Malachi speaks of the crisis in relation between son and father (1:6):

> A son honors his father, and a servant his master. If I am a father, where is the honor due me? If I am a master, where is the respect due me?

The passage goes on to accuse the priests of disrespect in the way they go about the sacrifices. Malachi returns to the domestic relation in 2:10:

> Have we not all one father? Did not one God create us? Why do we profane the covenant of our fathers by breaking faith with one another?

And the discussion turns to marriage with foreigners and divorces in Israel. The issues take on a distinctive postexilic application. But the implication that the problem announced in Hosea is still present cannot be missed.

The point that Hosea makes — that YHWH is still relevant for postexilic Israel — is clear. The postexilic situation is not the perfect end-time. It is filled with sin and needs the continued cleansing and judgment of God. Yet God's continued love for the people may be discerned there just as it was in the eighth century.

The Effect of the Frame

What is the effect of the frame for understanding the Book of the Twelve? Darr has shown how the frame of "rebellious children" provides

---

[8] Hosea 9–14 constitutes theological reflection of the highest order in regard to YHWH's love for Israel in the beginning. But treating Hos 4–14 and Zech 9–14 as an inner frame for the Twelve would have to be the subject for another paper.

[9] Malachi 2:11 speaks of YHWH's love for his sanctuary.

[10] As Isa 1:2–3 and 63:8–64:12 do in terms of father and children.

a new dimension in which to hear Isaiah's message. The frame of the love of God for Israel affects the Book of the Twelve in the same way.

The internal themes of the Day of YHWH (and YHWH's action against the nations) and of the restoration of the temple in Jerusalem receive a softer context from Hosea's presentation.

On the other hand, the domestic setting gives the whole a depth of feeling, both positive and negative, that moves beyond the other terms. This is particularly true in Malachi, in which God's love for Israel contrasts with "hate" for Edom. This contrast highlights Israel's survival through wars versus the destruction of countries like Edom over the same period. Some providential hand must have made that possible. Yet at the end, surviving Jews show little sense of gratitude or wonder. They go about "business as usual," with priests cheating on the quality of animals for sacrifice, husbands divorcing their wives, and all cheating on their taxes (tithes) for the temple.

While the similarities in these texts' referent to the love of God for Israel are plain, the contrasts are equally clear. While Malachi's exhortations and accusations are realistic and close to home in the postexilic situation of Palestinian Jews, Hosea's writing is theoretical. It lacks the specificity to the eighth century of Amos's preaching. It is therefore evident that the frame places the relevance of the Twelve in the world of Malachi, not that of Hosea. The Twelve was intended to be read and applied in the fifth century, not the eighth.

Nogalski has pulled together the evidence that the last verses of Malachi were intended to close the Twelve, the Prophets, and even the canon of Law and Prophets. He concludes that Malachi was composed for its position in the Book of the Twelve.[11] Is it also possible that Hos 1–3 was composed for its position? I have indicated, based on the second level of superscriptions ("the word of YHWH"), that both Hosea and Malachi belonged to a previously existing group of four books. The placement of the books of the frame suggests a subject for the Twelve: they are to speak to the survival of a remnant during the troubles of the eighth to the sixth centuries and to the wonder of the beginning restoration in Jerusalem in the late-sixth and middle-fifth centuries. How

---

[11] Many scholars, as Nogalski notes, have thought of Mal 3:22–24 (Eng., 4:4–6) as a secondary addition for the time when Malachi was the last book of the Prophets, or of the Law and the Prophets. In any case, these verses stand somewhat separate from the rest of the book. This grouping does question, however, Nogalski's understanding of Hosea as the anchor of a "deuteronomistic group of books" of eighth-century prophets.

can this be true when much in Palestine was obliterated by Assyrian and Babylonian armies? Malachi 1:2–4 responds that the wonderful and improbable love of YHWH for the people is the answer.

Change or No Change in YHWH?

A significant summary of the Book of the Twelve is Mal 2:17–3:18. The key statement is 3:6: "Indeed I, YHWH, have not changed, so you, sons of Jacob, you have not been destroyed." That is what the Book of the Twelve is about; the verse serves as a summary interpretation of the relation of YHWH and his people over the eighth to fifth centuries. Outwardly everything has changed. The political and social structures in the Near East have changed radically. Israel and Judah are no longer kingdoms or autonomous peoples. Most of Judah is in Babylonian exile or scattered around the Near East. A very small remnant remains in Jerusalem and its environs. They have no king. Twelve tribes no longer exist.

Hosea 1–3 and Mal 1 insist that the love and compassion of God for the people have not changed. But troubled times lead the people to say that it is no longer possible to distinguish between the fate of those who keep the ways of God and those who do not. They imply that God, in allowing this to come to pass, has lost moral integrity (Mal 2:17b and 3:14).

The Twelve struggles with whether God has changed. Joel 2:12–14 and Jonah 4:2 cite Exod 34:6 (see also Deut 7:9).[12] This is the basic dogma being tested.

YHWH, YHWH, a God of compassion and grace (רחום וחנון) slow to anger, abounding in love and faithfulness (חסד ואמת) br maintaining love (חסד) to thousands, forgiving guilt [or transgression], rebellion, and sin yet he certainly does not acquit (נקה), placing punishment for the guilt of the fathers on the children and the children's children, up to the third and fourth [generation]. (Exod 34:6–7; see Nah 1:2–3)

Joel 2:12–14 quotes the passage in appealing for the people to repent and turn to God, with the hope that God will turn toward them. And Joel adds, "and he repents of the evil (ונחם על הרעה). Who knows? Will he turn and repent?"

---

[12] "And you shall know that YHWH your God, he is God. The faithful God, keeping his covenant and the loyalty (החסד) to those loving him (אהביו) and keeping his commandments to a thousand generations but repaying those hating him to their face to their destruction. He will not delay toward those hating him to his face. He will repay them..." (Deut. 7:9–10; translation is mine).

When Jonah (4:2) cites this verse, he also includes this last line. Where did this line come from? Exodus 32:12 and 14 provide parallels. God has seen the people's apostasy, and true to God's proclaimed nature tells Moses that he intends to show his anger by destroying them (32:10). Moses pleads for him to "turn (שוב) from his anger, change his mind (הנחם) concerning the bad thing (הרעה) for his people" (32:14). "So YHWH changed his mind [repented] concerning the bad thing that he had thought to do to his people."

Both Joel and Jonah have read Exod 34:6 in light of 32:12–14. Joel sees the reprieve as a possibility depending on repentance. Jonah sees it as a fact for Nineveh based on its repentance. But the Twelve is aware that the judgment meant for Palestine, Israel, and Jerusalem had not been turned aside. Yet Hosea and Malachi proclaim the continued love of God and thus his continued claim on his people. God has in fact not changed. The old rules still apply.

Malachi 3:6, while insisting on the unchangeable nature of God, echoes Joel in accusing and exhorting the people, "You have turned (סרתם) away from my decrees and have not kept them. Turn (שובו) to me and I will turn (אשובה) to you." Both Joel and Malachi echo Jer 3:12, 14, 22, and other verses.

The God who chooses Israel, loves her, and does everything to try to rehabilitate her is still the God of justice and righteousness. Judeans have still not given up their evil ways.

> So I will come near you for judgment. I will be quick to testify against sorcerers, adulterers, and perjurers, and those who defraud laborers of their wages, who oppress the widows and the orphans, and deprive aliens of justice, who do not fear me. I, YHWH, do not change. (Mal 3:5–6)

The prophetic proclamations of Amos and Micah are confirmed. But the other side of that divine nature accounts for Israel's survival. "So you, children of Jacob, have not been destroyed" (Mal 3:6b). "Ever since the times of your forefathers you have turned away from my decrees and have not kept them" (Mal 3:7a). Hosea 2, Hos 4–14, and Zech 9–14 have dealt with these apostasies. Now Mal 3:7b renews the appeal of Joel 2:12: "Return to me and I will return to you."

Conclusion

By asserting God's unchangeable nature in terms of Exod 34:6 and God's unswerving commitment, or love, for Israel, a terrible discrepancy has been established. For Israel is recognized as disloyal and unrighteous.

Joel and Jonah recognize that, in the eighth century, this is not new. Torah also had to deal with this issue when Israel made the golden calf. There was frightful retribution, but not all were killed. God changed his mind (נחם) about wiping them all out. God dealt with that situation by making a distinction between the current generation and the one to come, distancing himself from the guilty survivors and turning to a new generation. Hosea 3:4–5 pictures a similar solution to the eighth-century apostasy:

> For the Israelites will dwell many days
>   without king and without prince,
>   without sacrifice and without altar,
>   without ephod and without teraphim.
> Afterward Israelites will turn (ישבו)
>   and seek YHWH their God and David their king.

Malachi pictures a different solution. God responds to a complaint that the emphasis on the constant, unchanging love of God removes the incentive for obeying God.

> "It is futile to serve God. What did we gain [profit] by carrying out his require-ments and going about like mourners before the Lord Almighty when now we call the arrogant blessed. Certainly evildoers prosper, and even those who chal-lenge God escape." Then those who feared the Lord talked with each other, and the Lord listened and heard. A scroll of remembrance was written in his pres-ence concerning those who feared the Lord and honored his name. "They will be mine," says the Lord Almighty, "in the day when I make up my treasured pos-session. I will spare them, just as a man spares his son who serves him. And you will see the distinction between the righteous and the wicked, between those who serve God and those who do not. Surely the day is coming, it will burn like a furnace. All the arrogant and every evildoer will be stubble, and that day that is coming will set them on fire," says the Lord Almighty. "Not a root nor a branch will be left to them. But for you who revere my name the sun of righteousness will rise with healing in its wings." (Mal 3:14–20 [Eng., 3:14–4:2])

The solution is to distinguish righteous and wicked and to treat them accordingly. There is an opportunity for repentance and turning to God. But ultimately there will be separation. For all of God's patience and love, the principle remains: God cannot and will not clear the guilty, even in Israel.

Torah continues to be applicable. God continues to send the prophet "to turn the hearts of the children to their fathers." Alternatively, the threat of further judgment (curse) remains (Mal 3:22–24 [4:4–6]).

While the core of the Twelve deals with the terrible wars of the eighth to the sixth centuries and God's involvement, and with the rupture in the relation between Israel/Judah and God, a part of the book asks about the future of God's relation to the people. What happens to election? What happens to covenant relations in these circumstances?

Much has obviously changed since the eighth century. There is no king, no kingdom. The people are not in "the land." The holy city is in ruins, and there is no temple. Does the relationship between YHWH and people have relevance? Does it have a future?

The work of Haggai and Zechariah, in calling for a restoration of the temple, implies a positive answer. But the theoretical answer, the theological answer, to the questions remain. The question of the validity of Torah in the new situation is also open. The frame of the Twelve — Hos 1–3 and Malachi — speaks to these issues.

These texts find answers based on Torah, as do Joel and Jonah. They state unequivocally the continuing, unchanging love of God for the people (Mal 1 and Hos 3). Malachi asserts that this unchanging nature of God accounts for the survival of Israelites (3:6). But the texts also state God's unequivocal requirement for loyalty and devotion, for justice and righteousness, as spelled out in Torah. Those who do not fit these categories cannot be a part of the people of God. Israelites have fallen short in the past and judgment has come upon them. Malachi reports that the postexilic community is no better. So how is the tension to be resolved?

All agree that repentance and change on the part of the people can resolve these difficulties. Hosea 3:4–5 suggests a parallel between the godless period of the eighth to the six centuries and the wilderness generation described in Torah. God will destroy some from the rest of that generation. Hope lies in the possibility of repentance and commitment by a later generation (Deuteronomy).

Malachi sees the need for a continuing process of rooting out the unbelieving, nonconforming element, while assuring that God will recognize the reverent, obedient, conforming core and reward them accordingly (Mal 3:6–21 [Eng., 3:6–4:3]). In either case, God's nature has not changed; nor has God's commitment to gather a people. Torah still applies, as does the assurance of continued prophetic guidance.

Index of Scripture References

Compiled with the aid of Melanie Greer Nogalski.
All Hebrew Bible citations follow MT numbering.

Index of Authors Cited

Compiled with the aid of Melanie Greer Nogalski.

R